MOOR PARK:
The Grosvenor Legacy

Martyn Pedrick

Riverside Books

ISBN 0 9515427 0 2
Moor Park: The Grosvenor Legacy. (hbk)

First published 1989

Published by
RIVERSIDE BOOKS
12, Sandy Lodge Road, Rickmansworth, Herts WD3 1LJ

Typeset by Footnote Graphics,
Warminster, Wiltshire

Printed in Great Britain by
Vine and Gorfin Ltd,
Exmouth, Devon

Publishers Note
The maps are based upon the Ordnance Survey (scale 1:7200) maps with the permission of the Controller of HMSO. © Crown Copyright
Pages from the 1919 and 1959 Auction Documents are reproduced by kind permission of the owners

Contents

Owners of Moor Park and the Manor

Abbey of St Alban's

Sir Ralph de Boteler (1456)

George Nevil, Archbishop of York (confiscated 1471)

Granted by the Crown to John de Vere in 1472

Returned to the Crown 1513–1524 when it was granted to Cardinal Wolsey, upon whose fall it was granted temporarily to:

John Russell, first Earl of Bedford (1529–1551)

The Crown and the Duchy of Lancaster, after holding it 1551–1576 granted it to:

Francis, 2nd Earl of Bedford (1576)

Edward, 3rd Earl of Bedford

Lucy, widow of the 3rd Earl sold in 1626 to:

William, 3rd Earl of Pembroke, on whose death in 1630 it passed to Philip, the 4th Earl who, in 1631 sold:

The MANOR to:	The PARK to:
Sir Chas Harbord, who sold in 1655 to:	Robert Carey, Earl of Monmouth followed in 1649 by:
	Henry, Earl of Monmouth, who sold in 1652 to:
Sir Richard Franklin, who sold in 1672 to:	Sir Richard Franklin, who sold in 1663 to:
	James, first Duke of Ormande, who sold in 1670 to:
Sir William Bucknall, from whom it passed in turn to:	
Sir John Bucknall (d. 1711)	James, Duke of Monmouth, after whose execution in 1685 it was granted to his widow, who sold in 1720 to:
William Bucknall (d. 1746)	Benjamin Styles, who died in 1739. Later, family trustees sold in 1754 to Lord Anson.
	On his death in 1762 Lord Anson was succeeded by Thomas Anson who sold in 1763 to:
	Sir Laurence Dundas, who was followed in 1781 by:
	Sir Thomas D. Dundas, who sold in 1785 to:
John Askell Bucknall (d. 1796)	Thomas Bates Rous (d. 1799) whose widow sold in 1801 to:
The Hon. William Grimston, (nephew – d. 1814)	Robert Williams who died in 1814 and was succeeded by:
The Hon. Harbottle Grimston (brother – d. 1823)	His son, also Robert Williams who sold in 1828 to:
Mrs Estcourt (sister – d. 1829)	Robert, second Earl Grosvenor who died in 1845 and was succeeded by his third son,
T. G. B. Estcourt (son – d. 1853)	
Rt. Hon. T. H. S. Sotheron Estcourt who sold in 1866 to:	
Robert, first Lord Ebury.	Robert, first Lord Ebury.

Foreword

This book is not intended to be the definitive history of Moor Park, neither have I set out to trace the lineage of its occupants for, by definition, lists of names and dates can make tedious reading.

Instead, I have attempted to tell the story of a manor less than twenty miles from central London, whose idyllic tranquility belies its chequered, and at times turbulent, past. But a story is nothing without people, and the owners, tenants and occupants of the old 'Manor of The More' have provided a rich vein of characters, all adding depth and colour to a tale which started with a few hundred acres. Between them, they experienced triumph, tribulation and tragedy, and at all times their story has been nothing short of remarkable.

There was Henry VIII, Wolsey, and Anne Boleyn. Later, the extravagant Duchess of Bedford, and the Pretender to the throne. Then proceeds from the South Sea Bubble furnished the building of the current mansion, and a subsequent owner received an £80,000 bill from a gardener called Capability Brown. Later came the cream of the aristocracy with the Grosvenors, and the creation of the Ebury title. Then the soap magnate, two Open champions, and Arnhem. All these, and many more besides, have contributed to the story of Moor Park. Not merely the 350 acres which now comprise the golf club, but the entire 3,000 acre manor which embraced large areas of Northwood and Rickmansworth.

It is now widely accepted as one of the top golf clubs in Europe, and enjoys a world-wide reputation. Even the 'nineteenth' is probably the most pretentious in the game. But that's always been the way of things, even back in the days when it was simply 'the Manor of The More. . . .'

The research was invariably interesting, often fascinating and, at times, frustrating – particularly when archives produced two or more differing versions of the same event. Where this has occurred, and I have been unable to ascertain fact from fiction, the alternatives are offered to the reader.

I have tried to write not a history book, but a book about *people* who have helped to make history. If I have succeeded, it is thanks to those who have so willingly offered their time, loaned me material, and given me encouragement while compiling this volume. They are legion, but those to whom special thanks are due include John Davies, Agnes Harwood, Victor de Peyrecave, John Edwards, Rickmansworth County Library, Rickmansworth Museum, Messrs Knight, Frank and Rutley, Bernard Thorpe & Partners, de Vere Hotels, and, of course, Bill Old.

I also gratefully acknowledge the works of the following authors, which proved invaluable during my research:

Susan Tweedsmuir – 'The Lilac and the Rose'
Alice Buchan – 'A Scrap Screen'.
Robert Bayne – 'Moor Park'
Hilary E. Armitage – 'A History of Moor Park'
W. A. G. Kemp – 'The Story of Northwood'

and various articles published in Country Life, Hertfordshire Countryside, Watford Observer, and The Sunday Times.

M.P.

This caricature of Robert Grosvenor, the first Lord Ebury, first appeared in Vanity Fair in April 1871, and is reproduced by courtesy of de Vere Hotels.

VANITY FAIR
LONDON, APRIL 15, 1871

'A common-prayer reformer.'
Lord Ebury.

CHAPTER ONE

Early Days At The Manor Of The More . . .

The story of Moor Park goes back almost to the dawn of history itself, with today's golfers tracing the steps of Neolithic man, his Bronze Age descendants and, more than a thousand years on, our comparatively sophisticated Roman conquerors.

Add a sprinkling of Royalty, a liberal helping of the aristocracy, throw in a handful of rebellious dissidents, add some society scandal for flavour, and you have a colourful and potent social cocktail which is stronger than most . . .

It was around three-thousand years B.C. that the story of Moor Park really began on a site just a few yards from the fifteenth tee on the High course. For centuries this mound has been known as Bathend Clump and is one of the highest points in Hertfordshire. It is also one of the most historic, for the discovery of traces of flint instruments and weapons provide irrefutable evidence that Stone Age man once colonised the Park.

A thousand years later, the neolithic brain progressed to discover that, by melting the ores of copper and tin together, man could produce bronze, thus providing historians with a snappy and commercial identity for a vital new age in human development. Traces of these historic Bronze Age instruments have also been discovered close to the Clump.

Later, it was the Romans. The main invasion came almost a century *after* Julius Caesar, and again, the views afforded by the high ground at Moor Park proved a decisive factor in the selection of a suitable site for an outpost. The Romans, however, opted to build on slightly lower land several hundred yards from the Clump. Although covered by undergrowth and surrounded by bushes, an original wall still remains behind the 17th tee on the West course and archeologists believe that it was once the site of a second-century Roman bath-house. Furthermore, it is thought that the original mosaic floor may still exist, although covered and protected by several feet of earth.

Excavations have also proved that the Romans constructed a pathway, or small road, from this site towards Bathend Clump. Remains of this can be seen clearly on the West course between the eighteenth tee and the seventeenth green. Then it disappears behind the seventeenth green but can be traced running the length of the fourteenth on the High, towards the fifteenth tee. Some sources suggest that the Clump was used by the Romans as a burial ground.

There is also evidence that Anglo-Saxon tribes, christians since the Roman invasion and noted for their farming achievements, were active on lower ground surrounding the Park around 400–600 AD, the early part of the Middle Ages more frequently termed the Dark Age.

Two hundred years later, the fabled King Offa II, a powerful and aggressive man, ruled over Mercia, an area embracing much of central and southern England. In the area now covered by south Hertfordshire were the two manors of Prichemareworde (Richmansworth) and Becceswurtha (Batchworth), and he is believed to have built some kind of base from which he could monitor his estates in this part of the country. The name he chose was the Manor of The More....

But Offa was hungry for more power and to increase his boundaries (according to legend) he offered the hand of his favourite daughter in marriage to Ethelburt, King of East Anglia. During the wedding feast Offa and Ethelburt had a difference of opinion which developed into a full-scale row. Offa, unable to control his temper, suddenly flew at his new son-in-law, killing him before the marriage had been consumated. His daughter, overcome by grief and the sight of her new husband dying at the hands of her father, was inconsolable. She shut herself off from the world, fell into decline, and died. Offa, filled with remorse, gave his manors of Prichemareworde, Becceswurtha, and The More to the Monastery of St Albans which he had recently founded, and he died two years later in AD 796.

The Manor of The More remained in the hands of the Abbey of St Albans for the next 400 years and little is known of its history during this period. The only legislation of note appears to have been imposed in 1090 when a clause was added to the deeds stating that the tenant must provide the Abbot of the Abbey with a sound and strong palfrey (saddle-horse) upon which he could ride whenever he visited the estate.

Later in 1182, the manor was exchanged by the Abbot of St Albans for two and a half hides of land in Horwood, in Buckinghamshire. (A hide is a measure of land, sufficient to support one family and its dependents, varying between 60 and 120 acres, depending upon the location). The new tenant was Adam Aignel, reputed to be of Norman extraction, who rented it from the Abbot at ten shillings a year. Aignel amended the name of his manor to 'La More', and it passed down to his son, grandson and great-grandson William Aignel, who died in 1364. There is no record of a manor house having been built during the Aignels' tenancy.

It seems that the estate at this time was fairly humble compared to the more opulent days which lay ahead, comprising only 40 acres of land, 18 acres of meadow land, and three acres of pasture. However, the Abbey steadily increased its hold, adding to the land whenever possible. By 1426 it had greatly increased in size and the new tenant, William Flete, obtained a licence to 'crennellate, enturret, and embattle with stones, lime and brik the The Manor of The More in Rickmaersworth'.

Thirty years later, the Manor of The More (now known simply as The More) was held by Ralph de Boteler, Lord of Sudeley, in Gloucestershire, who was an eminent statesman and confidante of King Henry VI. The

Abbot of St Albans Abbey, which still owned the land, saw de Boteler as a straight and honest man and took the opportunity to rid himself of the regular problem of rent arrears. In exchange for certain tenements by the Thames in London, he confirmed the manors of Ashley, Britwell, Batchworth, Eastbury and The More to de Boteler, free of all services with a token rent of one penny a year for each, in recognition of the fact it was held by the Abbot. Effectively, this was a type of early leasehold agreement and, although de Boteler was against it in principle, he eventually agreed.

Sir Ralph de Boteler eventually became Lord Chamberlain of the Household of Henry VI and was created Baron Sudeley in 1441. In 1455, the Battle of St Albans marked the start of the Wars of the Roses, and de Boteler was severely wounded. He mortgaged his manors to the Abbot of St Albans but retained his life interest in them for himself, his wife and his son. Later, when he lost his heir, he offered The More to the Abbey in return for £700 'plus the prayers of the Convent for himself, his wife and their dead son.' However, descendants of the de Botelers were to return to Moor Park two centuries later after adopting a subtle change of name....

CHAPTER TWO

An Era Of Extravagance And Lust

The roots of Moor Park as we know it today, and the history of the mansions which have housed Royalty and others of rank and privilege, begin with Sir Ralph de Boteler's successor, George Nevil, who is believed to have been granted the Manor of The More in 1460.

Nevil was well connected; his brother was Richard, Earl of Warwick, dubbed by his contemporaries as 'Warwick the King-maker' because of his apparent ability to determine who should, and who should not, rule the nation. In the Wars of the Roses, he first supported the House of York and overthrew Henry VI, declaring Edward IV as King. Some years later, a remarkable change of allegiance saw him join the Lancastrians, and restore Henry to the throne, albeit briefly.

Through his brother's influence, Nevil had been appointed Bishop of Exeter in 1459 at the age of twenty-four. The following year his hand was strengthened considerably with his appointment as Chancellor of England, a post which he held for eight years, and in 1464 he became the 52nd (and youngest ever) Archbishop of York.

On being granted the manor, Nevil immediately obtained from King Henry a licence allowing him to extend his land and enclose six hundred acres in the parishes of Rickmansworth and Watford, and shortly afterwards moved into a large and elaborate residence at The More. The site of this original palace was just off what is now Sandy Lodge Road, to the rear of what later became Moor Farm, and remains of the old moat can still be seen. Historians are divided over whether it was Flete, de Boteler or indeed Nevil who was responsible for building the first palace at The More.

Whether or not Nevil built the original is a matter of conjecture; if he didn't build it himself, then he certainly spent a vast sum enlarging and converting it into a splendid and ornate palace where he lived and entertained in lavish style. He also surrounded himself with close and trusted supporters for whom he created menial, but highly rewarding, positions. His extravagance is illustrated quite bluntly by Lord Lytton in his book 'Last of the Barons'....

'Every office that pomp could devise for a King's Court,' says the writer, 'was to be found in the household of this magnificent prelate.' He then lists the positions 'all emulously sought for and proudly held by gentlemen of the first blood and birth. His mansion was at once a court for middle life, a school for youth, and an asylum for age.'

Meanwhile, the Wars of the Roses continued to rage. In all, it devastated the kingdom over thirty years, accounting for the lives of sixty princes of the Royal family, plus half the nobility and gentry of England. Having overthrown Henry (with Warwick's support) in 1461, Edward of York became King Edward IV. Then, in 1470, Warwick quarrelled with Edward and, within twelve months, helped Henry regain the throne. Warwick was killed in the Battle of Barnet in 1471, and Henry VI was eventually overpowered by the Yorkists and died in the Tower of London the same year.

Having experienced Warwick's dramatic change of allegiance, King Edward was perhaps justified in doubting the sincerity of his brother, the Archbishop Nevil. Edward had already survived one plot the previous year when visiting The More, having been tipped off that one hundred armed men were in hiding, ready to attack and carry him off. The King escaped but remained silent about the affair, choosing instead to maintain a close watch on his Archbishop....

When Nevil received an invitation to visit Windsor shortly after King Edward had regained the throne in 1471, he saw it as a sign that he was once again in favour, and assumed that Edward was unaware that they were still conspiring against him.

It was Nevil's duty to reciprocate by inviting the King to The More, and Edward readily accepted. News of the visit aroused great excitement and gold plate, hidden away since the battles of Barnet and Tewkesbury the previous year, was produced for the sumptuous Royal banquet.

However, the King's suspicions that Nevil was plotting against the Crown were confirmed and, immediately after the banquet, the Archbishop was arrested for communicating with the exiled Earl of Oxford. He was imprisoned in Calais where he became ill, and he was brought home to die. Meanwhile, King Edward had seized his estates, including the Manor of The More, silver and gold worth a reported £20,000, and his mitre which was adorned with precious stones. The monarch had the jewels removed from the mitre and re-set in his own crown, where they remain to this day.

In 1475, the custody of the Park was granted to John Hawdeles, and later to Edward Gower, neither of whom made any notable contribution to its chequered history. It then passed into the hands of the Dean and Canons of St George's Chapel, Windsor, but at King Edward's request, they granted it back to him shortly before he died in 1483.

Students of history will be aware that Edward IV was succeeded by his twelve-year-old son who briefly inherited the royal mantle as Edward V before he and his younger brother were locked in the Tower and supposedly murdered by their uncle, who then assumed the throne as Richard III. But, as in the best story books, wicked Uncle Richard got his come-uppance just two years later, dying on the battlefield at Bosworth at the hands of Henry Tudor, Earl of Richmond. Henry was the heir to the House of Lancaster, and his prize for erasing the iniquitous Yorkist Richard was the throne and the title of King Henry VII, first of the Tudor monarchs.

The Manor of The More had remained the property of the Crown since the death of Edward IV two years earlier, and Henry saw it as the perfect reward for John de Vere, 13th Earl of Oxford, who had commanded the archers in the victory at Bosworth, which effectively marked the end of the Wars of the Roses. The More remained with de Vere for twenty-eight years and when he died childless in 1513, surviving his close friend Henry VII by four years, the manor again reverted to the Crown which now rested upon the head of yet another Henry....

The Rise And Fall Of A Cardinal:

During the sixteenth century, Hertfordshire estates had a remarkable instability of tenure, often changing hands at the whim of a monarch, and The More was no exception. The pattern was to continue with the advent of the Tudors, although during this period there are clearer reasons for the merry-go-round of occupants, providing a rich and colourful collage of historical fact and intriguing legend.

In 1515 The Manor of The More was granted by a young King Henry VIII to St Albans Abbey (the original owners), but it appears to have been little used until 1524 when the tenancy passed to the ambitious son of an Ipswich butcher! Determined to succeed in the Church, he had passed through Oxford University to become Rector of Lymington where, it is recorded, a justice threw him in the stocks for drunkenness.

This crapulent cleric was to become better known as Cardinal Thomas Wolsey, the King's Chancellor, advisor and personal friend, whose astonishing rise to a position of unequalled power is matched only by the speed and manner in which he fell from favour.

Wolsey was a brilliant scholar; at the age of thirty-six he was appointed to King Henry's Council, became Archbishop of York two years later and

King Henry VIII and Cardinal Wolsey: It was the ramifications over the first Royal divorce, after Henry had fallen in love with Anne Boleyn while visiting the Manor of The More, which led to Wolsey's downfall. (*National Portrait Gallery*).

the following year, in 1515, became Lord Chancellor as well as Cardinal and Papal Legate. At times his influence and strength exceeded even that of the King for, as Chancellor *and* Legate he administered affairs of both the Church and the State. He was effectively Pope in England and twice just missed the papal crown.

He celebrated his remarkable rise to power by building Hampton Court Palace in 1515 but, eleven years later, made a present of it to the King hoping to ingratiate himself still further to Henry by handsomely 'repaying' the gift of the Manor of The More.

Wolsey considerably altered the palace, making it more exquisite, with lavishly-appointed gardens. In order to achieve this he needed to extend his boundaries beyond what is now Watford gate (Sandy Lodge Road entrance) and achieved this by evicting one of his tenants, a farmer named Tolpott. He enclosed Tolpott's land, amounting to nearly two hundred acres, within his existing park, and through his new park he built a road linking Rickmansworth with Watford, now known as Tolpit's Lane.

It appears that Wolsey attempted to emulate even the Archbishop Nevil with his lavish lifestyle. His extravagance knew no limits, and it is recorded that his couch and table-cloth were decorated liberally with gold, and that he dined among the subtle perfumes of musk and sweet amber. His dishes were silver, and he drank only from gold or silver goblets.

King Henry was at this time experiencing major diplomatic problems with King Francis I of France and, despite many attempts, the monarchs had been unable to resolve their differences. Then Henry was persuaded to allow Wolsey to visit France as his emissary. The Cardinal succeeded where the King had failed and, in 1525, peace terms were signed between England and France at The More. This was known as The Treaty of The More, and it was from here in September 1525 that the proclamation of peace was issued. Wolsey's legendary greed appears to have been satisfied too, for the King's gratitude to his Cardinal totalled one hundred thousand gold crowns 'for great and reasonable service.'

This success endeared Wolsey still further to the King, who now visited The More frequently as the guest of his Cardinal. Indeed, it was here in 1529, during a month's stay with his Queen, Catherine of Aragon, that King Henry's attentions were first diverted by the lissom form of young Anne Boleyn, an attendant to the Royal household....

Anne, daughter of Norfolk landowner Sir Thomas Boleyn, was lady-in-waiting to Queen Catherine and it is thought to be during this visit to The More that Henry first declared his love for her. He recruited Wolsey to help persuade Catherine to agree to a divorce but, between them, they failed to overcome her resistance, and the dilemma which followed precipitated perhaps the greatest constitutional crisis in the nation's history.

It appears that this pressure from the King was rather more than Wolsey could stand. He was worried by Catherine's persistent refusals, and knew that Henry would see this as a sign of failure. He became perturbed about his own future, and would often throw himself into a chair, burying his face in his hands in silent reverie. On other occasions he would ease the tension by jumping on his horse and riding off at a fierce gallop 'to drive away the vapours that had gathered around him.' Both the armchair and

The ill-fated Anne Boleyn, the lady-in-waiting who became King Henry's second wife (*National Portrait Gallery*), and Sir John Russell, later to become the first Earl of Bedford, who succeeded Wolsey at The More. (*The British Library*).

the saddle remained with future owners of Moor Park until the manor was sold by auction in 1919.

Eventually, realising that Wolsey's shallow efforts at persuasion were getting him nowhere, Henry insisted that the Royal party should leave for Grafton, in Northamptonshire, and it was here that Catherine eventually agreed to let Henry divorce her. But Wolsey refused to sanction it, and Cardinal Campeggio was dispatched from Rome as a legate to hear the case. He went to see Wolsey at The More, where they decided upon their plan of action, and together they went to see the King. Meanwhile, personal letters between Henry and Anne Boleyn had gone missing, and Henry believed that these were now in the possession of Wolsey and Campeggio. Furthermore, the King had already intercepted letters from Wolsey to the Pope condemning the divorce....

Royal troopers were dispatched in pursuit of Campeggio, catching him at Calais, but he had already passed the letters to messengers who were hastening towards Rome and it is believed that, to this day, they remain in the archives of the Vatican.

This marked the beginning of the end for Wolsey. He was evicted from The More in disgrace, his seal of office of Lord Chancellor was removed together with its attendant privileges, and he was stripped of all his wealth. He was allowed to retain only the Archbishopric of York, and retired to his diocese where he attempted to rebuild his life and regain some of the popularity he had enjoyed with all classes. He wrote to several ministers and princes seeking their support, but the King's confidantes greatly distorted the contents of these letters, and Wolsey was arrested for high treason and summoned to London. After three days he reached Leicester Abbey where he died on November 29th, 1530, thus avoiding an ignominious death either at the gallows or on the block. His dying words, which have been frequently quoted, provide not only an accurate illustration of the regrets and disillusionment which had now consumed him, but also a fitting lament to his life:

> 'Had I but served my God with half the zeal I had served my King,
> He would not in mine age had left me naked to mine enemies.'

Historians, however, remember Cardinal Thomas Wolsey as a great ecclesiastical statesman of the Middle Ages. It is sad that he allowed his many fine qualities to be usurped by his greed, arrogance, and insatiable lust for power.

Having reclaimed the estate following Wolsey's demise in 1530, King Henry found it convenient to allow Catherine of Aragon to stay there briefly after banishing her from Windsor 'for her obstinacy' in 1531, while awaiting divorce proceedings. Her expulsion from the palace was accompanied by the order from Henry 'that she should see his face no more', and she spent the last five years of her life in Kimbolton Castle. She is buried in Peterborough Cathedral where a small plaque bearing the simple inscription 'Catherine Regina' is the only concession from total anonymity.

The Bedford Connection:

It was perhaps due to the influence of Thomas Cromwell, Wolsey's successor, that the King next granted both the manor and the Park, plus the Lordship of Rickmansworth, to Sir John Russell (afterwards the first Earl of Bedford) with an allowance of fourpence a day. Sir John, whose family country seat was nearby Chenies, resided at Batchworth Heath Lodge. He had been a strong supporter of Cromwell when he was in danger of being dragged down in the wake of Wolsey's fall from grace, and a close friendship developed beween them.

Russell was appointed Ranger of the royal estate, and in 1533 he wrote to Cromwell:

'Sir, the Park palings at The More are decaying and the deer are escaping, many are killed daily. I have felled two hundred oaks for this purpose, but I require money as the garden goeth to great ruin. . . .'

The letter bore the address 'Charley Wood', and contained a request for the King to increase his allowance to eightpence a day, with Russell offering to subsidise this by a further sixpence a day from his own purse. Poaching from the lakes and the moat was also rife, for he was forced to add: 'Also for keeping of fish thereof, if there be not a trusty fellow for the keeping of the garden there will be much displeasure and little fish left.'

It is recorded that, in the year that Russell wrote this note, the gardens were ruined and only 100 deer of the original 500 remained. In 1535 King Henry ordered that the Palace should be redecorated, refurnished and the grounds repaired, and for the next few years he and his respective Queens used it as a royal residence.

From records and accounts taken from books preserved in the Public Records office, as well as information gleaned from excavations, it is clear that it was now a fabulous and extravagant palace, comprising a base court, plus an inner court, in which were located the sumptuous Royal apartments.

In 1540, in an unfamiliar display of generosity to a former spouse, King Henry gave The Manor of The More to his fourth wife Anne of Cleves for life following their divorce, and during that year he visited The More with Katherine Howard, staying for three weeks. During 1542 many Privy Council meetings took place there, but after that Henry ceased to use it, and it is at this point that we find sharply conflicting reports about the fortunes of the old palace which is believed to have remained the property of Anne of Cleves until her death in 1557.

A comprehensive two-part article which appeared in Country Life in January 1912, refers to a twenty-nine page inventory taken in 1547 (the year of Henry's death) listing '125 tapestries, and carpets, beds and furniture of great richness.' However, in her booklet 'A History of Moor Park', Hilary E. Armitage claims that, from 1542, the Palace lay empty for fourteen years, that the Park became overgrown, and excavations showed that the building was inhabited by squatters and gypsies.

Henry was succeeded by his sickly ten-year-old son, Edward VI. With the government controlling the throne, the young boy was persuaded to nominate Lady Jane Grey as his successor but, after ruling for a few days, she was overthrown by Mary Tudor (daughter of Henry and Catherine of Aragon) and beheaded in 1554.

In 1556, when Queen Mary was busily reversing the religious changes instigated by her father, the Manor of The More was annexed to the Duchy of Lancaster, but she made little further contribution of note, other than to imprison Francis Russell, second Earl of Bedford, for refusing to conform to her staunchly Catholic beliefs. On her death in 1558 she was succeeded by her half-sister Elizabeth (Henry's daughter by Anne Boleyn) who freed Russell and invited him to become a Privy Councillor. The Queen later completed Russell's remarkable change in fortunes by granting to him and his heirs both the manor and the Park (now listed as 'Moore Park') at a rent of £120 per annum, with ultimate reversion to the monarchy.

It was during Elizabeth's reign, in 1568, that a survey was made of the estate. The only remaining trace states:

'The Great Park adjoining the Manor Place contains 830 acres, wooded chiefly by Maple and Hornbeam, with 415 deer and the Manor Place considerable decayed. The surveyors propose to dispark this and turn it into arable land. The little park containing two hundred acres is much overgrown with fern, it has 90 deer. The mansion is of brick, the chief buildings forming a square court, entered by a gate house with towers, the whole is moated. It is in a dilapidated state.'

The Earl died in 1585, surviving his two sons by a few years, and he was succeeded by his grandson, Edward. The third Earl of Bedford is described as a quiet, retiring man. He married in 1594 the daughter of Sir John Harington and both she and her mother were later appointed to the bedchamber of Queen Anne, wife of King James I, in preference to many other applicants sanctioned, and indeed preferred, by the monarch.

When the Queen died in 1619, Lucy Harington, the ebullient Countess of Bedford, retired after sixteen years in royal service and it is due to *her* influence, rather than that of the Earl, that Moor Park was about to see the dawn of a new era.

With the old palace now virtually uninhabitable, some historians tell us that the Earl and Countess embarked on the design and building of a new and elegant mansion. Although its exact position is not known, it is thought to have been on lower ground, about one-third of a mile in a North-easterly direction from the present mansion, near the Watford entrance to the Park. It was, according to deeds and other historical documents, occupied until 1825 (some 150 years *after* the building of the current mansion), when it was demolished.

The Bedfords' new home appears to have been of considerable size, with seventeen rooms, pleasure grounds, fish ponds, two stone lodges and a gamekeeper's cottage. The Duchess, who was notoriously extravagant, seems to have paid much attention to her gardens which were fabulous, and it is of these that Sir William Temple wrote so glowingly in 1685, some thirty years after his visit. (See Temple on Gardens)

But did the Bedfords really build a new mansion, or did they merely convert and modernise the inhabitable remains of the old one? Historical claims about its location place it uncomfortably close to the original palace occupied by Wolsey and company, and no remains have ever been found to suggest that it was a separate building. Certainly, the Duchess's new gardens must have considerably altered the appearance of the old palace, and this could well have convinced observers of the day that it was indeed a new mansion, albeit considerably smaller than the original. It would also account for the fact that no trace of another mansion has ever been found, and either this, or a Dower House, would have still have been in an acceptable state to house the Monmouths while they built their new mansion in 1670.

The Earl of Bedford died on May 3rd 1627 and his Countess three weeks later. He was interred in the family vault at Chenies, while she was laid to rest in Exton, Rutlandshire, the home of her ancestors, where she had been taken for health reasons following the death of her husband. This certain knowledge corrects two erroneous claims; the first, in Lodge's 'Illustrious Portraits' states that the Countess outlived the Earl for many years in widowhood, adding that she 'at last died, no-one knows when and no-one knows where.'

The second, and equally incongruous dismissal of her fate, appears in Whiffen's 'Memoirs of the House of Russell' where it is stated that 'It is altogether uncertain whether she was interred at Chenies or in Rutlandshire.'

An extract from the register of burials at Exton Parish Church clarifies the matter beyond doubt: '1627 – The Ladye Bedford buryed May 26th.'

The Demise Of A Pembroke:

The estate had been purchased the previous year by William Herbert, third Earl of Pembroke who, in 1626 was appointed Lord Chamberlain by Charles I in the first year of his reign and was also elected Chancellor of the University of Oxford, giving his name to Pembroke College.

His period of tenure, however, was to be tragically brief; while celebrating his fiftieth birthday with friends in 1630, one of his guests proposed a toast, congratulating him on having outlived the day which his tutor had predicted he would not survive. The prognosis proved to be alarmingly prophetic – after wining and dining he was, a few minutes before midnight, 'seized with a fit of apoplexy, fell back, and expired.' These words are borrowed from the Rev. Robert Bayne's text on Moor Park, first published in 1871, to which he adds the following erudite observation:

'Often a prophecy is its own fulfilment. The nervous system receives a shock, and never rallies. This melancholy event took place in the year 1630.'

Philip, the fourth Earl of Pembroke, was the younger brother of the unfortunate third Earl, William, and had been a great favourite of King James I who had died in 1625. He had a passion for dogs and horses – facets of his lifestyle which endeared him greatly to his King – and they had spent much time riding and hunting together. He was created Earl of Montgomery in 1605 in celebration of the baptism of the young Prince Charles, and later married Susan de Vere, a descendent of the brother of John de Vere who had owned The More 120 years earlier. Later, in the reign of Charles I, Philip was appointed Lord Chamberlain, but on the outbreak of the Civil War he abandoned the court and joined the rebels.

LEFT: Philip, fourth Earl of Pembroke, who inherited The More after his elder brother, the third Earl, died following a heavy drinking bout on his fiftieth birthday.
RIGHT: James Butler, first Duke of Ormande, who bought The More in 1663. He was descended from the de Boteler family who had owned the manor 200 years earlier. (*National Portrait Gallery*).

Philip's second wife was the Countess of Dorset who appears to have been something of a character. Described as 'the oldest and most independent courtier in the Kingdom' she had served in the court of Queen Elizabeth (which suggests she was probably older than her husband). Her services were also called upon by James I and Charles I before she decided to leave Pembroke 'after twenty years of ceaseless quarrelling.' Later, in the reign of Charles II, she was asked to approve the nomination of a Member of Parliament for the borough of Appleby, and assured herself a place among the great historical wits with the following terse reply:

> 'I have been bullied by a usurper, I have been neglected by a Court,
> But I will not be dictated to by a subject. Your man shan't stand.'
> Anne Dorset, Pembroke and Montgomery.

Until this point, the Park and the manor had been one estate but in 1631 Philip, fourth Earl of Pembroke, sold the manor to Charles Harbord, and the Park with the mansion to Robert Carey, later to be created first Earl of Monmouth. The estate was to remain divided for more than 20 years before the Park and the manor once again reverted to common ownership, albeit briefly. Later, they would be separated for over two hundred years.

Robert Carey – Rogue, Messenger And Earl:

Robert Carey was the third son of Henry, Lord Hunsden, son of Mary Boleyn (Queen Anne's elder sister) and therefore a cousin of Queen Elizabeth. Hunsden had been a firm favourite of the Queen, but later fell from favour and withdrew from Court. He had long felt that an Earldom had been due to him, but when he was eventually offered the title of Earl of Monmouth on his deathbed he must have found a perverse delight in declining it, saying that if he wasn't considered worthy of it while living, he didn't think himself worthy of it while dying!

Carey had from his early days distinguished himself in the Court of Elizabeth before he too, fell from favour with the crown by marrying against the Queen's wishes.

Clearly the man was a rascal and *roue* of some repute and enjoyed the better things in life, whether he could afford them or not! It appears that, through high living, he had occurred debts in excess of £1,000 and, in order to extracate himself from the financial mire, had found it necessary to marry one Elizabeth Trevanion, a widow of independent wealth. While his father was apparently undisturbed by his decision, the marriage offended influential friends and, more pertinently, the Queen. He was forced to withdraw from Court and adopt a low profile for a year, choosing to exile himself in Carlisle.

It seems, though, that Carey's fall from grace was shortlived, for the following year he returned to London, made a personal plea to the Queen, and was rewarded with the Wardency of the East Marches with the attendant purse of £500 per year. Later, his star ascended even more rapidly after he had played a vital role in the defeat of the Spanish Armada. But he was also a man of peace, and was forced to draw upon his considerable diplomatic skills to repair a rift between the Queen and the Earl of Essex, whose traditional seat was at Cassiobury. Like Carey and others, Essex had angered the virgin Queen by marrying against her wishes, and it was only through Carey's talents as a mediator that Essex was restored to royal favour.

On Queen Elizabeth's demise and ultimate death in 1603, Carey had received the news within minutes from his sister Lady Scrope, who was attending the Royal chamber at the time. This early intelligence gave him an advantage over his rivals, enabling him to ride immediately from London to Edinburgh to inform King James of Elizabeth's death. Despite falling heavily from his horse, and losing much blood, he arrived at Holyrood House on the third night when the King was in bed. On gaining admittance to the Royal chamber, he dropped to one knee and hailed James as King of England, Scotland, France and Ireland. The only proof he had was a sapphire ring given by James to Lady Scrope with orders that it should be returned to him by messenger as an incontrovertable sign of Elizabeth's death.

James rewarded Sir Robert and Lady Carey with positions of influence within his Court, but the power which Carey had gained following his dash to Scotland had inflamed his rivals. In 1631, six years after James's death, they succeeded in removing Sir Robert and his wife from every position of honour in the Court with a remarkable display of character assassination. Then, according to Bayne's history of 1871, they retired to The More 'to meditate on the vanity of the world.'

The Careys' self-imposed retirement didn't last long; they were soon returned to partial favour – largely as a reward for the remarkable care they had taken over King James's sickly and rickety son, who had now become King Charles I. He had been unable to walk or talk at the age of four and, while other courtiers had dreaded having charge of the Prince, fearing that he might die while in their custody, Lady Carey attended him with love and encouragement. The King, clearly a man of limited patience, believed his son to be tongue-tied and wanted to cut the string beneath the tongue to ease his attempts at speech. He was also keen to put the prince in iron-clad boots to strengthen his legs.

Lady Carey, with the support of the Queen, was vehemently against such radical treatment, and was eventually proved right. In his autobiography, Sir Robert Carey records 'Prince Charles grew daily more and more in health and strength, both of body and mind, to the amazement of many who knew his weakness when she first took charge of him.'

As a sign of his appreciation, James bestowed the title of Lord Leppington upon Robert Carey and later, King Charles I created him the first Earl of Monmouth, the very title which his father had shunned on his death-bed. Sir Robert died at Moor Park in 1639 at the age of 80, and was buried in Rickmansworth Church, as were his wife (who died in 1641) and family. His elder son, the second Earl of Monmouth, sold the park in 1652 to Sir Richard Franklin who, three years later, also bought the manor.

The More was purchased from Franklin in 1663 by James Butler, 12th Earl and First Duke of Ormonde, and it is at this stage that we find history throwing up a few coincidences. Butler's forebears were the 'de Botelers' and Sir Ralph de Boteler had held the Manor of The More over 200 years earlier. Then came the subtle change of name from Boteler to Butler and we find that the *seventh* Earl (Sir Thomas Butler) had a daughter who married Sir William Boleyn of Blickling in Norfolk. Sir William's son, later to become Sir Thomas Boleyn, was the father of two daughters, Anne and Mary. The unfortunate Anne became enmeshed with Henry VIII and was subsequently beheaded, while Mary married William Carey, had a son Henry (Lord Hunsdon), whose own son Robert Carey, later to become first Earl of Monmouth, had been a recent occupant of Moor Park.

The Duke of Ormande (whose eldest son took the title of Lord Butler of More Park) sold the Park and mansion in 1670 to James Fitzroy Scott, first Duke of Monmouth (not to be confused with the Earl), and a new chapter was about to begin....

CHAPTER THREE

Monmouth: Soldier, Builder And Pretender

James Fitzroy Scott was the eldest and first bastard son of the dissolute and rampant King Charles II. His mother was Lucy Walters and he was born in Rotterdam in 1649. His father, then heir to the throne, had fled to France while King Charles I had elected to remain in England and face the Parliamentary uprising led by Cromwell, only to be beheaded the same year.

It was widely rumoured that some form of secret marriage had taken place between Charles and Lucy while in France. The certificates of proof had been stolen by emissaries from Rome to ensure that, should the child elect to support the Protestant faith, no evidence of the marriage would exist and he would be discredited as a bastard.

After the restoration of his father to the throne in 1660 following the Civil War, James was brought to London by Henrietta Maria, the Queen Dowager (widow of Charles I) and, despite his young age, was favoured with positions of influence in preference to many eminent and more deserving statesmen. In 1661, at the age of twelve, a marriage was contracted with the ten-year-old Anna Scott, daughter of the Duke of Buccleuch, ironically, the man who is supposed to have been instrumental in blocking his path to the throne by stealing evidence of his father's marriage. Some reports claim that James and Anna were married in 1663, but most historians seem to agree that the ceremony was conducted in the King's Chamber of Whitehall Palace by the Archbishop of Canterbury two years later, when he was sixteen and she was fourteen. But by now James was known to be a staunch Protestant and, without proof to the contrary, he was exposed as illigitimate, thus forfeiting his right to the throne.

Having, therefore, no official name of his own, it was the bastard James who took his wife's name of Scott at the marriage ceremony, but to make the match more acceptable, King Charles immediately created him first Duke of Monmouth.

It is certain that his Duchess was no beauty. She was dumpy and walked with a slight limp, and it is highly probable that the new Duke had found more attraction in her fortune than in her face. At the age of ten she had acceded to the title of Countess of Buccleuch in her own right, thus becoming one of the wealthiest – and most eligible – heiresses in the

The man of the mansion: James Fitzroy Scott, Duke of Monmouth and bastard son of King Charles II, who was beheaded at the age of thirty-six (*National Portrait Gallery*), and his wife Anna, taken from a sketch by Peter Lely, circa 1670.

country. However, they were seen still to be children, and on the evening of their marriage, King Charles wrote to his sister, the Duchess of Orleans: 'This being James's marriage day, I am going to sup with them, where we intend to dance and see them a-bed together, but the ceremony shall stop there for they are both too young to lie all night together.'

Neither were they allowed free access to Anna's considerable financial resources. Instead, they were allowed 'pocket-money' of £1,200 per year, and the new Duchess inflamed her husband when, as an early sign of extravagances still to come, she spent her entire year's allowance on a pair of diamond ear-rings. However, in spite of her lack of looks and her legendary spending sprees, history recalls her as 'a lively woman, shrewd, intelligent and sharp-tongued' with an acute sense of survival which was to serve her well in later years.

The Duke, however, appeared to be the complete antithesis of his wife. It is reported that he was handsome, brave and excelled at all sports. When he became of age in 1670, his father appointed him Captain-General of all the King's Forces, and it was at this time that he purchased Moor Park and is supposed to have moved into the mansion built by the Duke and Duchess of Bedford while planning his new home. But, as related earlier, no signs have been found to support the claim that the Bedfords built a *new* mansion, and it is likely that they converted an existing part of the original palace. It was probably this, or perhaps a Lodge or Dower House, that was to become the Monmouth's temporary home while they built their own mansion on the present site. Later claims that the Bedford's house was occupied until it was pulled down as recently as 1825, seem to support the view that it was a mistaken reference to an additional property on the estate, and not a mansion of great architectural or historical importance.

It is pertinent that the period between the occupation of the Bedfords (which ended in 1626) and the purchase by James, Duke of Monmouth (1670) was a particularly stormy time. Britain had been ravaged by two Civil Wars, the Plague and the Fire of London, in addition to a string of overseas conflicts, and owners changed so rapidly that the old palace, despite additions and repairs (probably undertaken by the Bedfords) which justified its being described in 1631 as 'lately built' must have fallen into grave disrepair, for when Monmouth came to build later in the 1670s, he abandoned all ideas of trying to restore the crumbling edifice, opting instead to commence building on a new site.

Although the Monmouth's extravagant new home was to provide the basis for the current Moor Park mansion, it has since been extensively altered and little of its early background is known, although at the time it was applauded as one of the nation's best examples of Stuart brickwork.

The original design has been attributed to Wren, but there is little foundation for this claim. At this time he would have been too committed to the building of St Paul's Cathedral and the rebuilding of London after the great fire of 1666 to have concerned himself with work in the country. Other sources suggest it could be the work of Drew but, despite exhaustive searches over three centuries, no conclusive evidence has been presented.

Surprisingly, it seems that not only is the architect of Monmouth's mansion unknown, but there also appears to be no record of the house itself! Even in Chauncy's history of 1700, where many estates and mansions of Hertfordshire are listed, there is no reference to Moor Park.

Monmouth was rarely at home during the early years of his ownership of the Park. His professional duties as Captain-General of the King's Forces made heavy demands on his time to battle with the Dutch, the French or the Scots, and it is accepted that he distinguished himself both as a military tactician, and as a courageous leader of men. He was also remarkably humane; after defeating the Covenanters at Bothwell Bridge in 1679, he refused his men permission to pursue and slay the vanquished army. Later, when he was challenged about his decision by King Charles, it is claimed that he retorted: 'I cannot kill men in cold blood. That's work only for butchers.'

These protracted periods away from home prevented him from supervising work on the new mansion, and that is almost certainly why he elected to grant power of Attorney to Sir Philip Fox, allowing him to make whatever building arrangements necessary, including the removal of the crumbling, decaying part of the palace which had once been the home of Nevil, Wolsey *et al.*

It is worth noting that it was shortly after Monmouth took over the Park that Sir Richard Franklin, who nine years earlier had sold the Park and the Bedford's 'mansion' to the Duke of Ormande, now decided to dispose of the manor. It is recorded that he sold it in 1672 to Sir William Bucknall, in whose family it was to remain under various names and guises, until the Park and the manor were restored to common ownership by the first Lord Ebury in 1866.

Apart from his military skills, Monmouth was now seen as leader of the Protestant cause and clashed frequently with his uncle (later to become King James II) over religion. He was involved in the Popish plot (with Titus Oates) and the Rye House plot, both designed bring pressure on his father, King Charles II, to overthrow Catholicism in England.

Both conspiracies failed and he fled to Toddington in Bedfordshire where he was eventually discovered while being given sanctuary by Lady Wentworth, unaware at this stage that Monmouth was having a salacious affair with her fourteen-year-old daughter, Lady Henrietta. He was forgiven by his father, the King, after writing a letter of penitence, but he was banished from the Court and retired (supposedly) in peace at Moor Park. However, it was later discovered that he was still plotting against the Catholic regime, and he was forced to flee the mansion and escape to Holland. Any remorse he may have felt at abandoning his wife and family was clearly shortlived, for it is known that while in exile he led a rich and frivolous existence with the young Lady Henrietta Wentworth, who had now become his mistress, much to the fury of her mother!

Earlier this century, during repairs to the mansion, a false wall was found concealing a secret passage to the basement. From here a tunnel was discovered and, what is thought to be its exit, is still visible among a clump of bushes some two hundred yards from the mansion, between the fourteenth and fifteenth fairways on the West course. This was almost certainly his escape route, although it is possible that he fled through a brick drainage culvert which is visible just a few yards away...

After the death of his father, Charles II, in 1685, Monmouth's Uncle became King James II, and the Duke conspired to invade England and capture the throne which he now considered to be his birthright. He landed at Lyme Regis with only eighty-two followers, and his token rebellion was crushed by the Royalists at Sedgemoor, culminating with his imprisonment in the Tower of London. There seems little doubt that his wife and family were with him in the Tower, but on this point historians are again divided. Hilary Armitage (in 'A History of Moor Park') suggests that Monmouth was allowed their company as a privilege, but Bayne, writing in 1871, claims that they too, were incarcerated by a warrant 'which committed an innocent and much-wronged woman to prison for the faults of a man who had for years abandoned her and her children.' Altogether the Monmouths had six children, but the first died while still a child, and two others in infancy, one in the Tower.**

His efforts to claim the crown had earned Monmouth the title of 'Pretender to the Throne' and, together with many of his followers, he was tried and sentenced to death by the infamous Judge George Jeffreys at the Bloody Assize of 1685. Following the trial, James Fitzroy Scott, first Duke of Monmouth, was beheaded at the age of thirty-six. Jeffreys, who was

****The Third Option...**

There is yet another claim that, upon hearing of the Duke of Monmouth's landing at Lyme Regis, King James snatched his children and imprisoned them in the Tower. The Duchess, always a close friend of the King, went with them, but was not held against her will, being free to come and go as she wished. The Duke saw his wife in the Tower only twice after his defeat and capture at Sedgemore, but declined her attempts at a reconciliation before he died, stating that he still loved Lady Henrietta.

This source (writer Christine Sheppard) claims that Anna threw a fit of hysterics on the morning of the Duke's execution, but recovered enough to breakfast with the King in Whitehall. All estates and favours which had been previously withdrawn from the Monmouths, were later restored to her, and the Duchess and her children returned to Moor Park in 1686.

only thirty-seven, earned himself a reputation as an arrogant man whose sentences were of merciless severity. Few tears were shed when, with no little irony, he died as a prisoner in the Tower three years later.

Shortly after Monmouth's death, it appears that King James may have regretted his hasty action in imprisoning the Duchess and her children for, as compensation for his harsh treatment, he granted the 'Park of Moore' with its mansion, to her and her heirs forever.

But the Duchess seems to have been unmoved by the extravagance of the King's gesture. Legend would have us believe that, still seething over her husband's death and her own incarceration in the Tower, she had all the oak trees in the Park pollarded, supposedly so the King could not use them to build ships for his navy. Such, at least, is the traditional story, and even until the last century, there were still signs that the old oaks had been beheaded. However, the Duchess must have known that to destroy ten times as many trees would not have had the slightest effect on the building of a single man-of-war. Furthermore, it is most unlikely that she would have taken such action as revenge for the execution of a husband who had virtually abandoned her....

Meanwhile, Lady Henrietta Wentworth, having already rejected fortune and privilege in favour of an extended dalliance with the Duke, fell into decline and died nine months after his execution, supposedly of a broken heart.

In 1688 Anna, Monmouth's widow, married Charles, the third Lord Cornwallis and a favourite of William and Mary, who had been invited to rule jointly after James II had been forced to flee to France earlier the same year. Anna bore Cornwallis three children, survived him and, in 1720, elected to spend her last years in Dalkeith, Scotland, having agreed to sell Moor Park to Benjamin Heskin Styles.

A New Look For The Mansion And Gardens:

The new owner's wealth came from the South Sea Trading Company, the infamous get-rich-quick investment institution whose bubble burst, plunging thousands into financial ruin. The company was established in 1711 to relieve the nation's troubled exchequer. A group of wealthy merchants was induced to buy up the floating national dent of £10 million on a

The Cost of Education...

In the early 1700s, education for children of workers on the Moor Park estate was non-existent. The need to teach them the basics of reading and writing was recognised by local churchman John James, and in 1711 he issued an appeal for money which would enable him to open a school. It is recorded that twenty-three people responded with amounts ranging from £8 given by the Duchess of Monmouth (widow of the beheaded Duke) down to five shillings. A sum in excess of £15 was amassed to meet the bills for the first quarter, and the school was duly opened.

government guarantee of six per cent interest and a right to a monopoly of trade in the South Seas.

Despite warnings of its fragility by such financial luminaries as Sir Robert Walpole, it produced an unparalleled number of speculators and shares rose dramatically until a single £200 bond was quoted at £1,000. Styles' brother-in-law Sir John Eyles was a sub-governor of the South Sea company and he therefore had inside knowledge of its limited life. Styles invested his entire fortune, but was tipped off by the governors *before* the bubble burst, enabling him to sell out at a huge profit. He appeared unconcerned that the very dealings which had amassed his fortune had plunged thousands of families into ruin, and his action was probably one of the earliest examples of what is today termed 'insider dealing'.

Styles spent over £150,000 to change dramatically the appearance of Monmouth's mansion, employing Italian Giacomo Leoni to work on the exterior. Leoni re-fronted it, largely as it is today, encasing the entire edifice in Portland stone with a magnificent portico supported by Corinthian columns. He added two wings, comprising a chapel and offices linked to the mansion by collonades in the Tuscan style. Tragically, sixty years later, the collonades were to be torn down in an astonishing display of vandalism by a future owner.

Initially, Styles retained designer-artist Sir James Thornhill to oversee the entire project and also to work on the interior. He also commissioned the famous Italian artist Amiconi to paint the four scenes from Ovid's Metamorphoses, still to be seen in the main hall. (See 'Paintings and Decor').

Because of the vast amount invested in the house itself, it is unlikely that Styles paid much attention to the gardens, and they weren't too ambitious. In any event, they were later to be completely re-designed at vast expense by Admiral Lord Anson.

Styles died at Moor Park in 1739, aged 63, and was buried 'in linen' in the chapel of Moor Park which was never consecrated, and it was eventually pulled down with the collonades. His wife died the following year, but the mansion remained in the Styles family until 1754, with its dignified and stately majesty standing, somewhat peversely, as a monument to one of the most ill-advised and fraudulent financial ventures in the nation's history.

The Sailor, The Gardener And The Vandal:

The new owner of Moor Park was Admiral of the Fleet Lord Anson, who bought it from the Court of Chancery (Styles's trustees). Anson had now retired following a triumphant life at sea, and is probably best remembered, together with Lord Warren, for emaciating the French fleet at the battle of Cape Finisterre in May 1747. The nation celebrated, and George II rewarded him with a peerage and, ultimately, the title of Admiral and Commander-in-Chief of His Majesty's Fleets. Anson had earlier endeared himself to the crown by relieving the Spaniards of £500,000 worth of treasure during the four-year encounter which historians have dubbed as the War of Jenkin's Ear! (Hostilities erupted in 1742 after a Spanish raiding party had boarded a British merchant vessel captained by Robert

The two sides of Lord Anson:
LEFT: A formal study of the land-lover who employed Capability Brown to design the parkland around Moor Park mansion (*National Portrait Gallery*)
RIGHT: History will remember him as the Commander-in-Chief of the King's fleet who defeated the French at Cap Finnistere in 1747.

Jenkins, and cut off his ear). Anson was also responsible, but somewhat less remembered, for introducing the turtle to this country in 1752!

However, in spite of his successes at sea and his popularity at Court, Anson was a man of simple tastes and habits, and would shun the gaiety and high life normally associated with a man of his social standing. Indeed, it is claimed he was so retiring in his manner, that one cynic was moved to suggest that 'while Anson might have been *round* the world, he's never been *in* it!'

Now, at the age of 57 and suffering ill health, he purchased Moor Park as a retirement home, and immediately spent £80,000 on a dramatic re-organisation of the entire park and gardens.

His advisor was Launcelot 'Capability' Brown, a horticultural svengali who had risen from kitchen garden-boy to head gardener at Stowe Park, the home of the Marquis of Buckingham. He worked on many splendid gardens for the aristocracy, and eventually became head gardener at Windsor Castle and Hampton Court. His methods were revolutionary, dispensing with the formal character of symmetry. With little respect for tradition, he swept away generations of horticultural care as he raised mounds, introduced shrubs, plants and even animals from overseas, and planted trees where no other would have dared. He laid out extensive fruit and kitchen gardens and, at Lord Anson's behest, cultivated the celebrated Moor Park apricot, which he had brought back from the East. (The parent tree, incidentally, survived until 1840).

But some of his best work was the planning of 25 acres to the south-east of the house which later became known as the Pleasure Gardens. It was, in effect, a large amphitheatre, with valuable trees and shrubs flanking a water lily lake well stocked with wild fowl.

The south-east front featured an ionic temple which overlooked the lake and was dedicated to the four winds, aptly named Temple Of The Winds, which he built from Portland Stone to match the mansion. In the latter years of his life, Anson would retire to his Temple and gaze for hours across the lake, to the mansion below, surrounded by the Park. Here, he would regail visitors with tales from the sea, and his battles, and after one visit his great friend, lexiographer and wit Dr Samuel Johnson, was moved to write:

> 'A grateful mind I praise. All to the winds he owed
> And so upon the winds, a Temple he bestowed.'

Between them, Anson and Brown destroyed totally the garden created by the Duchess of Bedford, and of which Sir William Temple had written so glowingly in 1685. In any event, this was now old, and probably overgrown.

But it would seem that Brown's capabilities did not impress everyone! Horace Walpole, a celebrated writer and wit of his day, visiting in 1760, was openly contemptuous of it ... 'I was not much struck with it after all the miracles I had heard that Brown had performed there. He has undulated the horizon in so many artificial mole-hills that it is full of unnatural, as if it was done with a rule and compasses.' However, it matured later to become widely admired.

The Temple of the Winds, built by Anson as a tribute to the elements after he had retired from the sea. It was torn down by builders around 1930.

Walpole's appreciation of horticulture clearly fell considerably short of his understanding of literature. He had already inspected the Bedfords' magnificent gardens, but remained unmoved, suggesting that 'any man might design and build as sweet a garden who had been born in and never stirred out of Holborn.'

Lord Anson died in 1762 at the age of 65. In about 1930, The Temple of The Winds was tragically torn down by builders erecting new houses in what is now Temple Gardens, and parts of the old columns can still be seen in the garden of a house built on the site. However, the lake still remains, albeit considerably less ornamental than it was in Anson's day. But Anson may know this, for several people today believe they have seen his ghost walking near the site of the old Temple. . . .

During Anson's ownership, the house had fallen into neglect and, on his death, it passed to his brother, Thomas Anson. In 1763, Thomas Anson sold it to Sir Lawrence Dundas, who had spent eleven years as Commissary-General and Contractor to the Army, and had amassed a considerable fortune victualling the troops for campaigns in Europe, America and India.

Dundas greatly enhanced the interior of the mansion with expensive tapestries and furniture, and commissioned J. P. Cipriani to paint Robert Adam's ornate ceiling in the tapestry gallery (now the main dining room). It is known that this room was greatly admired by the artistically-aware King George IV who, as the young Prince of Wales, was frequently entertained by Sir Lawrence and his family at Moor Park.

Anson's Pleasure Gardens, built for him by Capability Brown, with the Temple of the Winds in the background, before the development of Temple Gardens. (*Copyright Country Life*).

The Crystal Dining Room (left) as it was shown in a Moor Park brochure in the 1940s, showing clearly the ceiling which was designed by Robert Adam, and painted by Cipriani. It was originally used as a Tapestry Gallery.

A study of Robert Adam, (right) attributed to the artist G. Willison circa 1775, about the time the Adam brothers were commissioned to design and build Rickmansworth Lodge for Sir Lawrence Dundas. (*National Portrait Gallery*).

Dundas also commissioned the Adam brothers to build Rickmansworth Lodge, set in delightfully-informal gardens which stretched down to the banks of the River Colne. The Lodge still stands immediately opposite the Rickmansworth entrance to the Park, although it is surrounded by more recent development, and its once-ornate thatched roof has long been replaced by tiles.

Its purpose was two-fold; the small half-moon window at first floor level enabled the Lodge-keeper to challenge the authenticity of visitors before allowing them access to the Park and mansion. At the rear of the Lodge, they built a tea-room, with a high-pitched octagonal roof, and the gently undulating lawns suggest that it might at one time have been a duckery. The Lodge is a classic example of the work of the Adam brothers, and is a listed building. However, in the 1960s, it was sympathetically extended in the Adam style by a local builder, and it is a testimony to his craftsmanship that this new work is also governed by a protection order.

On Sir Lawrence's death in 1781, the estate passed to his son, Sir Thomas Dundas who, in 1785 sold Moor Park to Thomas Bates-Rous.

You Take The High Road...

In Daniel Patterson's 'New and Accurate Descriptions of all the Direct and Principal Roads in England and Wales' printed in 1794, the route from London to Rickmansworth is recorded thus: 'Paddington – Kilburn – Hyde – Edgware – Stanmore – Hatch End to Pinner Green, where, beyond the windmill you turn right over the common to Northwood, Bacher Heath and Rickmansworth.'

Rickmansworth Lodge, or the Thatched House as it was known, from the rear, prior to the development of Moor Lane.

Moor Park mansion as it looked before Rous tore down the collanades.

If ever one man vandalised a stately home of unequalled beauty and architectural merit, then it was Thomas Bates-Rouse, a director of the East India Company. He destroyed much of Styles's work by pulling down the collonades, and the wings containing the chapel and offices. He built large kitchens underground, and did much to wreck the symmetry of the mansion.

Why? Nobody knows for sure, but one account suggests that he was short of money and hoped to improve his situation by selling the materials. In reality, this claim can be virtually discounted, since it is unlikely that a director of such a prominent and successful company would find himself in such a dire financial situation. In any event, he would have been able to raise a considerable amount by using the mansion as collateral ... It is recorded, however, that he regretted his actions to the last, and attempted to atone for his error of judgement by building the Orangery, which is now the professional's shop.

Bates-Rouse died old and childless in 1799 (he is buried in Rickmansworth churchyard) and in 1801 it was sold by his widow to 66-year-old Robert Williams.

Williams was extremely popular with all who met him and worked for him. He was MP for Dorchester, and a successful banker and shipowner. When he died at Moor Park in the winter of 1814, a heavy fall of snow prevented his body being taken back to be buried in the family vault in Dorchester, and he was consequently interred in Rickmansworth Church.

The estate passed to his son, also Robert Williams, who succeeded his father as MP for Dorchester. His mother moved from the mansion to Moor House, which some reports have erroneously claimed was the elegant mansion supposedly built by the Duchess of Bedford in 1620. Whether it was a Lodge, or Dower House is uncertain, but she was to be its last occupant, for it was destined to be pulled down after her death....

The younger Robert Williams made several alterations and improvements to both the mansion and the estate, but reports that it was Williams, and *not* Sir Lawrence Dundas, who built Rickmansworth Lodge can be totally discounted. Robert Adam died in 1792 and, while Williams was a man of some influence, even he would have wilted at the challenge of commissioning work from someone who had expired 22 years earlier! However, there is little doubt that Williams *did* spend a considerable sum on improving the estate, and it seems that he invested more than he could afford. Funds became rapidly diminished, enforcing a return to Dorchester and, in 1825, the estate was once again offered for sale.

During 1826–27 many farms on the manor passed into new hands, but the Park and mansion remained unsold until 1828 when it was bought by Robert, the second Earl of Grosvenor, later to become the first Marquis of Westminster, and with this transaction, another chapter in Moor Park's history unfolds....

CHAPTER FOUR

The Grosvenors And The Ebury Title

The 'Le Grosveneur' family is one of unbroken male descent from the time of the Norman conquest, and their motto 'Nobilitatis Virtue non Stemmacharacter' (Virtue, not pedigree, is the characteristic of nobility) can be seen on their coat of arms over the front portico of the mansion.

Robert, the second Earl, made considerable alterations to the grounds, enlarging and redesigning the gardens at the rear of the house with such a strong Latin flavour that were named 'the Italian gardens.' He also built the North terrace which, for generations has been known as 'Wolsey's Walk', although there is little to suggest that the venerable Cardinal ever made a habit of gracing this particular area of the Park. The terrace, once flanked by one of Capability Brown's magnificent copper beech trees which split and had to be removed many years ago, is adjacent to what is now the short 13th on the West course. Sadly, its wide promenade, the stone balustrades, statues and steps pay little homage to the age of opulence in which they were conceived and built. Today, the pieces of scarred, cracked and crumbling masonry stand only as a monument to vandalism or, perhaps worse, the apathy of man.

Even the stone seats at either end of the terrace, which date from the William and Mary period and were moved there from another site in the Park, are in an extremely sad state. The large bronze vases which adorned

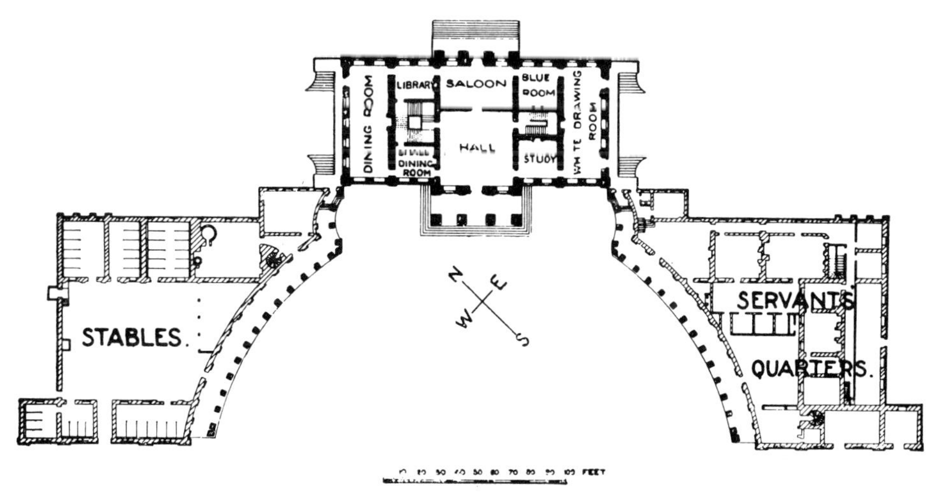

A plan of the manion as rebuilt by Benjamin Styles in 1720.

Robert, the second Earl of Grosvenor, later to become the first Marquis of Westminster, purchased Moor Park in 1828, and was father of the first Lord Ebury. These sketches, complete with deletion marks, were early roughs prepared for a sculpture of the Earl by the artist F. Chantry. (*National Portrait Gallery*).

the terrace wall for one hundred years disappeared without trace during the war, and the once-ornate fountain-statue of Neptune, carved in London in 1785 but installed by the Grosvenors some years later, lies in ruin, its cracked and headless body half-hidden by weeds.

The Earl also devoted his attention to Anson's pleasure garden, encompassing it with a terrace wall and adding several more valuable and ornamental trees from abroad. It was also Grosvenor who built the large ornamental archway at Batchworth Heath, the principal entrance to the Park, although the huge iron gates have long since disappeared.

The North terrace, which can still be seen adjacent to the short 13th on the West course, was just one of many innovations and improvements introduced to Moor Park by the Grosvenors. (*Copyright Country Life*).

The second Earl was elevated to the title of first Marquis of Westminster as part of the coronation celebrations of William IV in 1831. When he died in 1845, the Moor Park estate passed to his third and youngest son, Lord Robert Grosvenor. It is here, with the man destined to become the first Lord Ebury, that we start perhaps the most significant chapter in the history of Moor Park....

Born in 1801, Robert Grosvenor's life was to span nearly all of the nineteenth century during which he earned the reputation of being 'a statesman, philanthropist, good landlord and friend of great influence.'

However, it would appear that this future pillar of society was something of a rake in his early days. Born at Millbank House, between Westminster and Vauxhall Bridge, he was educated at Westminster School and Christ Church, Oxford, and soon learned to use his good looks and dashing personality to advantage.

He became an attractive and fashionable target for both single and married society ladies of the day and historians suggest that, as a young man, much of his life was dedicated to the pursuit of pleasure. Even before his University days, his penchant for high living had earned him the nick-name 'Reveller Bob' from members of his family. However, his lifestyle was to change dramatically in later years....

Robert was born into a life of politics and, as a young man of 24, he was chosen as one of the diplomatic aides to represent Britain at the crowning of the new Czar of Russia. Later, he represented first Shaftesbury, and then Chester, in Parliament.

He married the Hon Charlotte Arbuthnot Wellesley, niece of the Duke of Wellington, at St George's Church, Hanover Square, in 1831, the same year in which his father had become first Marquis of Westminster. But the marriage did more than merely curtail his frivolous activities – it was to link the Grosvenor name to one of the most infamous scandals to involve 19th-century aristocracy....

Charlotte's father was Sir Henry Wellesley, Britain's Ambassador to Spain. He was one of four brothers – Richard (the Marquis) and Arthur (the Duke of Wellington who defeated Napoleon at Waterloo) were older, while Gerald, who took Holy Orders, was two years his junior.

It appears that Henry and Gerald Wellesley were seen as highly eligible suitors to two attractive sisters, the Ladies Charlotte and Emily Cadogan. Henry married the Lady Charlotte and, in a frenetic five-year period, they had four children – three boys and a daughter who was also named Charlotte. Gerald completed the Wellesley-Cadogan foursome by marrying Lady Emily.

A Drive to Remember

On June 16th, 1833, Grosvenor held a magnificent fete to honour the visit of King William IV and Queen Adelaide. The event was attended by 20,000 people who mingled with the invited nobility on a cloudless summer's day. The Royal party toured the house, and later drove along a drive specially constructed for the occasion. This was later known as 'King's Drive', but is now sadly hidden beneath fairways.

The Italian Gardens at the rear of the mansion were introduced shortly after the Earl of Grosvenor purchased Moor Park and remained a feature of the grounds until the estate was sold in 1919. This photograph was taken in 1912. (*Copyright Country Life*).

It seems, however, that life with the enormously wealthy but notoriously staid Wellesley men soon began to lose some of its appeal for the sisters, particularly Lady Charlotte. She became involved in an amorous dalliance on the side, and the young child Charlotte and her brothers, acutely sensible to their parents discord, were suddenly removed from their Grosvenor House home in Mayfair (now the site of a hotel) to a large house in Putney, where they were placed in the charge of a nanny.

At first, the Wellesleys were able to smother rumours of the indiscretion, but Lady Charlotte clearly found the charms of her amorata quite irresistible. In 1809, barely two years after baby Charlotte was born, the news leaked out and London society was stunned by the revelation that Lady Charlotte Wellesley had taken a lover. The subject of her amorous indiscretion was the dashing Henry Paget, created Marquis of Anglesey following his successful exploits at Waterloo. The clandestine affair had already lasted well over two years, with Lady Charlotte meeting Paget in Half Moon Street, Mayfair, from where they would take a cab to borrowed rooms in Mount Street.

Society, however, was surprisingly sympathetic towards Lady Charlotte, perhaps understanding her need to find an outlet for her emotions after the frustrations of living with Sir Henry Wellesley, later described as 'a replica in marble.'

Paget was clearly a man of social nerve as well as sexual appetite. He was also cited as correspondent in the divorce of Emily, Lady Charlotte's sister, and was busily engaged in divorcing his own wife at the time. It is also extremely possible, because of the timing of the affair, that the young Charlotte, later to become the first Lady Ebury and reside at Moor Park, was not the child of Wellesley, but the bastard offspring of the liaison between Lady Charlotte and the rampant Paget, Earl of Anglesey.

Even with this knowledge, Sir Henry Wellesley showed compassion to the last. When Lady Charlotte arrived at her former home in Curzon Street penniless, bedraggled and pregnant with Paget's child (after Paget had been sent abroad on the Walcheren Expedition), he offered to take her back. She accepted temporary refuge, but declined his more permanent offer, and Lady Charlotte eventually divorced Wellesley to become Lady Anglesey.

Whether or not the first Lady Ebury was base-born is a matter of conjecture. It is clear, however, that she recalled vividly the knowing winks and whispered innuendos of the Wellesley's servants, and the possibility was magnified throughout her life by the certain knowledge that she was the daughter of a society adulteress.

When her brothers were sent to Ireland to be educated, the young Charlotte remained at home and was pushed along a chain of governesses. Later, she travelled with her father to Madrid when he was appointed Ambassador to Spain. When her father married again, this time to Georgiana, sister of the Marquis of Salisbury, she found herself partially rejected by her new stepmother who appeared unable to accept a child of such scandalous heredity. However, in later years they became very close and Charlotte entertained both her mother and her stepmother, albeit separately!

By the age of seventeen, she had developed into a most attractive young woman, no doubt inheriting something of her mother's dazzling beauty.

Waterloo hero Henry Paget, later to become first Earl of Anglesey, whose passionate affair with the mother of the first Lady Ebury shocked society and cast doubts upon her parentage. (*National Portrait Gallery*).

She was slightly built, with long light reddish curls and blue eyes. She was also a most accomplished dancer and her stepmother, seeing the chance to rid herself of an embarrassment, decided it would be in everyone's interest if she were married off swiftly. She was consequently offered on the marriage market long before she was ready, by way of hunt balls and county ensembles, but always closely chaperoned.

By now, Charlotte's sheltered upbringing was beginning to show. With her natural shyness she found it difficult to make friends and, while there were several offers of marriage, none was deemed suitable. At the age of 21, she was sent to Vienna to broaden her outlook and, although names were never revealed, it is believed that this is where she had her first disastrous love affair.

It was while in Vienna that she was first introduced to Robert Grosvenor in 1829, and he decided immediately that they should marry. When Charlotte returned from Vienna, she was invited to the Grosvenor's home at Eaton, near Chester, where she made a great impression on the family.

A Pony-tale...

Charges for passing through turnpike gates were unpopular – particularly with blacksmith Alfred Hodgkisson, reputed to be the strongest man in Hertfordshire. His forge was next to Ye Olde Greene Manne on Batchworth Heath and, when passing through the old 'Qu'ferry Turnpike' on Kewferry Hill, he would hoist his pony onto his shoulders and *carry* it through the gate to avoid paying a toll.

Grosvenor admired Anson's Pleasure Garden, and greatly improved the appearance by encompassing it with a stone wall, remains of which are still evident behind the first tee on the High course. Access was by a pathway, part of which was replaced by tennis courts in the 1920s. (*Copyright Country Life*).

After their marriage in 1831, the 'young Grosvenors' (as they were now called), moved into 35, Park Street, W.1. and this was to be their home for the next fourteen years. It is known that Charlotte would secretly entertain her profligate mother, Lady Anglesey, at this address, but there is no record of her ever having visited Moor Park.

Life for the young Grosvenors was fun. They were popular at parties, and the extrovert Robert was such an enthusiastic and capable partipant in 'lounge theatricals', that one influential onlooker expressed regret that he had not become an actor!

The Rake's Progress:

It was at this stage that Robert Grosvenor's career began to take off. He held various posts in the Royal Household during two separate periods (1830–4 and 1846–7) and in 1837, as a Privy Councillor, was among those summoned to witness Queen Victoria's accession to the throne. Throughout his political life he was a staunch Liberal, and supported the administrations of Canning, Goderich, Wellington, Grey and Melbourne. He was eventually raised to the peerage by Lord Melbourne in 1857 as Baron Ebury of Ebury Manor in Middlesex.

The derivation of the Ebury title goes back to the late seventeenth century when one of the Grosvenors – Sir Thomas – contributed greatly to the family fortune by marrying Miss Mary Davies, heiress to the manor of Ebury. This embraced much of west London, particularly the more fashionable areas of Belgravia and Pimlico which, in turn, furnished the title of Marquis of Westminster bestowed upon the Earl of Grosvenor in 1831.

A Journalist Remembers...

Writing in the West Herts and Watford Observer (26.9.1941) F. H. Barnes records that Queen Victoria, Prince Albert and the Queen Dowager (Queen Adelaide, widow of William IV who was then residing at Cassiobury) and several others of the Royal family visited Grosvenor at Moor Park. He also describes Grosvenor (who became the first Lord Ebury when he was raised to the peerage on 10th September, 1857) as 'a moral and ecclesiastical reformer, a churchman of the evangelical type, and a steady supporter of the Liberal party. He also showed a very commendable interest in the welfare of the neighbourhood.'

NOTE: Frank H. Barnes joined the editorial staff of the Watford Observer in 1896, became editor shortly after the First World War, and remained there until October 1941 – just a month after this article appeared. As a young reporter he landed perhaps the greatest scoop in the paper's history when he was tipped off about an inquest at Leavesden hospital. The inquest heralded the trial and ultimate execution at St Albans of Mary Ansell who was found guilty of poisoning her mentally-ill sister in order to gain insurance proceeds of £22.10s.0d to pay for her own wedding. The case captured the interest of newspapers across the world.

Barnes died at 64.

Robert Grosvenor, third son of the Earl, and the man destined to become the first Lord Ebury.

Robert and Charlotte Grosvenor moved into Moor Park in 1845, on the death of the Marquis of Westminster, and inherited much of the furniture which had been originally bought by the Dundas family who had last occupied the mansion sixty years earlier. Surprisingly, although much of it was built by the fabled Robert Adam, it was not to the Grosvenors' taste and it was found in the attic in 1922 wrapped in copies of The Times dated 1845. Although much of it was shipped to America, it was bought back for the nation by a philanthropist dealer, and is now in Kenwood House.

New furniture was bought, new fittings for oil and gas lamps replaced the Adam torchères, a billiard table and harmonium were installed and 'a hideous druggett of red and yellow felt' was laid in the hall. Racks for billiard cues and croquet mallets stood beneath Amiconi's paintings of the 'Loves of Jupiter', and it seemed that the mansion was once again geared to echo to the sound of fun and laughter – this time from the Grosvenors' seven children Robert, Tommy, Norman, Algy, Dick and the two girls named after the Queen and Prince Consort, Victoria and Albertine.

When they moved into Moor Park, the eldest of the Grosvenor offspring, yet another Robert, was nearly twelve years old. Known simply as 'Bo', he was the natural heir to the Ebury estate, but it would be a further forty-eight years before he would inherit the mansion and accede to the title. Later, in July 1867, at the age of thirty-three, he married the Hon Emilie White, daughter of the first Lord Annaly, and they were to have five children of their own.

The Grosvenor's second son, Tommy, went into the diplomatic service and while in China he met and married American socialite Sophie Wells Williams from Boston. At first, Lady Charlotte was horrified at the idea of American blood mingling with that of the Grosvenor aristocracy, but eventually she relented and Sophie was accepted as one of the family. After Tommy's death from pneumonia in Petersburgh at a tragically young age, Sophie remained with the Grosvenors both at Moor Park and in London, throughout her life, and was to become a firm favourite with her entourage of nephews and nieces.

Norman, their third son and Charlotte's favourite, was a brilliant musician. After a long engagement, he married Caroline Stuart Wortley, a talented young painter and writer. After being stifled for several years at Moor Park, they broke the mold by moving, at their own instigation, to a house in Green Street, Mayfair, where they could paint, compose and entertain their musician friends. The decision met with approval from Lady Ebury on the understanding that they conducted their lives in London 'without contravening the conventions of their class.' Later, with two growing daughters, Susan (who became Baroness Tweedsmuir) and Margaret, they found the house too small and moved to 30, Upper Grosvenor Street. Sadly, the Norman Grosvenors were married for only seventeen years before he died of inoperable cancer.

The Grosvenors' two younger sons were Algy, who at one time served as an officer in the Rifle Brigade, and Dick, who became a barrister. The two daughters of the marriage, Victoria ('Siss') and Albertine, known simply as 'B', could not have been more different. Victoria, the elder of the two by twelve years, was obese, robust and strong-willed, while her sister was slightly-built, with fragile health and a permanent limp.

Victoria's great love was to drive her ponies and trap through the Park at high speed. She adored horses and was frequently at odds with her brothers over her apparent domination of the stables, and her insistence that the animals should not be overworked. She had a powerful personality but, as a Grosvenor daughter, had little or no responsibility. This clearly rankled with her, and she appears to have spent much of her

I am the Very Model...

Sir William S. Gilbert, whose comic operettas written with Sir Arthur Sullivan are universally known, was a great friend of the Grosvenor family in general, and of the music-loving Norman in particular. Apart from being a brilliant lyricist, Gilbert was also a highly competent artist and his impromptu sketch of 'Norman Resting' captures the subject to perfection. The drawing remained a valued piece of trivia among the Grosvenor art collection for years.

time locked in verbal battle with Emilie (who was the wife of Robert and liked to be called Minnie) probably over the behaviour of the children, for whom Victoria had little or no time. Albertine, on the other hand, was far less aggressive, but is remembered for being 'quietly obstinate.' Both spoke fluent French and Italian, but they were not well read. There were never any books lying around the Grosvenor home, merely volumes standing regimented but unopened on shelves, behind metal grilles.

The large dining room, photographed during the time of the second Lord Ebury, showing the magnificent carved stone fireplace which 'disappeared' during alterations. (*Copyright Country Life*).

On their father's death in 1893, neither sister was keen to remain under the new regime at Moor Park, and they shocked the family by announcing that they were leaving England to become missionaries in Japan and Assyria. It took some persuasive talking to convince them that, with Victoria's weight problem and Albertine's failing health and poor mobility, their christian intentions might be more wisely directed closer to home. Instead, they moved temporarily into the Thatched House (Rickmansworth Lodge) and later took a house in Cheyne Walk where they remained until their deaths, a year apart, in 1913 and 1914.

The seven Grosvenor children appear to have spent most of their time together, revelling in the freedom of their surroundings which were so different from London. It was a life of opulence, a life of plenty and, in future years, a life that would have to be geared to cater for a new generation of little Grosvenors who, like their parents before them, would chase each other up the cedar staircase, and gallop around the galleried landing of the mansion....

The days of opulence and taste: The main hall as it was in 1912, during the ownership of the second Lord Ebury. The saddle, to the right of the central doorway, once belonged to Cardinal Wolsey. (*Copyright Country Life*).

Before he became the first Lord Ebury, Lord Robert Grosvenor clearly enjoyed life as head of his own mini-kingdom. He always dressed immaculately, mostly in black, with a high white collar, and insisted upon being referred to as 'His Lordship' behind his back or simply 'Lordship' to his face. He would lead family prayers in the hall before breakfast each

morning, demanding that all staff must attend, with the exception of the most junior kitchen maid whose task was to remain alert to the food on the stove. When relaxing, he showed a preference for whist or billiards but, while he had a reputation for being good-humoured, he was also notoriously strict with his children.

Caroline Stuart Wortley, who later married Norman, Charlotte's favourite son, wrote about 'the meek way in which the five sons and two daughters spent the day in each other's company, sat for three lengthy meals around the dining room table, and at night received their bedroom candlesticks from their father, and finished the day talking in front of their bedroom fires, all without rebelling.'

This severity seemed to dilute their natural bouyancy; as the years passed there seemed to be far less spontaneous fun, as though all seven were perhaps in fear of incurring his Lordship's wrath. Only in the harshest winter, when the lake in Anson's Pleasure Garden had frozen over, would the Grosvenor boys really appear to unwind and enjoy themselves. They would brush the ice and spend hours figure-skating, each upright with his arms folded in classic pose....

Her Enigmatic Ladyship

But it wasn't only the former *bon viveur* Robert Grosvenor whose lifestyle had undergone a total transformation. Charlotte, whose dislike of the grandeur life had already made her more serious in her attitude, now became even more frugal in her expenditure. For some years she had tried, with considerable success, to strengthen the serious side of Robert's nature at the expense of his natural levity. Perhaps, with the passing of the old Earl, she had been affected by the realisation that they were now guardians of great and untapped wealth; whatever the reason, she over-reacted, becoming withdrawn and stifled by a shroud of solemnity of her own making. She desperately neeed people, but would never let herself go; it was almost as though the shame of her mother's past was forbidding her to enjoy the position of influence and privilege in which she now found herself. Her two abiding passions were her religion and, later in life, her grandchildren, and these accounted for a large part of her day. Apart from these, she found little solace in anything but fresh air, her garden and homeopathy. Even her love for music which, with her laughter, she had brought to the Grosvenor household many years earlier, was silenced,

Read All About It...

It would appear that the safety of 'Lord Ebury's Railway', linking his estate with Watford, was giving cause for concern in its inaugural year. In the first issue of the Watford Observer, published on January 24th, 1863, there appears under the heading 'Rickmansworth' the following item:

'The Railway – We have heard all kinds of vague rumours in reference to this circuitous route; we cannot believe half of them. Let our nervous friends take courage, the bridge has been rendered secure, or the company would not run a train.'

A close study of one of the two magnificent side tables which were a feature of the Eburys' hall, showing the ornate carving and gilt-work. (*Copyright Country Life*).

presumably because she now regarded it as too frivolous. Indeed, so serious minded did she eventually become, that Disraeli was moved to write: 'Lady Ebury said she lived for climate and the affections, two good things, but this is not much to build a character on.'

Her style of dress was always black, simple and practical, far removed from the high fashions favoured by her social contemporaries. Later, she even started to ration heating and light, insisting that fresh air was as good in the house as out of it. She was liberal with fruit and vegetables, but became frugal with meat rations, and before long, laughter too, was in short supply...

Lady Ebury's apparent frugality is something of an enigma. She was loved by the entire family and it is unlikely that anyone whose lifestyle was conducted in a miserly fashion would have commanded such respect. An answer is offered by her grand-daughter Susan, Baroness Tweedsmuir

The Urban Mr Lomas...

Like many other prominent properties on the manor, the Ebury's home at Moor Park came under the administration (such as it was) of Rickmansworth 'Council' who would meet in the church vestry. But things progressed in 1884 when the town said goodbye to Vestry administration and became a Parish Council, with local solicitor Henry Lomas as its first clerk. A man of vision, he immediately campaigned for Urban status, and the town was upgraded four years later. This meant that, for the first time, councillors were elected by ballot rather than by a show of hands which had been the case under Parish legislation. Fittingly, Lomas was appointed as first clerk of the new Rickmansworth U.D.C.

(daughter of Norman and Caroline Grosvenor), in her book 'The Lilac and the Rose': 'Her austere black clothes were fashioned for hard and long wear, for all her spare money went secretly to the poor. Her whole life was lived unobtrusively for others, and was illumined by a religion which glowed through her daily actions like sunshine through a fine stained-glass window.'

However, these tales of thriftiness among the Grosvenor family are confirmed by the Eburys' *great*-grandaughter Alice Buchan, who recounts that His Lordship would call family meetings to discuss expenditure; bedroom fires were banned from March to October, pieces of coal in bedroom scuttles were counted, and Charlotte was limited to only one oil lamp in the white lounge (now the main bar) where the ladies would gather after dinner, often tripping over the stools in the gloom.

The period of self-imposed austerity reached a farcical level when Albertine, the younger of the two Grosvenor sisters, was ordered to abandon her canary because it was consuming too much bird-seed!

By the time he was bestowed with the title of the first Lord Ebury in 1857, Robert Grosvenor had succumbed totally to his wife's influence. He had become deeply religious and completed the transition from 'a wild young man in the highest fashion of his day' to a dedicated Low Churchman. It was due largely to his influence and benevolence that Holy Trinity Church, Northwood, had already been built ...

When the new church was due to be consecrated by the Bishop of London in January 1854, a particularly heavy snowstorm delayed the clergy bearing the official forms of service, forcing the Bishop to improvise. The missing minister eventually arrived, frozen and bedraggled, halfway through the service and it transpired he had, quite literally, been stuck in the snow, and parishioners had to dig him out. It seems that the tight restraints which his Lordship imposed upon his own family didn't apply outside, for the following day over one hundred 'helpers' were dined in the Orangery at Moor Park.

Lord Ebury adopted Holy Trinity in preference to Rickmansworth Parish Church, and would insist that his family and staff attended every Sunday morning service. At 11 am. precisely he would turn to ensure that there were no absentees from the pews reserved for Moor Park retainers.

Differing religious views have a sad history of precipitating wars, revolutions and assassinations. Even in the Grosvenor household, the subject could be relied upon to detonate nothing less than fierce debate. Lord Ebury's support of the Low Church was most distressing to his wife

Fair Rickmansworth...

In 1862, the population of Rickmansworth (which included large areas of the Ebury estate) was recorded as less than 5,000. It was seen as a typically English market town, if somewhat isolated, with two turnpike roads linking it to the main supply towns of Watford and Uxbridge. It boasted three fairs a year (cattle events in July and November, and a 'statute' fair in September) when merchandise and amusement stalls would be a feature of Church Street, stretching from the High Street to Bury Lane.

Charlotte and their two daughters Victoria and Albertine, all of whom were dedicated to the doctrine of the High Church. Ebury would defend his views against a broadside from the three women and would delight in infuriating them further by insisting that the minister from Northwood should be summoned to Moor Park to hold a personal communion for him.

However, they must have found common ground somewhere, for Victoria was a keen supporter of Holy Trinity, where she played the organ and conducted the choir for many years.

One of Ebury's few unrealised ambitions was to undertake a complete revision of the Prayer Book, but he came up against strong opposition from the Church who felt that the style of his suggested changes was far too radical. He was also a noted Parliamentary campaigner and successfully fought for the Ten Hours Factory Bill, and also proposed and carried (after a tough battle) the Bill restricting County elections to one day. He also introduced the Bill prohibiting payment of voters' expenses by candidates.

It appears, though, that he was sadly out of touch with the views of the electorate on one major issue. His attempt to enforce observation of the Sabbath by banning all Sunday trading and closing the pubs caused riots in London, during which the windows of his town house were smashed by a hostile crowd.

But Ebury's concern for the morals of the nation were more than matched by his interest in the well-being of those closer to home, which extended far beyond merely their spiritual development. He was acutely aware of the need for basic education and, in 1861, he built Holy Trinity Church School. It remained the only elementary school for children aged between five and fourteen in Northwood until the opening of Half Mile Lane Infants School in 1899. Half-mile Lane was subsequently known as Clifton Road, Church Road, and now, the High Street. The school closed in 1975.

The Park was freely open to anyone who wished to walk through its thickly-wooded acres, and Lord Ebury would host regular 'Harvest Home' dinners for around 90 agricultural workers each September. He also willingly opened his grounds for Horticultural Shows and other local gatherings.

The Train Now Standing...

The first Lord Ebury actively supported the call for better communications for Rickmansworth, and he is credited with fathering the idea of a rail link with Watford. Opened in 1862, 'Lord Ebury's Railway' was built and owned by the London and N.W. Railway Company, and provided a single track between Church Street and Watford High Street for which travellers were charged the sum of sixpence ha'penny. Development of the Metropolitan railway necessitated the building of the current Rickmansworth station in 1887, and the line was eventually closed in 1952. The defunct station became a clothing factory, then a printing works before being demolished in 1970 to make way for development of the Skidmore Way council estate. Plans for a similar link between Rickmansworth and Uxbridge were proposed a little later, but got no further than the drawing-board.

The Manor Comes Home

In 1866, he bought the *Manor* from the Rt Hon T. H. S. Sotheron Estcourt, to reunite the two parts of the estate for the first time since 1663 – two hundred and three years. He had always shown a keen interest in the history of the Park and mansion and had amassed a number of historical documents, letters and manuscripts. In 1870, he entrusted these to a Rickmansworth parson, the Rev. Robert Bayne, thus enabling him to write in 1871 an accurate history of the estate.

He was a keen sportsman ... he loved cricket and, until Northwood Cricket Club took over its current ground at the beginning of this century, matches were played at Park Farm and also on Lord Ebury's pitch at Moor Park. He also ran his own cricket team which comprised his family, estate workers and servants.

Perhaps more pertinently, he was aware of the increasing popularity of golf. In the 1880s, he had his own private course designed and laid out in the parkland surrounding the mansion. But by now he was an old man, and it is unlikely, therefore, that he could claim credit for being first to tee off on any Moor Park course. That unique distinction is more likely to have been claimed by his son, Robert. (See the chapter on Golf).

By 1880, Charlotte, Lady Ebury, had become a frail lady of 73 with failing sight. Although she lived for another eleven years, she did not enjoy good health and was convinced to the last that the aristocracy had never forgiven her for the amorous philanderings of her mother. She is buried in the churchyard of Holy Trinity, Northwood, which she and her husband had built over 30 years earlier.

Remarkably, Lord Ebury declined to attend his wife's funeral, claiming that the weather was too cold. Afterwards, mourners returned to Moor Park to find that he had remained in the mansion and read the burial service to a 'congregation' of two – his sister-in-law and the kitchenmaid!

Lord Ebury died in 1893 aged 92, having survived his wife by two years, and was buried alongside her in Holy Trinity churchyard. Until the end, he remained a dignified and compassionate statesman who had time to talk to anyone, pauper or potentate, never varying his display of impeccable manners.

If there was one minor criticism levelled at him during his lifetime, it was that he seemed to know everyone in a position of influence, and would adopt a fierce and almost tribal loyalty towards them. His apologetic defence to this charge was that the aristocratic world was so small that it was almost impossible *not* to be related to everyone in it...

The Second Lord Ebury

He was succeeded by his eldest son, Lord Robert Grosvenor, who was 59 years old by the time he acceded to the title of the second Lord Ebury. He was born at the family home at Eaton, Cheshire, and later educated at Harrow and King's College, London, after which he served with both the Life Guards and the Cheshire Yeomanry, retiring with the rank of Captain.

Later, he sat as a Liberal M.P. from 1865–1874, thus combining his father's love of politics with an acute business brain which he channelled into banking and commerce. He was a noted Parliamentary orator, delivering his speeches with controlled power, and always in perfect English. In later years, he was to split with the Liberal Party in favour of the Tories. For the period immediately prior to the First World War, he was chairman of the West Herts Conservative Party. His commercial interests were broad and, in addition to a thirty-seven year spell as chairman of the Army and Navy Stores, he held directorships with the Havana Cigar and Tobacco Company, Webley and Scott, and Van Den Burghs Ltd.

Another aspect of the main hall (*Copyright Country Life*).

He was also a great benefactor to local communities, and did much to help put the embryonic Northwood on the map by building Kewferry Road and providing land for broadening development around the Sandy Lodge area. Rickmansworth also benefitted greatly from his philanthropic nature. In 1902 he built Ebury Hall, primarily for the use of social functions organised by the Church, and six years later gave two acres for the building of Rickmansworth recreation ground.

He loved all sport but, for the second Lord Ebury, golf was the all-consuming passion. When returning to Moor Park from the House of Lords, or a business meeting in London, he would be met by his coach at Northwood station (Sandy Lodge Halt had not yet been built, and even when it was, the Eburys refused to use it!) and be driven to the Batchworth Heath entrance of the Park. Regularly, he would pause to change his jacket and his shoes, remove his golf clubs from his coach, and play his way back to the mansion.

In later years, when his trips to London became less frequent, he would spend hours in his beloved Pleasure Gardens, gazing across the lake from Anson's Temple, marvelling at the colours of the strutting peacocks, and the white blanket of snowdrops which were an unforgettable feature to anyone who saw them. And in harsh winters, when the lake had frozen over, he would ask to be pushed around on his specially-adapted ice-chair, his mind perhaps returning to a time, some seventy years earlier, when the five Grosvenor boys, tall, proud and erect, would skate their frustrations away...

Like his father, the second Ebury was a keen churchman, but opted to frequent St Mary the Virgin in Rickmansworth during his lifetime, rather than Holy Trinity in Northwood which had become the Eburys' family shrine.

By the time he acceded to the Ebury title in 1893, most of his five children had reached maturity, if not the age of majority. His son and heir, Robert Victor, was already 25, followed by Hughie, Maudie, Alice and Francis, who was just ten at the time. However, the jinx which had cost Lord Ebury two of his brothers – Tommy and Norman – in the prime of their lives, was about to strike again...

Northwood Awakes...

When Mount Vernon Hospital opened its current site in 1904, it's official name was The Country Branch of the North London Consumption Hospital. It was originally opened in Hampstead as a hospital 'for the relief of the Consumptive Poor', and later moved to larger premises, also in Hampstead, called Mount Vernon. The move to the Batchworth area of Northwood was prompted by the view that patients suffering from tuberculosis were 'better served by the fresh air of a country environment' and, with the aid of a £100,000 gift, the foundation stone was laid in 1902. The first secretary was W. J. Morton who, when not devoting himself to caring for the body at the Hospital, would dedicate himself to matters spiritual, caring for the soul at Holy Trinity Church where, as a successor to the Hon. Victoria Grosvenor, he was organist and choirmaster from 1914–18.
The hospital was converted to specialise in the treatment of malignant diseases in 1929, and ten years later was designated as a General Hospital. It was absorbed into the National health Service in 1946.

Robert Grosvenor, the second Lord Ebury. He acceded to the title in 1893 and continued to combine his passion for golf with his love of commerce and politics until his death in 1918.

Emilie, the second lady Ebury. They were married for 51 years and had five children.

His second son, Hughie, was a foreign diplomat and a compulsive gambler who had run into debt well over his head. Ebury bailed him out on the understanding that it was the first and last time. But to Hughie, it was an incurable disease. He continued gambling and again found himself in dire financial trouble. This time, rather than go to his father for help thus exposing his weakness, he took what he considered to be the honourable way out and shot himself in Vienna.

The second Lord Ebury died in 1918, the year after he and Lady Emilie celebrated their Golden wedding, and is buried in Holy Trinity churchyard with his wife and family. However, it is known that during his lifetime he had expressed a wish to be buried in the Temple of the Winds, the edifice built by Lord Anson and dedicated to the elements some 160 years earlier. Unfortunately for Ebury, the 'Temple' was unconsecrated ground, and ecclesiastical forces persuaded his family that it might be better, in his

In Case of Fire...

It was Dr W. Henderson of Basing House who suggested in 1869 that Rickmansworth should have a volunteer fire-fighting force. (Until then, the Parish overseers were responsible for tackling blazes, often with disastrous results.) A public meeting was called, and attended by interested parties from neighbouring towns, and the Rickmansworth volunteer brigade proved so successful that it was hailed as 'second only to London.'

Lordship's long-term spiritual interests at least, if he were to be buried in Northwood in the grounds of the Church built by his father.

On Lord Ebury's death, Lady Ebury remained at Moor Park for more than a year before moving to Batchworth House, on the corner of Harefield Road, with its rear entrance opposite the White Bear. Part of the original boundary wall can still be seen.

Moor Park had now become the property of Lord Robert Victor Grosvenor, who took the title of the third Baron Ebury, and it was he who put the entire manor, embracing 3,000 acres, up for auction in September 1919. Shortly afterwards, Moor Park, together with the mansion, was purchased for a fraction of its true value by Lord Leverhulme, the industrialist who founded Port Sunlight on the Mersey, and represented the Wirral constituency as a Liberal from 1906 until 1910.

It was just before Leverhulme stepped in to convert it to an American-style country club, that Susan Charlotte Grosvenor, (daughter of Norman and Caroline) returned to the place of her childhood for a sad, valedictory visit:

'A statue of Neptune, brown with age, with a pitcher in his hand from which water trickled, sat comfortably gazing in front of him, head engulfed in a Portugese laurel, whose embrace became more urgent as time went on. I parted the branches and looked at him as he sat, entirely hidden. My grown-up years rolled away for a moment as I gazed down at a basin full of brown water, stiff dead laurel leaves, and wriggling tadpoles. It was just the same as ever.'

The first two Lord Eburys will be remembered as statesmen who contributed greatly to the historical mystique and heritage of Moor Park; Robert Victor Grosvenor, the third Lord Ebury, will be remembered as the man who sold it, apparently because his American wife Florence Padelford, whom he had married in 1908, refused to live there. He died in 1921 aged fifty three, and was succeeded as the fourth Baron Ebury by his young brother Francis, a gutsy young man in the mold of his father and grandfather. Had he taken the title on the death of his father in 1918, then the decision might have been different...

Perhaps only temporarily, though, for the jinx which had taken the lives of three young Grosvenor men in two generations, claimed yet another when Francis was killed in hunting accident at the age of forty-eight.

The Tea-boy Tycoon...

Full marks to would-be newspaper tycoon Charles Duncan, owner and publisher of the Rickmansworth News which first appeared in 1896. Believing that Rickmansworth was nothing more than 'a sleepy hollow on the Ebury Estate' he decided to shake the townspeople out of their lethargy with the introduction of his eight-page weekly. He was only 19 years old, tall and thin with spectacles, and combined his job as editor with that of reporter, advertising manager and tea-boy. Remarkably, as a one-man band, he built the circulation to over 3,000 copies per week before he threw it in after eleven months, departing the town in search of a fresh challenge. The final edition of the Rickmansworth News appeared on July 15th, 1897.

The House Of Memories:

The layout of the mansion, and the use of its rooms, changed little under the three generations of Grosvenors who lived there. The main hall, the small and large dining rooms remained virtually untouched, apart from servicing and upkeep, and are used for the same purpose today. The rest of the ground floor has, by necessity, changed considerably in use, if not in appearance. The present cocktail bar was the Ebury library, the Thornhill Room was the Ebury's saloon, and the spike bar was known simply as the Blue Room.

RIGHT: The White Lounge, now the main bar, was usually the preserve of the ladies of the house. Most of the features, including the fireplace, have remained intact, but the false wall at the far end has been removed to expose the windows. (*Copyright Country Life*).

The white drawing room, which is now the lounge bar, still has many of the features which were evident in the Eburys' day, although the windows behind the present bar were obscured by a false wall featuring shelved display alcoves and decorative plasterwork.

The principal bedrooms were on the first floor, approached either by the cedar staircase on the left of the main hall, or the more austere flight of stone steps to the right. They were clearly recalled by Margaret Peyton-Jones, second daughter of Norman and Caroline Grosvenor, and grand-daughter of the first Lord Ebury, in her sister's book 'The Lilac and the Rose'.

"*Every evening after tea, Susie and I came down (from the second floor) to our mother's room before bed-time. I can vividly remember the look of the room, with its huge glowing fire (it seems to be always winter in my recollections) which I think cast more light on the furniture than the lamps or the soft yellow candle-light that was supposed to illumine the room. How well I can see the huge four-poster bed, the writing table in front of the sofa, at the end of the bed, the dainty, muslin-skirted dressing-table, on which reposed, among other things, the curling tongs which I so deeply envied, and of which I am supposed to have said to mother that 'when I'm grown up, and you dead, I shall have those tongs.*"

To the left of the fireplace was a door leading to a similar room occupied by the girls' omnipresent Aunt Sophie, widow of Tommy Grosvenor, 'which, owing to the kindess of its occupant, we invaded just as

BELOW: Loggers' wagons crossing Batchworth Heath, viewed from the main entrance to Moor Park. The teashop in the foreground is now the Prince of Wales public house which was reduced to half its size by a wartime bomb.

confidently as we did that of our mother.' The remaining rooms on the first floor were occupied either by members of the family, or used as spare bedrooms for the many guests of Lord and Lady Ebury.

The childrens' nursery-cum-playroom was on the second floor, on the northern corner of the building with four large windows on two sides, affording views either of the gardens at the rear of the mansion, or across the valley towards Rickmansworth. From the nursery ran a long wide passage to the other end of the house, with another passage leading off to the right. It was here that the two Grosvenor sisters, Victoria and Albertine, lived in a suite of rooms during their latter days at Moor Park. Further along the passage were two or three box rooms, with connecting doors, where the young girls would ferret among old trunks, searching for the treasures of childhood, blissfully unaware of the value of the Adam furniture which was neatly stacked at one end, protected by copies of The Times since 1845...

Even towards the end of the Ebury occupation, the mansion employed an indoor staff of around twenty. They included the butler, valet, ladies' maid, housekeeper, linen maid, two housemaids, cook, kitchen maid, hall-porter, first and second coachmen, two footmen, odd-man, two stable-lads and two laundry-maids. The estate also employed eighteen gardeners, including three specialists who tended the kitchen garden, which was located to the rear of the seventh green on the High course, and was reached from the mansion by a gravel pathway. Much of the kitchen garden area was taken by the glasshouses in which were cultivated grapes, peaches, figs and apricots. Soft fruit was there in abundance too, and the storage sheds where the produce was kept were later dismantled and used for housing tractors and other agricultural machinery in the area now occupied by the green-keeping staff.

The estate also employed a farm bailiff, responsible for dairy supplies etc, who lived in a picturesque old farmhouse on the site of Home Farm. The Ebury's gamekeeper, responsible mostly for pheasant, partridge, rabbit and hare, lived in Watford Lodge, now home of the head green-keeper.

The Fuzzy Photographer ...

Around the turn of the century a pioneer photographer with a cloudy lens published a book of a dozen fairly uninspiring photographs of Moor Park and the mansion. His name was Alvin Langdon Coburn and his book is remarkable, not for the poor quality of his work or the absence of any explanatory text, but because he somehow managed to persuade Emilie, the second Lady Ebury, to contribute a foreword!

For historical background, she draws heavily from Bayne's book of Moor Park, written in 1871, but she shows some nice touches of her own: '... a mere seventeen miles from London, while Watford, a town of some 45,000 inhabitants, is almost at its gates. The deer wander about its glades, undisturbed by the noise of motor cars which now pass so frequently outside the paling which surrounds the Park.'

It is also clear that she enjoyed living there. Describing the hall, she writes: 'It is very splendid with solid marble doorways and paved with marble.... In fact the decorations and arrangements of the interior remind one more of a Genoese palace than of an English country house.'

A Grosvenor's Requiem:

'It is now a golf club and the Park has rows of villas which make it unrecognisable. Luckily, I do not have to see these changes, and I still believe that were I to wander up the drive from Rickmansworth, or down from the Batchworth Heath Lodge, I should find everything as I left it, perhaps a little dustier, a little more faded, with ghosts for inhabitants. But if, as time goes on, I am forced to realise the changed aspect of things, I still have my memories; the terrace on a night in June, with the great house behind us humming with life, the wide canopy of stars above us, the lights of Watford in the distance, the occasional rumble of the North-Western Railway breaking the deep stillness. The freshness of the Spring mornings, the beauty of the flowering shrubs, the scent of azaleas, of lilacs, syringas and roses. The wonderful coolness of the hall as one came in out of the glare of an August sun. These, and many other memories, will stay with me until I die, and perhaps afterwards – who knows?'

– Caroline, wife of Norman Grosvenor
and daughter-in-law of the first Lord Ebury.

Did ever golf club have a nineteenth hole
So sumptuous as this?
Did ever golf club have so fine a hall?
Venetian decor, 1732.
And yonder dome is not a dome at all
But painted in the semblance of a dome.
The sculptured figures are all done in paint
That lean towards us with so rapt a look –
How skilfully the artist takes us in.

What Georgian wit classic Gods have heard
Who now must listen to the golfer's tale
Of holes in one, and how I missed that putt,
Hooked at the seventh, sliced across the tenth,
But ended on the seventeenth all square.
Ye gods, ye gods, how comical we are!
Would Jove have been appointed Captain here?
See how exclusive thy estate, Moor Park.

From 'Metroland' by Sir John Betjeman
– Poet Laureate (1972–1984)

CHAPTER FIVE

The Rise Of Moor Park As A Golf Club

Mention Moor Park to anyone, and most of them will tell you it means just one thing.

Golf. With the added bonus of a rather special clubhouse.

The club as we know it today was formed in 1937, but the Park and the mansion have been synonymous with the game since the 1880s when the nation, reeling from a virulent strain of golf fever, saw a dramatic increase in the number of courses and clubs.

Suddenly, it seemed, golf was 'in', although its history stretches back over centuries, with the Scots and the Dutch still vying over the origins of the game. It was certainly played prior to the 15th century, and legend claims that the game was banned by King Henry VI in 1457 – the early days of the Wars of the Roses – because it was interfering with archery practice!

Sir Robert Grosvenor, the first Lord Ebury, recognised the social potential of the game and hacked a rough course through the parkland around the mansion, for the exclusive use of his family and a few favoured friends.

But Lord Ebury was already an old man, and preferred to concentrate his energies on billiards, a rubber of whist, or watching a game of cricket. However, the game held a considerably stronger appeal for his son and heir...

Robert, later to become the second Lord Ebury, really caught the golfing bug. After he acceded to the title and inherited Moor Park in 1893, he considerably improved the course by making it more testing, and also by paying heed to the condition of the greens and fairways.

To say that the course ran from the Batchworth Heath entrance to the Park, down to the Rickmansworth gate, and back again would be a gross over-simplification. It was contained in its entirety on the left side of the road as one drives through the Park from the Batchworth entrance, with the first tee located approximately halfway up the first fairway on the High. The first eight holes snaked down towards the River Colne before the course turned back up the hill, with the ninth tee positioned in the middle of what is now the Batchworth Hill roundabout! Golfers would then drive across a deep grass pit towards the green, which is now the fourth on the High course.

Shortly after the turn of the century, the public demand for golf exceeded the facilities available, and Ebury was persuaded to relax his edict governing the exclusivity of the course. By 1910, a selected number of influential and professional enthusiasts from Rickmansworth were allowed access to the nine holes furthest from the mansion, but always strictly by prior arrangement. Two years later, with his Lordship's consent, they formed Rickmansworth Golf Club with a membership limited to 65 golfers. Annual subscriptions were one guinea for men, and half a guinea for lady members.

It would appear that Ebury was impressed both by the manner in which the club was run, and also by the etiquette of members, for he soon lifted the nine-hole restriction allowing them access to the entire course.

In 'Newman's Guide to London Golf' dated 1913, Rickmansworth Golf Club is listed as a private course on Lord Ebury's Moor Park estate, but the reference to members having access to only nine holes has been deleted. No play was allowed on Sundays (almost certainly at Lord Ebury's insistence) and ladies were not allowed on the course after 2.pm. on Saturdays. Guests were allowed to play at the cost of one shilling a day, providing they were accompanied by a member. Access to all eighteen holes clearly enabled the club to extend its membership, for Newman records: 'Members: 65 men, 25 women. No vacancies.' Lockers were available in the clubhouse at an additional cost of half-a-crown per year. The course is described as being within easy access of both Rickmansworth stations, the cost of a return ticket from Euston being four shillings for first class, and two shillings for third class travel.

The clubhouse, which had been made available by Lord Ebury, was a timber structure resembling a small barn set in the expansive gardens of Rickmansworth Lodge, opposite Rickmansworth gate. The Lodge was then thatched, standing in splendid isolation among ornate gardens before the development of Moor Lane. From 1908, it had been the home of William Harwood, a former Army officer who had now become a keen and gifted member of the Eburys' horticultural staff with special responsibilities for tending to the Italian gardens. More pertinently, however, it was also the home of his young daughter, Agnes...

Agnes was just seven years old when the family moved to Moor Park. She had walked the Prince's Course at Deal with her Uncle at the age of four, owned her first golf club before she was five, and was taking the game seriously at six!

The Ice Age...

At least two ice-wells remain beneath the fairways of Moor Park – one between the pond and the 15th green on the High course, and another just off the 14th fairway on the West. These wells, thought to be at least 250 years old, are deep brick-lined vaults where large chunks of ice (taken from the lakes) were stored. The more ice that was stored, the lower the temperature became, giving it an underground refrigeration effect, and it is believed that game and sides of venison were stored in this manner to prevent them from becoming rancid.

By her twelfth birthday, she was playing to a handicap of ten, and was invited to partner Lord Ebury in a foursomes match against the two Misses Barnes, society friends from Chorleywood. She clearly performed well, for she was soon to become his Lordship's favourite partner, frequently playing twice a week. Playing regularly in such august company gave her something of an awesome reputation by the time she reached her teens, and Rickmansworth golfers would constantly seek her as a partner, often tempting her with the promise of half-a-crown. On the occasions she relented, the money was invariably spent on buying Woodbines for the troops.

With the indelible memory of childhood, 'Aggie' Harwood clearly recalled those days almost eighty years later. Not so much the drives, the chips, the putts, or even whether games were won or lost; more the things that are an inherent part of a young girl's life. Important and lasting memories 'like riding around the course in an open buggy, with clubs strapped to each side, pulled by a pony called Kitty with a coat like black velvet...'

Lord Ebury, she recalled, was crazy about the game. He was an excellent player and a demanding partner – even for a twelve-year-old. Poor shots are a fundamental part of every golfer's repertoire, but there was never the slightest suggestion of temper or bad language. Indeed, his only concession to disappointment on the course – whether reacting to a shot by himself or his partner – was to remove a silk handkerchief from his pocket and chew on it for a few seconds. And always, after the game, the gardener's daughter was invited into the mansion to join his Lordship and other well-heeled guests for tea.

Five Holes in One...

Aggie Harwood's remarkable golfing achievements would still challenge the best club players in the land today. Apart from playing to a handicap of ten at the age of twelve, she shot an astonishing eight-under-par 68 around Lord Ebury's private course in 1918, at the age of seventeen. She was offered the courtesy of the course by Lord Leverhulme and his company from 1922 and, twelve months later, she won the Civil Service championships playing off scratch. That title, won in 1923, is especially memorable for her, coming at the same time that her lifelong friend Kitty Godfree caused a major upset by beating Helen Wills to win the Ladies singles title at Wimbledon!

In a life which spanned almost eighty years of competitive golf, she has five holes-in-one to her name and her impressive list of partners include such legendary players as Tom Fernie, the former professional at Royal Lytham, and Henry Cotton. On one occasion she bumped into Sandy Herd as he was returning from an Open Championship. She helped him with his luggage and he handed her the putter he had used in the tournament. She has continued to use it for over sixty years!

The same year – 1923 – marked another unique double, for not only did Moor Park appoint Sandy Herd as its first professional, it also marked Arthur G. Havers Open championship victory at Troon. Havers was eventually to succeed Herd in 1946.

A young Aggie Harwood showing the style which saw her break the Rickmansworth course record at the age of 17 with an eight-under-par 68. She played the round with Lord Ebury, little more than two months before his death, and he was thrilled by the performance of his young protegee.

Miss Harwood remembers him with a genuine warmth and fondness. 'He was a classic aristocrat, one of the old brigade. I got on very well with him, although I would never speak to him unless he started the conversation.' Such was the way of things in those days, even for the young golfing partner of a member of the aristocracy...

It appears typical of Ebury that he never took anyone's company, even that of a child, for granted. On the day before she was invited to partner his Lordship, a note would be delivered to her mother, asking: 'If Agnes is unengaged tomorrow, would she like to play...?' Later, when she was sixteen, the invitation was addressed to Aggie herself.

When, a few months after her sixteenth birthday, she joined the Civil Service, Lord Ebury's partnership with Agnes seemed stymied. He tried others, but they clearly fell short of the standard and companionship he had enjoyed with his young favourite, so he decided to resolve the problem in the most logical manner. Being a man of some social and political clout, he went to Miss Harwood's boss and negotiated her release from Whitehall for one afternoon a week for the vital purpose of playing golf!

RICKMANSWORTH GOLF CLUB.

18 HOLES.

Player's Name ....Agnes Harwood....

Signature of Marker ....Ebury....

No.	Length of Holes Yards.	Bogey.	(*a*)	Strokes.	No.	Length of Holes Yards.	Bogey.	(*a*)	Strokes.
10	283	5	+	5	1	299	4	+	4
11	380	5	−	6	2	92	3	+	2
12	204	4	0	3	3	236	4	+	3
13	217	4	+	3	4	261	4	0	4
14	368	5	−	5	5	234	4	+	3
15	445	6	0	6	6	218	4	+	4
16	289	4	+	4	7	99	3	+	2
17	293	4	+	3	8	200	4	+	2
18	283	4	+	4	9	362	5	0	5
	Out	41	5 up	39		Home	35	7 up	29
							Out		39

(a) Here if a Hole is 12 up

Won: Lost: Halved: TOTAL 68

Put + — o HANDICAP

Date..August 22 1918... NETT

No Competitions, except unlimited ones, to be started before 10 o'clock. All Competitions must be played over the whole Course when available.

Aggie Harwood's record breaking round at Rickmansworth in 1918 although, by today's standards, the bogey strokes could be described as generous.

So, at the end of every Thursday morning, she could close her books, lock her filing cabinet, and take a train to Northwood station where she would be met by Lord Ebury's coach, complete with sandwiches and drinks to compensate for her missed luncheon.

Lord Ebury's death in 1918 sounded a warning bell for the golfers of Rickmansworth. His heir, Robert Victor Grosvenor, decided to dispose of the estate and it was put up for auction the following year. However, it wasn't until late in 1920 that soap-magnate Lord Leverhulme actually took possession of the Park, and the widowed Lady Ebury allowed Rickmansworth Golf Club to use the course until the Grosvenor family officially relinquished ownership.

William Lever, the first Viscount Leverhulme, was a shrewd and successful industrialist. He founded the soap manufacturing company of Lever Brothers, later to become Unilever and, in 1888, built Port Sunlight in Cheshire as a model village for the working classes. But, by 1919, his role in the company had become minimal, and Moor Park offered a fresh challenge which would occupy both his time and his mind. The popular tale that Leverhulme bought the estate because he had been refused membership of Rickmansworth Golf Club is appealing, but untrue.

Despite his advancing years, his flair for business told him that his latest acquisition offered rich pickings, and he formed Moor Park Ltd to sell land for development on the fringes of the estate. This provided the new company with funds to convert the mansion into a clubhouse, and also to employ top golf course architect Harry Colt to construct three new courses – the High, the East and the West. Then, after adding six hard tennis courts, six grass courts and a croquet lawn, Moor Park Club was officially opened in May 1923.

Although the club had an elected committee, it was run as a business by Leverhulme, and it operated very much along the lines of an American country club, with a Dormy House, liveried porters and page boys.

Harry Colt's work decimated much of Ebury's original course, and was a long and laboured operation. By the time the new club was due to open in the Spring of 1923, only one of the three courses was in play, forcing the

Refreshing the Greens...

The method of providing water for Moor Park's 54 greens has changed little since the system was devised and installed in 1923. The only source is the pond built by Lord Anson adjacent to Temple Gardens and the water is gravity-forced through a network of underground iron pipes, although many of these had to be re-laid when the East and West courses were redesigned in 1937, to make provision for what is now the Rickmansworth municiple course. The pond beside the 15th green feeds Anson's pond via a four-inch stoneware pipe, although it is likely that this was constructed after the original work was completed.

The only concession to present-day technology is the pumping system which tops up Anson's pond from the River Colne whenever the water level becomes dangerously low. The pump is located in the old game larder in the grounds of Watford Lodge, the home of Moor Park's head greenkeeper.

Lord Leverhulme, who saw Moor Park as a sporting hobby and also as a commercial opportunity.

committee to restrict membership. In order to maintain interest at a high level, they instead issued terms of provisional membership for the period May 1923–April 1924, regretting that the other two courses would not be ready until July, and even then 'the greens may be in a rough condition for a month or two.' Full membership, offering golf, tennis and croquet, was ten guineas for both ladies and gentlemen and, for members wishing to play golf only, the subscription was a mere nine guineas.

The First Professional

The year 1923 is particularly significant because it marked the appointment of the club's first professional, Sandy Herd, who came to Moor Park from Coombe Hill at Kingston-upon-Thames. Prior to joining Coombe Hill in 1911, he had been attached to Huddersfield Golf Club.

Herd's pedigree was unquestionable, having finished in the top six in the Open championship on no less than thirteen occasions. His historic victory at Hoylake in 1902 was the first with the revolutionary new Haskell ball, but his achievement is all the more creditable since he was one of the few players to break the stranglehold of the fabled 'triumverate' – Harry Vardon, James Braid and John H. Taylor – who between them landed sixteen Open titles. He finished runner-up on four occasions, was third twice, fourth twice, fifth three times, and sixth once.

Herd is remembered as a popular and charming man whose memory is perpetuated in the lounge bar by a bronze sculpture presented in 1935 to mark his fiftieth year in the game. One of his own fondest memories was playing the High course on his seventieth birthday in seventy strokes!

Herd retired in 1946 to be followed by Arthur G. Havers, coincidentally the man who had succeeded him at Coombe Hill twenty-three years earlier. He was later to move to Sandy Lodge before coming to Moor Park.

Havers, too, was a tournament player of the highest quality. He won the Open championship at Troon in 1923, the last Briton to take the title before a barren period of ten years ended with Henry Cotton's first Open victory in 1934. Havers had already sounded a warning of things to come in 1921, when he came fourth at St Andrews and, in 1932, he finished third behind Americans Gene Sarazin and Macdonald Smith at Princes, after moving to Sandy Lodge. He doubtless found some consolation in this defeat, for he was awarded the Tooting Bec Cup, presented annually for the best single round by a British golfer, after shooting a sixty-eight. His consistent performances throughout the 1920s had also made him a natural selection for the inaugural Ryder Cup match, played at Worcester, Massachusetts in 1927. For the record the U.S.A. won by nine-and-a-half to two-and-a-half.

By the time Lord Leverhulme died in 1925, aged seventy-four, he had seen his dream of Moor Park Club become a reality, and had also instigated a programme of development which was beginning to encroach upon the hallowed gardens of the Park itself. It was eventually to lead to the wanton destruction of Lord Anson's Temple of the Winds, built in the 18th-century from Portland stone, and a feature of the Pleasure Gardens designed by Capability Brown.

But, by 1937, Rickmansworth Urban District Council decided it was time to halt this sort of speculative development before it became totally out of hand. They bluntly refused a request from Moor Park Ltd to develop more land, and the Council safeguarded the future by stepping in and buying 350 acres, including the mansion.

Rickmansworth U.D.C., later to become part of Three Rivers District Council, granted a forty-year lease to a new company formed by members and known as Moor Park Golf Club Ltd. The founder and driving force behind the new organisation was Charles H. Falloon who steered the club through its embryonic days, and eventually saw his dream of a private members club become a reality. He became chairman of the Company and was, for 21 years, also chairman of the Moor Park Golf Club. In 1946, he was elected President of the club, an office which he held until his death in 1959.

The purchase by Rickmansworth U.D.C. in 1937 marked many changes. In return for the 40-year lease, the Council insisted that one course should be made available to members of the public. Hence the old East course became Rickmansworth municipal course, Moor Park retained the High and West and, for a while, the Dormy House became self-contained flats.

If there was one thing which alarmed members more than the sudden loss of one complete course, it was the fear that their hallowed ground was to be invaded by outsiders. This, they decided, necessitated a swift re-designing of the East and West courses to ensure, as far as possible, that the ubiquitous Mr and Mrs Public were limited to the perimeters of the Park. Previously, the East course had been fairly central, with three holes – the first, tenth and eighteenth – all within full view of the clubhouse. For members to be subjected to the sight of strangers, many of whom were

Sandy Herd (right) with the fabled triumverate of John H. Taylor, James Braid and Harry Vardon who won sixteen Open championships between them. (*Hulton-Deutsch*).

HE(A)RD AT THE TELEPHONE.

"A'M MUSTER HERD, 307, PUT ME ON TO 314. . . . . YOU THERE, MUSTER HILTON? A WEEL, WHA' SAID DECADENCE? A'M SANDY HERD, YE KEN"

Before the 1902 Open Championship at Hoylake, Sandy Herd was harshly criticised by former champion Harold Hilton for his 'decadent' approach to the game. Herd came up with the perfect answer, winning with a round of 307, seven shots ahead of Hilton. This cartoon, showing Braid, Taylor and Vardon peering through the window, is reproduced from 'Golf Illustrated' dated June 13th, 1902.

Sandy Herd's Open Championship Record:

(*Finishing sixth or better*).

1892: Joint runner-up to the amateur Harold Hilton in the first Open championship to be played at Muirfield. It was also the first Open to be played over seventy-two holes. Score: 308.

1893: Third behind Willie Auchterlonie (322) and Johnny Laidlay (324) at Prestwick. Score: 325.

1895: Runner-up to J. H. Taylor (322) at St Andrews. Score: 326.

1896: Fifth at Muirfield after Vardon had beaten Taylor [both 316) in a play-off. Score: 320, with Braid in sixth place, three strokes behind.

1897: Fifth at Hoylake, three strokes behind Braid (second with 315) and two ahead of Harry Vardon (sixth with 320).

1901: Fifth again with a score of 325, with the triumverate of Braid (309), Vardon (312) and Taylor (313) taking first three places for the second year running.

1902: Won the Open championship at Hoylake with a score of 307, beating both Vardon and Braid (joint runners-up) by one stroke, and Taylor (sixth) by a further six strokes.

1903: Fourth at Prestwick behind the Vardon brothers Harry (300) and Tom (306), with Jack White (308) third. Score: 309.

1908: Fourth again at Prestwick, eleven shots behind the winner, James Braid (291).

1910: Shared third place with Harold Hilton (both 304) at Sandwich, just one stroke behind Harry Vardon (winner after a play-off) and Arnaud Massy.

1912: Sixth at Muirfield after Ted Ray (295), Vardon (299) and Braid (303) had taken the first three places. Score: 309.

1920: Almost a fairy-tale ending . . . second at Deal with 305, two shots behind George Duncan.

hackers and most of whom would be improperly dressed, was clearly unthinkable...

These three holes, all at the rear of the clubhouse, are now part of the West course; the first has become the sixteenth, the tenth is now the eighteenth, and the old eighteenth is the fifteenth.

At this stage we can correct a myth about the old East course, which is popularly thought to have been for the exclusive use of Lady members. This was not the case, but the misunderstanding may have arisen through the fact that *restricted* lady members had full use of the East course at all times, but were bound by certain conditions governing their access to the West and the High courses.

Then there was the putting green – surely one of the largest and most lovingly-tended in Britain. It stretched from the back of the mansion to the perimeter wall of the north terrace (Wolsey's Walk), with long approaches to each hole, every one individually mowed, almost ironed, like perfect miniature fairways through the plush and weedless lawns.

Arthur Havers with the trophy after winning the Open Championship at Troon in 1923. He later became the professional at Sandy Lodge Golf Club before succeeding Sandy Herd at Moor Park in 1946.

OPPOSITE: *Copyright Henry Longhurst/The Sunday Times, 21 August 1932.*

While not accepted as a full championship course Moor Park has, over the years, hosted many memorable competitions, with the Bob Hope Classic and the Four Stars pro-celebrity tournaments figuring among the most recent. But there are few, if any, that can compete with the classic head-to-head between American Walter Hagen and Archie Compston during the week prior to the Open championship at Sandwich in 1928.

Hagen had already won the 1922 Open at Sandwich, finished runner-up to Arthur Havers at Troon in 1923, and reclaimed his title in 1924 at Hoylake. Archie Compston had been runner-up to Jim Barnes (U.S.A.) at Prestwick in 1925. Now, as part of the warm-up before the big event, Hagen and Compston were to play a 72-hole exhibition match, doubtless with a fistful of dollars on the side.

It is now part of golfing folk-lore that Compston won by 18 and 17, thought to be the heaviest defeat ever inflicted on the American during his career. But Hagen had the last word when it really mattered. The following week at Sandwich, he won the third of his four Open championships, beating the great Gene Sarazin by two strokes, with Archie Compston one shot behind in third place! Compston, who was unattached at the time, later followed the path of Sandy Herd and Arthur Havers to Coombe Hill. He was also personally 'adopted' as private professional to the Prince of Wales, and featured in the infamous incident which led to His Royal Highness withdrawing the 'Royal' prefix from The Berkshire Golf Club.

The Day War Broke Out

The army of golfers playing their regular morning round on the first Sunday of September 1939, teed off in the peaceful late summer sun, and returned to the clubhouse after eighteen holes to find Britain was at war.

The outbreak of hostilities disrupted most things, and the serene splendour of golf at Moor Park was no exception. Like many other large houses, the mansion was requisitioned for the duration of the war, and immediately became the headquarters of the Territorial Army and the A.T.S. Around the clubhouse, recreational golf bags gave way to protective sand-bags and, where hopeful caddies had once lingered on the steps of the portico, uniformed sentries now stood erect, caressing not the hickory shaft of the brassie or the niblick, but the polished oak butt of a Lee-Enfield rifle.

A Bark From The Past...

Golfers finding themselves in the light rough between the 16th and 17th fairways on the High course may well have found their ball close to what appears to be a gravestone for a dog named Paddy, dated 1860. Animal lovers need not fret – the stone doesn't mark the burial place for an Ebury pet; instead, it was retrieved from the Italian garden, and is now used as a cover for nothing more sinister than a drainage culvert!

Homes of London Golf—V.

THE THREE COURSES AT MOOR PARK

COLOURFUL HISTORY OF THE "MANOR OF THE MORE"

MAGNIFICENT CLUBHOUSE

By HENRY LONGHURST

Of all the distressing circumstances attendant upon the depression under which we labour, not the least unfortunate has been the gradual disappearance of that sure evidence of prosperity, the old-fashioned country mansion. A crumb of consolation, however, is found when a particularly noble example escapes the usual fate of becoming the local lunatic asylum and blossoms forth with renewed vigour into a golf club.

Whatever the quality of the golf it might offer, any description of Moor Park, as a golf club, would turn naturally to its mansion clubhouse. A massive, incongruous pile, it stands as a permanent memorial to the solid magnificence of a by-gone age. Long carriage drives lead down to it from over the hills; lawns, gardens and terraces surround it, and anything which is not vast of its kind, be it a tree or a modern motor-car, seems dwarfed beside it.

Moor Park is a place of great historical associations, though its appearance to-day is somewhat different to what it was in the past. What was good enough for Cardinal Wolsey and Henry VIII was not good enough for a Mr. Styles at the beginning of the last century, and he covered the house with a complete facing of Portland stone.

Its Early Reputation

As far as the golf is concerned—and there are three courses—Moor Park has been distinctly unlucky. It is like the dog which was once given a bad name, and those who have not been there recently are liable not to realise how good it really is. The trouble was, as anyone there will admit, that it was opened for public competition play too soon. It was not thoroughly drained at the time and conditions became very bad, and it left in the minds of those who saw it a bad impression, which very soon afterwards ceased to be justified.

It is a regrettable but established fact that no one is quicker than the average golfer to pass on a derogatory opinion either of a course or a player, without being sure of the information upon which it is based, and Moor Park has suffered in this respect for many years. The High course is excellent golf and a fine test of the game, though its peaceful beauty on an August evening is so overcoming as to make a fair judgment a little difficult.

The West course is not quite so long and is different in character from the High. Its lay-out is rather on the lines favoured in America, with narrow, closely guarded greens which call for an accurately placed drive.

Both courses are "park" golf of an unusual order, retaining its virtues, but without most of its vices. Here is none of the flat, tree-dodging golf of the average park course, abominably wet and weary. Trees there are in plenty, of unequalled size and majesty, but if they get in our way we have always deserved it. Views of great sweeps of country stretch out below, and the bracken and "whins" which thrive in several places all help to dispel the illusion that we are playing in a park.

What Might Have Been

The third course is only a matter of some five thousand yards, but is, I am told, "great fun." It certainly looks it. But one cannot entirely suppress a sneaking regret that, with all the resources available, they did not take their courage in both hands and do what no one in England has yet dared to do, that is, build just one real tigers' course, on the lines of Oakmont or Pine Valley; a course of huge "carries" and huge bunkers, where a good shot goes to certain safety and a bad one to certain damnation.

There was, after all, plenty of room, and such a course would have seemed only a fitting adjunct to such a clubhouse. However, it was not to be—and doubtless most of the twelve hundred members would shudder at the thought of it. The High course is long enough for most people.

Sandy Herd

Not the least of Moor Park's assets is Sandy Herd, who has been with the club ever since it opened in 1923, and whose accomplishments need no repeating here.

In its comparatively short existence Moor Park has been the scene of one or two historic encounters, of which the most notable was, of course, that in which Archie Compston beat Walter Hagen by 18 and 17 over seventy-two holes. A few days later Hagen, characteristically undeterred, won the Open Championship at Royal St. George's.

Since then nothing of very great note has occurred at the club, but it will have a chance to come back into its own next month when the finals of the Professional Championship are to be held there. To those who passed judgment on it seven or eight years ago it will be, I venture to prophesy, a revelation, and to those who have never seen it before a great delight.

MOOR PARK CLUB

Near RICKMANSWORTH.

Station: Moor Park and Sandy Lodge (Metropolitan Railway). Club Bus meets all Trains. **Telephone: Rickmansworth 26.**
Accommodation in the Dormy House available for a limited number.

Open Amateur Golf Meeting

FOR THE

MOOR PARK CHALLENGE BOWL

with PRIZE value £10 10 0 *and a* SCRATCH PRIZE value £10 10 0

Saturday, 11th October, 1930

On the High and West Courses.

36 HOLES MEDAL PLAY. Open to Members of recognised Golf Clubs. Handicaps limited to 12.
Entrance Fee **5/-**. Optional Sweeps **5/-** on 36 Holes, and **2/6** on each 18.
Entries close at 6 p.m. on Wednesday, 8th October, 1930.

CONDITIONS.

1. Competitors must play under their lowest Handicap at any Club, and forward the usual certificate from the Club Secretary.
2. Competitors may choose their own partners.
3. Starting times will be allotted as near as possible to those asked for.
4. Competitors will be made Honorary Members of the Club from Wednesday, 8th October, to Saturday, 11th October.
5. The Committee reserve the right to refuse any entry, make any change they think desirable, also to settle all questions that may arise, and their decision must be accepted as final.
6. No competitor to take more than one Prize.
7. Ties will be decided on the last 9, 6 or 3 holes on the High Course.

High Water...

To the right of the sixth green on the High course – one of the highest points in the county – there is an ancient artesian well which even today can provide water a mere four feet below the fairway. It is thought that this, together with a pond which once stretched from this site to Batchworth Hill, provided a source of irrigation for Moor Park's comprehensive and well-stocked kitchen garden, which was sited behind the remains of the old wall alongside the eighth fairway.

For several months, however, life remained fairly quiet for the military occupants of Moor Park, with the main enemy action coming from sporadic attempts to destroy the railway line at Watford and, on one occasion, from a bomber dumping its bombs on the course, blasting three large craters in the fairway of the twelfth on the West!

It is interesting to note that parts of the course remained open during the war, with members who had joined the armed forces volunteering to assist with the upkeep of greens and fairways during their periods of leave. Members wishing to play had the use of the small municipal clubhouse at Rickmansworth gate, and servicemen and women were allowed to retain their membership for a nominal £1 per year between 1939–45.

It wasn't until the latter stages of the war that Moor Park mansion was able to make its most important contribution. In February, 1944, it became the headquarters of the 1st Airborne Corps, which was part of the 21st Army Group. It was a move which was to link irrevocably the name of Moor Park with one of the most heroic, if ill-prepared operations in the history of the war.

Arnhem.

Or, as it was known in the planning stages on 1944, 'Operation Market Garden', code-name for a massive combined air and ground offensive to liberate the Dutch, which included capturing a vital bridge in the small town, mediaeval pride of the Netherlands now immortalised by both book and film.

The commanding officer was Lt-General F. A. M. Browning, or 'Boy' Browning as he was known among his contemporaries. He was a man with a proven military record although, before the war, he was better known in social circles as 'Mister' Daphne du Maurier, husband of the best selling author. But it is doubtful whether du Maurier herself ever penned a more chillingly-accurate aphorism than Browning who, expressing his misgivings to Montgomery, prophesied: 'I fear we might be going a bridge too far...'

The British assault was to be led by a golf-loving Scot Major-General R. E. Urquhart, who had no previous experience of airborne operations, and tended to suffer from air-sickness, both of which, with the benefit of hindsight, could be read as somewhat ominous signs.

During the planning of the operation, Urquhart was based in a caravan sited close to the mansion, overlooking the green fairways hoping, no doubt, that they would provide him with inspiration and good fortune. When, on September 15th – the day before the raid – his famous 'Red Devils' were being briefed at airfields prior to their departure, Urquhart relaxed by playing a few holes of golf...

It's all history now; how it was planned in sparsely-furnished rooms in the mansion, the inadequate time to prepare, the heavy German armaments, the differences of opinion before the raid, and the recriminations afterwards. Perhaps statistics alone should sit in judgement on the operation; they record that, of a total strength of 10,000 men, there were 8,000 casualties.

Military golfer . . . Major-General Robert E. Urquhart seen on his return to Britain after escaping from captivity following the Arnhem offensive. During the planning of 'Operation Market Garden' he lived in a caravan overlooking the course and played golf the day before departing for the raid. (*Copyright Hulton-Deutsch*).

Significantly, perhaps, it was not until twenty-one years later that a memorial ceremony was held at Moor Park for those of the 1st Airborne who had died at Arnhem, and a plaque was unveiled in the portico, adjacent to the main entrance, by Sir Richard Gale.

In 1945, the club was returned to members and, despite the lengthy period of post-war austerity, things seemed to run pretty much as they had before the rantings of a power-crazed Austrian psychopath punctuated the more serious business of the Handicap committee, the House committee, the Membership committee *et al*. . .

Sandy Herd retired in 1946 after a long and distinguished career as a club and tournament professional. His successor, Arthur Havers, spent eleven years at the club and, in 1957, Pat Keen became Moor Park's third professional. He was succeeded in 1965 by Ross Whitehead.

The First Accounts

Accounts for year ended April 30th, 1938:

To Rent:	800					
Rates:	483	12s.	8d.			
Insurances:	26	17s.	4d.	1310	10s.	0d.
Wages (Courses)	3367	4s.	0d.			
,, (Tennis & Gdns)	827	2s.	4d.	4194	6s.	4d.
Clinkers, Sand and Fertiliser:				213	5s.	8d.
Repairs, Renewals and Golf Tools:				301	19s.	0d.
Professional's Retaining Fee:				100	0s.	0d.
Repairs, Renewals and Tennis Tools:	52	18s.	6d.			
Tennis Upkeep:	49	4s.	6d.	102	3s.	0d.
Tractor Running and Upkeep:				205	7s.	2d.
Tractor Hire:				146	0s.	0d.
Gardens and Upkeep (net):				27	16s.	10d.
Sundries:				58	9s.	8d.
Revenue A/c Recoverable From Rickmansworth UDC:				200	0s.	0d.
				£6859	17s.	8d.

A copy of the first year's accounts taken from the Moor Park Golf Club ledger

By 1939, Rickmansworth UDC had increased their contribution (or share) to £1,500, (presumably to cover the Rent and Rates which are now listed at £1,578.10s.0d.)

The wages bill had increased by less than £200, and the accounts included 'Reserve for Sheds – £100.'

The accounts continued to total between six and eight thousand pounds throughout the war years, and it is interesting to note that in 1945, the Professional's retaining fee was increased from £100 to £260.

An Editor Remembers:

Writing in the Moor Park members' booklet, which was circulated in the late 1940s and early 1950s, the late E. M. Cockell (a former Editor of 'Golf Illustrated') writes:

My Ideal Golf Club:

Moor Park is almost my ideal club. Since I am resident in London my ideal club must be within easy stages of London. Moor Park is that. Situated on the southern border of Hertfordshire, Moor Park is easily accessible from Baker Street on the Metropolitan. The journey takes no more than thirty minutes and the service of trains could not be bettered. There is a station at Moor Park, a short distance from the Club, and a taxi-service operates between the Club-house and the station on Saturday and Sunday between 9am and 1.30.pm. At other times, taxis can be booked, to meet trains, through the receptionist. The club is also easily accessible by road.

Then my ideal club must have an adequate club-house. By an adequate club-house, I mean a place wherein I can find comfort; where I can get good food, well cooked and properly served; where, after strenuous exercise, the appointments do not limit me to the washing of my face and hands; and where, be the weather too inclement for outdoor sports, I can enjoy a rubber of bridge or a game of billiards.

Moor Park can offer this and more ... (he then goes on to cover the history of the club-house in some detail) ... Needless to say, this mansion club-house is equipped and appointed throughout to satisfy the most fastidious club-man that ever lived.

Next, my ideal club must provide me with two golf-courses. These courses must be of the true sea-side variety, cut through the bellies of big sand hills with hummocky fairways carpeted with those fine grasses which seem to thrive by the sea. The lay-out of these courses must be intelligent. They must not just ask me to slog: they must set me a problem for my tee-shot, and another for my second, and their greens must be so moulded as to make of putting an art and not a mere mechanical trundling of the ball along a flat expanse.

Only in its failure to provide me with sea-side golf does Moor Park fall short of my ideal. But it does the next best thing. It offers golf on gravel soil, which means dry-footed golf at all seasons of the year. Its two courses are as I want them. The big one measures 6,602 yards and has a standard scratch score allowment of 73 (par 72), whilst the smaller one is two shots easier. Both are of a highly intelligent order, offering a fine test for highest class of player. Always they are in fine shape with greens that do make of putting an art.

My ideal club must have attached to it a first-class professional, and, in this respect Moor Park is fortunate in having Arthur Havers, an ex-champion and a man of particular charm and personality. My ideal club must provide me with recreation apart from golf. Moor Park has nine grass and six hard courts for tennis, besides being the headquarters of the Hertfordshire Lawn Tennis Association and the venue for the Association's official matches.

Finally, I want in my club a spirit of good fellowship with an atmosphere of friendliness, and I have always found that combination at Moor Park.

RIGHT: A detail from the club brochure printed in the 1940s. Appealing, but inaccurate, for the current mansion was never the home of Cardinal Wolsey. A later reprint of this booklet shows that the entrance fees and subscriptions were revised on May 1st, 1950 to the levels shown here.

MOOR PARK CLUB is situated on the borders of Hertfordshire and Middlesex in perhaps the most beautiful surroundings that can be obtained anywhere within a reasonable distance of London. It is only 17 miles from Marble Arch. The Club Grounds are in most attractive undulating parkland, high up, from which fine views are obtained of the surrounding country towards Rickmansworth, Pinner and Watford. + + +

There are three eighteen hole Golf Courses, all centred from the Club House itself, and the Club provides fifteen Grass and Hard Tennis Courts. Leading Golf Professionals have declared Moor Park to be one of the most attractive Golf Courses in the United Kingdom. + + +

There is a frequent train service from Baker Street and Marylebone, and through trains to the City (approximately ten minutes interval at the popular hours). By road Moor Park is approached from London through Edgware Road and either *via* Stanmore or Pinner and Northwood —a thirty minutes run.

The Club House, once the home of Cardinal Wolsey, is of great historic interest and well worthy of a visit. +

FULL MEMBERS (Including golf and tennis).

	£ s d
Entrance Fee	15.15.0
Subscription	15.15.0
Compounded sub., per annum:	17.17.0

FIVE-DAY MEMBERS (Including golf and tennis)

	£	s	d
Entrance Fee	7	7	0
Subscription	8	8	0
Compounded sub. per annum:	9	9	0

FULL TENNIS MEMBERS:

	£	s	d
Entrance Fee	6	6	0
Subscription	6	6	0
Compounded sub. per annum:	7	7	0

NON-PLAYING MEMBERS:

	£	s	d
Entrance Fee	5	5	0
Subscription	5	5	0
Compounded sub. per annum:	6	6	0

MOOR PARK CLUB

Terms of Provisional Membership

For the period ending 30th April, 1924.

THE Committee of MOOR PARK CLUB are prepared to receive applications for provisional Membership of the Club for the period ending 30th April, 1924. There will be no obligation on persons who join for the above period to become permanent members, nor will there be any obligation on the Committee to elect for permanent membership those who now join. On the other hand, those who are elected as above will receive preferential consideration if they apply for permanent membership when the Committee announce the terms as to entrance fees and annual subscriptions on which permanent members will be elected.

Subject to other things being equal, preference will be given to applicants who hold debentures in Moor Park Limited of the nominal value of £200, and after the above period, and subject as above, preference will also be given to residents on the Moor Park Estate.

The Committee are enrolling members for the above period only now, because although one Golf Course has been completed for some months and has been already in play, the second and third courses will not be ready for play until July, and then the greens may be in a rough condition for a month or two.

It is not expected that the Grass Tennis Courts will be available for play until July, and even then the courts may be in a somewhat indifferent condition for this season's play, although every effort is being taken to lay turf which will be playable upon this year if the weather conditions improve. The four Hard Courts will be ready for play in May.

The same remarks apply to the two Croquet Lawns as to the Grass Tennis Courts.

The alterations to the Mansion House to fit it for the purposes of a Club House with all the usual Club House conveniences will be completed in ample time for the opening of the Club, which it is hoped will be in the week commencing 13th May. Due notice of the exact date will be sent to all who are elected members for the above period.

No Entrance Fees will be payable for the period ending 30th April, 1924. The terms of subscription for that period will be as follows :—

(A) FOR FULL MEMBERS (including Golf, Tennis and Croquet).
Gentlemen and Ladies £10 10 0

(B) FOR FULL MEMBERS PLAYING GOLF ONLY.
Gentlemen and Ladies £9 9 0

Ladies may, however, pay a subscription of £7 7 0 in Section (A) and £6 6 0 in Section (B) if they prefer, in which case they will not be allowed to play on the long Golf Course on Saturdays, Sundays, Bank Holidays, Christmas Day, Good Friday, or Competition Days.

RESTRICTED MEMBERS. A restricted Member shall not play Golf, unless introduced as a Visitor by a full Member, on Saturdays, Sundays, Bank Holidays, Christmas Day, Good Friday, or Competition Days, nor shall he introduce a visitor to play Golf on these days. No restriction as to Tennis or Croquet or use of the Club House.

(C) For Restricted Members Playing Golf, Tennis and Croquet.
Gentlemen and Ladies £6 6 0

(D) For Restricted Members Playing Golf only.
Gentlemen and Ladies £5 5 0

(E) FOR TENNIS AND CROQUET SECTIONS ONLY. (No restriction as to days).

Gentlemen and Ladies £4 4 0
Ladies being the wives or daughters of Full Members in Section (A) £2 2 0

Form of Application is attached.

MOOR PARK HOUSES ONE SERVANT LESS

THE principle which has been kept in mind in the planning of the houses which are to be built on the Estate, is that utility and beauty will always blend well together. Here, where the best of nature's gifts are lavished on the green and sheltered uplands, homes

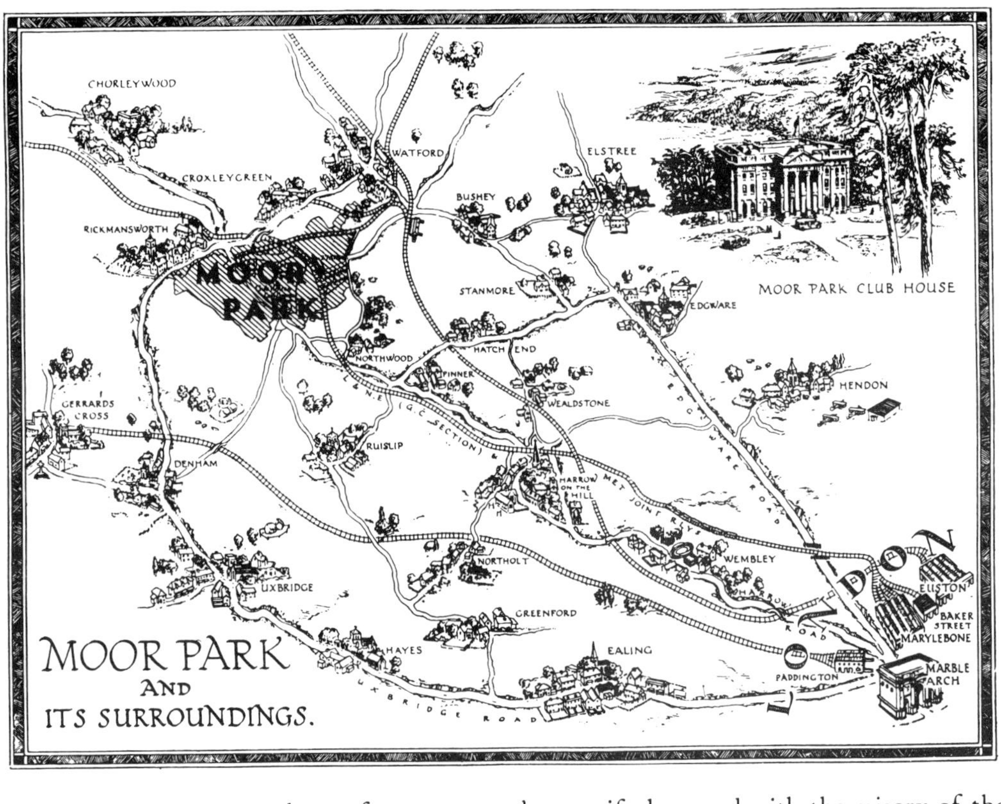

will breathe the atmosphere of contentment. Houses constructed to last a century without the need for anything more than minor repairs, fitted with every modern device that changes domestic work from an offensive drudgery into a matter for pride and pleasure, will frame a picture of comfort and ease.

Gas cookers, gas heaters for kitchen and bath, deep teak sinks with constant hot water and plate-rack above. Heated linen cupboards, hot towel rails and glazed tiles for the bathroom, wooden stair-rods, lacquered taps, glass finger-plates and door-knobs—only the housewife harassed with the misery of the bad, old conditions knows how much these seeming trifles mean. If a servantless house be an unattainable ideal, these houses at least mean one servant less. There is not one of them at which the spirit of muddle would not shake a doubtful head.

Details from a 1924 housing brochure advertising new homes at Moor Park. At this time there were still 1.3 million women in domestic service, earning an average of £1 per week. Only 4,000 people in Britain were earning in excess of £8,000 per annum. An average middle-class income was between £8 and £9 per week, whilst a miner's average weekly wage was around £3.16s.

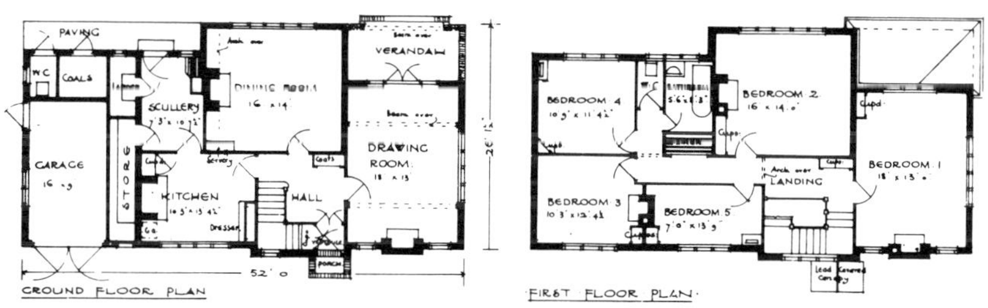

Design No. 9. *This compact and roomy house, with garage and spacious verandah, is constructed as follows. Foundations and surface : Cement concrete. Walls : Brick face cavity walling up to first floor, solid walling and cement roughcast above, with "half timber" finish to gable as shown. Solid pitch-pine posts to verandah and beams in drawing-room. Roof covered with Broseley pattern tiles on boarding. Windows : Solid frames, steel casements, and lead-lights. Joinery and fittings of good quality throughout; hanging cupboards in all bedrooms, and landing ; also dresser and store cupboard in kitchen and servery between dining-room and kitchen. Drainage connection to main sewer ; water supply from main in road. Electric-light wiring throughout, left for fixing fittings Gas laid on to gas cooker and to two gas fires in bedrooms. Hot-water supply to sink, bath, and lavatory basin. Internal decoration, painting and distemper, in shades to match purchaser's selection.*

The site enclosed with fence to side and back, and with oak trellis fencing and gate to the front. The illustration shows the garden front elevation.

It should be noted that the size of the sites upon which these houses are built may be varied to the purchaser's requirements with a slight alteration in price.

The price of this house is £3,200 including fencing, drains, and all fittings shown.

Easy terms of payment can be arranged

C.1924 Moor Park Estate
Details of houses for sale, and accompanying article, reproduced from an advertising brochure.

CHAPTER SIX

The Mansion: Paintings And Decor

Sir James Thornhill (1675–1734) was the man chosen by Benjamin Styles to enlarge and completely change the look of the mansion after he had purchased it from Anna, widow of the Duke of Monmouth, in 1720. It was a decision which Styles later regretted, for a major row over the standard and cost of Thornhill's work led to court cases over payment, and it is not clear exactly who was responsible for completing various parts of the work after the two men had fallen out.

The choice of Thornhill as 'architect and surveyor' wasn't surprising. He combined his architectural skills with decorative painting and politics, and had gained a reputation as a stylist of considerable individuality for his work on the interior of the dome in St Paul's Cathedral, which he had decorated with scenes from the life of the prolific apostle. It seems that he was also a believer of keeping artistic talent in the family, for his daughter married William Hogarth, the celebrated eighteenth-century painter and engraver.

Thornhill was charged with the overall responsibility for the design of both the exterior and interior of the Moor Park mansion, and worked closely in the early stages with Giacomo Leoni who is credited with having designed and erected the portico and the Corinthian pillars. Two additional bays were added to each side, and the style of the front was reproduced at the rear of the building with an engaged portico supported by matching columns. The entire mansion was encased in Portland stone, which is reputed to have cost around £14,000 in transportation charges from the London wharfs.

Much of the exterior work was completed by 1725, when Styles signed a separate agreement, worth £3,100, for Thornhill to paint eight canvases for the hall on the theme of Historic Virtues. It was the question of these paintings, rather than his architecture, which led to the row with Styles, but there are varying reports over the incidents which precipitated the parting of the ways. The official version appears to be simply that Thornhill worked throughout 1726 and 1727 on his canvases but, when they were completed, Styles, with the reputation of a man who wanted every penny to count, simply refused to pay more than £800.

The ceiling of the main hall, with its painted false dome, is thought to be the only example of Thornhill's work which remains in the mansion. (*Copyright Country Life*).

However, more detail is offered by Alice Buchan, great-granddaughter of the first Lord Ebury, in her book 'A Scrap Screen'. It appears that Styles was unimpressed with the quality of the paintings, claiming that they 'were poorly executed and would fade and deaden with time.'

Thornhill, somewhat miffed by this assault on his reputation, wrote in reply that 'a little varnish laid on by the most ordinary hand would refresh and recover them', but he refused, unless paid more, to undertake the job himself.

Styles dismissed Thornhill and refused to part with any more money, not only for the canvases, but also for other work already completed and approved, which had exceeded the original estimate. Thornhill had been forced to dip into his own pocket to pay his workers and, with a justifiable grievance, sued Styles for the remainder of the money. The case was settled out of court on the strength of a promise by Styles in 1728, but it appears to have erupted again in 1730, when the verdict was in Thornhill's favour.

It was probably in the early 1730s when Thornhill's paintings from the hall were torn down and replaced by the story of Io and Argus by Venetian artist Jacopo Amiconi, who had arrived in Britain in 1729. In fact, it is thought that the only work by Thornhill that remains in the mansion is the painted ceiling in the main hall, with its imitation dome copied from St Peters in Rome.

As a professional architect, painter and politician, Sir James Thornhill clearly succeeded in seeing himself as others saw him. The portrait on the left is by William Hogarth, his son-in-law, (*The British Library*) while the version on the right is a self-portrait. (*National Portrait Gallery*).

The four paintings by Amiconi, which replaced Thornhill's original decor, are taken from Ovid's Metamorphoses and tell the story of how the peacock got the 'eyes' in its tail. They are considered to be among the finest of his surviving works.

To say that the story behind the paintings is complex in the extreme, is understating the case, and it is perhaps as well that Amiconi has always been judged for the brilliance of his painting, rather than for his abilities as an illustrator of Roman mythology which is obscure enough in the written word, let alone the brush.

From the left, as one enters the mansion, they depict:

1. **JUPITER AND I0**: Jupiter, King of the Gods, falling in love with the nymph Io, with a curtain hiding their activities from the prying eyes of Jupiter's suspicious wife, Juno, Queen of the Goddesses. To avert suspicion, Jupiter turns Io into a cow which Juno, knowing all is not well, immediately demands as a gift. Juno, apparently knowing a thing or two, puts the cow in the charge of Argus, who had a hundred eyes, only ever closing two at a time so he could watch everything around him. But, missing his lover, Jupiter sends Mercury, the winged messenger, to rescue Io ...

2. **MERCURY PLAYING TO ARGUS**: Disguised as a shepherd, Mercury plays on the pipes to lull Argus to sleep while Io, the cow, watches from behind.

3. **MERCURY SLAYING ARGUS**: Argus sleeps, and Jupiter cuts off his head...

4. **JUNO RECEIVING THE HEAD OF ARGUS**: Still with us? The scenario reaches a gripping climax as Juno takes Argus's eyes and places them in the tail of her bird, the peacock.

The decorative plasterwork surrounding the four paintings is by Bagutti and Artari, two of many Italian artists and craftsmen drafted in to work on the mansion after Thornhill's departure.

The richly-decorated saloon, now the Thornhill Room, as it looked in the early part of the century, with candles either side of the doorway. (*Copyright Country Life*).

The dining room, to the left of the main hall, was originally a ballroom. Sir Lawrence Dundas, the art-lover who bought the mansion in 1763, converted it into a tapestry gallery, and employed Robert Adam to design the ornate ceiling which was afterwards painted by J. C. Cipriani.

One of the more confusing features of the mansion is the fact that the Thornhill Room, originally called the saloon, contains none of Thornhill's work. Experts now believe that the ceiling, featuring a painting of the Aurora (dawn) with the Chariot of the Sun preceded by the morning star, was painted for Anna, the Duchess of Monmouth, by Antonio Verrio prior to his return to Italy in 1707. Much of the detail is missed in a cursory glance, but a concentrated study of the work shows the planets and constellations being put to flight, while Olympian Gods watch from the clouds above. The work is a copy of Guido Rene's masterpiece in the Ruspigliosi Palace, in Rome.

It is likely that the walls were simply decorated by tapestries in Anna's days, because the four paintings depicting the seasons are clearly later works. The first three – Spring, Summer and Autumn – are thought to be by Francesco Sleker, but the style of Winter appears to differ from the rest and the true origin of this work is unknown.

The belief that Sleker was probably responsible for three of the paintings in the Thornhill Room is fuelled by the fact that his name appears on some of the canvases decorating the main stairway, most of which depict mythological tales of the beginning of the seasons. At least, they were all *thought* to have been the work of Sleker, sometimes spelt 'Sleter'...

When restoration and conservation work started on the four principal canvases in 1981, experts were struck by the quality and similarity to Amiconi's work in the main hall. The gallery of paintings on the staircase are dated 1732, adding credence to the theory that they may have been the result of a collaboration between Sleker and Amiconi. The two artists are believed to have pooled their talents some years later when painting canvases for the gallery at Mereworth Castle, in Kent. Work on the restoration of the principal paintings was halted several times through lack of funds in the 1980s, but commenced again in earnest in 1989.

For the mythologically-minded, the paintings on the stairway depict the fable of Proserpine, the young daughter of Ceres, who was carried off by Pluto, King of the Underworld. While a distraught Ceres searched for her daughter, all her crops died, apparently through lack of water. Then she met Arethusa, a water nymph, who claimed to have seen the missing girl with Pluto, somewhere beneath the earth. Ceres appealed to the all-powerful Jupiter, King of the Gods, for the return of her daughter but, because Proserpine had eaten seven pomegranate seeds, she was condemned to spend six months of each year living with Pluto. Such, it seems, was the heavy price one had to pay for stealing fruit in those days...

The paintings are (from the top of the landing):

1. **PLUTO COMING ACROSS PROSERPINE**: Shows Cupid aiming at Pluto, under the guidance of his mother, Venus.

2. **PLUTO PLUNGING UNDERGROUND**: Cyane, watching, wept so much that she became a lake.

3. **THE WATER NYMPH**: Almost certainly Arethusa.

4. **THE JUDGEMENT OF PARIS**: Signed and dated by F. Sleker in 1732.

5. **BOY CHANGED TO LIZARD**: Ceres, presumably still hunting for her daughter, rests at a cottage. A young boy is rude to her and she throws her drink at him, changing him into a lizard.

6. **CERES TALKING TO ARETHUSA**: Self-explanatory.

7. **CERES PLEADING WITH JUPITER** for the return of Proserpine.

The grisailles around the open gallery represent various characters in classical mythology. They are: Apollo (Sun-God); Iside (Isis, the Egyptian Goddess); Ercole (Hercules); Flora (Goddess of Spring); Zingara (Gipsy); Baccanale (Worshipper of Bacchus, the God of wine); Amazone (One of the tribe of the fabled female warriors) and Sileno (Tutor of Bacchus).

RIGHT: The extravagantly-decorated gallery, showing the grisailles depicting figures from classical mythology and the fine decorative plasterwork. (*Copyright Country Life*).

The top of the cedar staircase, illuminated by ornamental gas lamps, showing the door leading to the gallery. (*Copyright Country Life*).

Temple On Gardens

Sir William Temple was a seventeenth-century statesman and author of some considerable social standing and influence. In 1655, at the age of twenty-seven, he married Dorothy Osborne, a cousin of the Franklins who had bought the Park and the mansion in 1652 and, at the time of Miss Osborne's marriage to Temple, had just completed the purchase of the manor.

Although it is claimed that Miss Osborne was not on the best of terms with the Franklins, she and Temple accepted the invitation to spend their honeymoon at Moor Park. It was during this visit that Temple, an accepted expert on matters horticultural, first saw the magnificent gardens which had been so carefully and extravagantly laid out by the Duchess of Bedford more than thirty years earlier. Indeed, so vivid was the impression of his visit, that he was moved to name his own house – Moor Park in Surrey – after the Franklins' Hertfordshire home.

Indeed, he still recalled its splendour in 1685, exactly thirty years later, when he penned a memorable and oft-quoted tribute to the Duchess of

Bedford's work. Temple died in 1699, aged 71, but his description of the Moor park gardens was included in a folio edition of his works printed in 1740:

RIGHT: Rome Guthrie's artistic impression of the Duchess of Bedford's gardens at Moor Park, which were so highly praised by Sir William Temple. There is no doubt that they existed, but where?

> 'The perfectest figure of a garden I ever saw, either at Home or Abroad, was that of Moor Park in Hartfordshire, when I knew it about Thirty years ago. It was made by the Countess of Bedford, esteemed among the great Wits of the Time, and celebrated by Doctor Donne; and with very great Cares, excellent Contrivance, and much Cost; but greater Sums may be thrown away without Effect or Honour, if there want Sense in Proportion to Money, or if nature not be followed; which I take to be the great Rule in this, and perhaps in every Thing else, as far as the Conduct not only of our Lives, but our Governments.
>
> And whether the greatest of Mortal Men should attempt the forcing of Nature may be judged, by observing how seldom God Almighty does it Himself, by so few, true and undisputed Miracles, as we see or hear of in the World. For my own part, I know not three wiser Precepts for the Conduct either of Princes or Private Man than:
>
> *Servare Modum, Finemque tueri, Naturamque sequi.*
>
> Because I take the garden I have named to have been in all Kinds the most beautiful and perfect, at least in the Figure and Disposition, that I have ever seen, I will describe it as a model to those that meet with such a Situation, and are above the Regards of common Expence.
>
> It lies on the Side of a Hill, (upon which the House stands) but not very steep. The Length of the House, where the best Rooms and of most Use or Pleasure are, lies upon the Breadth of the Garden, the Great Parlour opens into the Middle of a Terras Gravel-Walk that lies even with it, and which may be, as I remember, about three hundred Paces long, and broad in Proportion; the border set with Standard Laurels, and at large Distances, which have the Beauty of Orange-Trees out of Flower and Fruit.
>
> From this Walk are Three Descents by many Stone Steps, in the Middle and at each End, into a very large Parterre. This is divided into Quarters by Gravel-Walks, and adorned with Two Fountains and Eight Statues in the several Quarters; at the end of the Terras-Walk are two Summer-Houses, and the Sides of the Parterre are ranged with two large Cloisters, open to the garden, upon Arches of Stone, and ending with two other Summer-Houses even with the Cloisters, which are paved with Stone and designed for Walks of Shade, there being none other in the whole Parterre.
>
> Over these two Cloisters are two Terraces covered with Lead, and fenced with Balusters; and the Passage into these Airy Walks is out of the two Summer-Houses, at the end of the first Terras-Walk. The Cloister facing South is covered with Vines, and would have been proper with an Orange-House, and the other for Myrtles, or other more common Greens; and had, I doubt not, been cast for that Purpose, if this Piece of Gardening had been then in as much Vogue as it is now.
>
> From the Middle of this Parterre is a Descent by many Steps flying each side of a Grotto that lies between them (covered with Lead and Flat)

into the Lower Garden, which is all Fruit Trees ranged about several Quarters of a Wilderness which is very Shady; the Walks here are all Green, the Grotto embellish'd with Figures of Shell-Rockwork, Fountains and Waterworks. If the Hill had not ended with the lower Garden, and the Wall not bounded by a common Way that goes through the Park, they might have added a Third Quarter of all Greens; but this Want is supplied by a Garden on the other Side of the House, which is all of that Sort, very Wild, Shady and adorned with rough Rock-work and Fountains.

This was Moor-Park, when I was acquainted with it, and the sweetest Place, I think, that I have seen in my Life, either before or since, at Home or Abroad. What it is now I can give little Account, having passed through several hands that have made great Changes in Gardens as well as Houses; but the Remembrance of what it was is too pleasant ever to forget, and therefore I do not believe to have mistaken the Figure of it, which may serve for a Pattern to the best Gardens of our Manner, and that are most proper for our Country and Climate.

And whoever observes the work upon the best Indian gowns, or the painting upon their best screens or purcellans, will find their beauty is all of this kind (that is) without order. But I should hardly advise any of these attempts in the figure of gardens among us; they are the adventures of too hard achievement for any common hands, and though there may be more honour if they succeed well, yet there is more dishonour if they fail, and 'tis twenty to one they will; whereas in regular figures, 'tis hard to make any great and remarkable faults.'

This account of the of the Duchess of Bedford's gardens inspired the accompanying illustration by Rome Guthrie which appeared in 'Country Life' in January 1912.

Northwood Awakes...

When, in 1887, the Metropolitan line was extended from Pinner to Rickmansworth, Northwood got its first station. However, a critic wrote to the 'Financial News' complaining that the new line was so little used, and the countryside so boring, that he considered the extension to be 'unnecessary, a waste of money, and doomed to failure.' This unleashed an avalanche of replies including one which pointed out that, as a result of the Metropolitan line reaching Northwood, his company had been involved in the sale of 53 individual building plots close to Northwood station. This land, varying in size from one-quarter to one-and-a-half-acres, was part of the Eastbury estate. Earlier in the same year, in anticipation of the popularity of Northwood and 'Metroland', the remarkably-named Frederick Murray Maxwell Hallowell Carew had bought 762 acres of the Eastbury estate, and this marked the beginning of building in Northwood on a large scale.

CHAPTER SEVEN

The Sale Of The Ebury Estate

When Lord Ebury's estate came under the auctioneer's hammer on the morning of Thursday, 11th Sepember, 1919, it marked more than simply the end of an era. Not only did it fragment the manor, it also dispelled forever the aura of mystique and grandeur which had enveloped first the old palace, and then the mansion, for five hundred years.

Now the Eburys had gone, and with their departure, the magic of Moor Park seemed to evaporate too. Now there was an almost chilling emptiness about the mansion as mere mortals, after two centuries of veneration for its occupants, felt strangely exposed without the presence of their omniscient leader.

The sale was conducted by Messrs Knight Frank and Rutley in auction rooms in Hanover Square, ironically within bidding distance of St George's Church where the Grosvenors, later to become the Eburys, were married.

The entire estate, embracing almost three thousand acres of Rickmansworth and Northwood, was divided into eighty-three lots. Inevitably, perhaps, the thirty-six bedroom mansion, with its ten reception rooms, 400-acre deer park, 250 acres of woodland and Home Farm, was Lot Number One. Strangely, it attracted few bidders, and was still on the books at the end of the auction. Later, Lord Leverhulme negotiated for it by private treaty and is reputed to have bought it in its entirety for the knockdown price – even in those days – of £250,000.

Also at the top end of the sale were ten major residences, including three Dower Houses to the estate. The remainder included ten farms, various lakes, shooting grounds, development land, smallholdings, several cottages, Sandy Lodge Golf course and two public houses.

Batchworth House, Money Hill House and Batchworth Heath House were the Dower Houses. Lady Ebury, on moving out of the mansion following Lord Ebury's death in 1918, opted to live in Batchworth House (see Lot 39), an imposing residence of seven main bedrooms, a further four attic bedrooms, and a gardener's cottage. The frontage of the house was most attractive, overlooking well-maintained and colourful gardens, with several acres of parkland. The rear entrance, used by tradesmen and servants, was opposite the White Bear public house, and part of the

Supplement to "Country Life."

COUNTRY LIFE

THE JOURNAL FOR ALL INTERESTED IN COUNTRY LIFE AND COUNTRY PURSUITS.

VOL. XLV. No. 1170 [REGISTERED AT THE G.P.O. AS A NEWSPAPER.] *SATURDAY, JUNE 7th, 1919.* Published Weekly, Price ONE SHILLING. Subscription Price per annum, Post Free. Inland and Canadian, 60s. Foreign, 74s.

WALTON & LEE AND KNIGHT, FRANK & RUTLEY

LONDON, EDINBURGH AND GLASGOW.

THE GARDEN FRONT.

EAST CORNER OF THE HALL.

BY DIRECTION OF THE RIGHT HON. LORD EBURY.

HERTFORDSHIRE

On the borders of Middlesex, and about eighteen miles from the Marble Arch.

Close to the two railway stations at Rickmansworth (joint Met. Ry. and G.C. Ry. and L. & N.W. Ry.), adjacent to Watford on the north-east, and to Northwood on the south, and with Sandy Lodge Station on the Estate.

THE HISTORICAL, RESIDENTIAL, AGRICULTURAL, AND SPORTING ESTATE OF

MOOR PARK

including a stately Mansion seated in matured gardens and pleasure grounds, and surrounded by a finely-timbered DEER PARK about 500 acres in extent.

The Residence contains a handsome suite of nine reception rooms, about 36 bedrooms, complete domestic offices, and laundry. The DECORATIONS of the principal ground floor apartments and main staircase are by

SIR JAMES THORNHILL, AMICONI, and CIPRIANI.

Three lodges, garage, stabling, home farm, and walled gardens. Company's water. Gravel subsoil.

The Estate includes ten good residences, TEN CAPITAL DAIRY AND MIXED FARMS, a large number of small holdings, building land adjoining the towns of Rickmansworth, Watford, and Northwood, building sites, cottages, two licensed houses, allotments and market gardens, about

240 ACRES OF WOODLAND,

principally oak. Gravel pits, land with valuable gravel deposits close to the Grand Junction Canal, the Sandy Lodge golf course and Batchworth Lake, the whole extending to nearly

3,000 ACRES

For SALE by AUCTION at an early date.

Solicitors: Messrs. BOODLE, HATFIELD & CO., 53, Davies Street, Berkeley Square, W. 1.

Land Agent: HENRY B. COUCHMAN, Esq., Rickmansworth.

Auctioneers: Messrs. WALTON & LEE and KNIGHT, FRANK and RUTLEY, 20, Hanover Square, London, W. 1.

WALTON & LEE, AND KNIGHT, FRANK & RUTLEY,
20, Hanover Square, W. 1.
100, Princes Street, Edinburgh.
78, St. Vincent Street, Glasgow.

Telephones:
3066 Mayfair (4 lines).
146 Central, Edinburgh.
2716 „ Glasgow.

'*Country Life*' carried the announcement of the sale of Moor Park estate in June, 1919, three months prior to the auction.

original high wall which flanked the kitchen garden, is still visible on the corner of Harefield Road. After Lady Ebury's death Batchworth House was pulled down to make way for the small housing estate which now occupies the site.

Money Hill House, at Mill End (Lot 68) was an imposing seven-bedroom residence, with maids' quarters, standing in grounds of twenty-one acres. It was let on an annual agreement to local soft-drinks manufacturers Franklin and Sons at an annual rent of £48.10s.0d. It had once been the home of local socialite Lady Ellen Lambert.

But the most interesting by far of the three Dower Houses is Batchworth Heath House (Lot 26), overlooking Batchworth Common, with grounds of nearly 120 acres. At the time of the auction, the house was occupied by W. J. Morton, although part of the land had been let, under a separate agreement, to the farming Nichols family. Earlier, Batchworth Heath House had been the home of noted diplomat Sir Robert Moirer, who did much to foster a greater understanding between Russia and Britain during his period as Ambassador to Russia from 1884. A close friend of the Grosvenor family, he was a frequent visitor to Moor Park in his latter days, and he died in November 1893, surviving Lord Ebury by little more than two weeks. He, too, is buried at Northwood, and his funeral was attended by many leading statesmen, with floral tributes from both Queen Victoria and the Czar of Russia.

Unfortunately, many of the records of the 1919 auction have been lost, and it has been confirmed that many documents relating to the sale were destroyed in 1952, having been considered to be of no further interest. Even vital copies of local newspapers dated 20th and 27th September 1919, which should have recorded details of the sale, are missing from the National Newspaper Library.

However, it seems clear that Lord Leverhulme's purchase extended beyond merely the Park and the mansion for, in May 1923, coinciding with the opening of his new Moor Park Club, he offered both Batchworth Hill House (see Lot 34) and Frogmore House (see Lot 43) for sale. Batchworth Hill House, which was also known as Moor Park Farmhouse, had been the home of the second Lord Ebury's youngest son Francis, later to become the fourth Lord Ebury. It is known that the development of Moor Park Club was a private venture by Leverhulme, and that he was losing the battle to open his three golf courses on time. Was he perhaps running out of money...?

Many of the working farms on the estate were sold to existing tenants, some of whom were able to reap a fat profit in later years by selling large areas of land for development. Two of the farms in particular – Grove Green Farm and Moor Farm – occupied prime sites within the Moor Park estate, located between the railway line and the golf course, and eventually made way for up-market development in Astons Road, Pembroke Road, Wolsey Road, Russell Road and Bedford Road etc ... Ebury's estate also embraced the Eastbury Farm area of Northwood, with an area called 'The Roughs' much favoured for shooting. This, however, was developed much later, for at the time of the auction, the name Batchworth Lane didn't exist. Instead, it was Claypit Lane which snaked down from Batchworth Heath, through farmland, over the railway and beyond Eastbury Farmhouse to an area where it is thought that bricks were once fired.

Eastbury Farm (Lot 17) has long since disappeared, making way for development of the Eastbury Farm estate in the 1950s and 1960s. The old farmhouse is still standing, however, and local historians believe that it may have been built on the foundations of the old Eastbury Manor House. Excavations have revealed huge slabs of stone which suggest that a formidable building, measuring about 100′ × 40′, once occupied the site. It is also thought that some of the original timbers were used in the building of the farmhouse. The ancient Manor of Eastbury, like the Manors of The More and Batchworth, was once owned by St Alban's Abbey, but there is no record of when the farm became absorbed by the 'Manor of The More'.

The sale of the Ebury estate must mark one of the few occasions when a golf course has been among the lots offered for auction. But members at Sandy Lodge (Lot 10), which occupied nearly 145 acres of the Ebury estate, need not have worried. The club, which was founded in 1910 with its course designed by Harry Vardon, had already been safeguarded by the granting of a 21-year lease. Hardly surprisingly, there were no takers for the leasehold interest, and Sandy Lodge Golf Club was included in the estate purchased after the auction by Lord Leverhulme. Later, in 1929, the club bought the freehold interest from the Leverhulme estate.

Public Houses:

Considering that both the first and second Lord Eburys were Godly men of remarkable temperance, it is perhaps surprising to learn that they allowed their estate to be surrounded by a plethora of pubs and beer-houses. The supposedly quiet market town of Rickmansworth claimed an astonishing twenty-one, with a further three in Batchworth and a handful in Northwood and Ducks Hill.

Only two of them, however, were included as part of the Ebury estate when it came under the auctioneer's hammer in 1919, and both were rented to Salter's, the Rickmansworth brewery.

One was the Rose and Crown (Lot 56), on the fringe of the manor in Woodcock Hill (now Harefield Road). An old timber-framed building

A Sign of Things To Come...

Hooligan behaviour at sporting events is nothing new. In 1890, three years after the opening of the Metropolitan line extension, it is reported that 'a crowd of Londoners who had journeyed to Northwood for the day' began hurling clumps of mud into the well on Batchworth Heath. There was a cricket match in progress at the time, and the cricketers retaliated with considerable enthusiasm. The result was a full-scale battle 'with a bare-back rider dispatched to inform the police of Rickmansworth and Watford.' The riot was eventually quelled, but only after many had been badly injured. Particular mention is made of a Mr W. Gristwood 'who intervened on the side of law and order and suffered concussion from a blow from a flying coconut.'

The 'Rose and Crown' in Woodcock Hill in the 1950s, long before the extensive alterations.

dating from the 17th-century, it is believed to have been originally an old forge. However, records show that in 1812 it was registered as a farm owned by William Lucas. Its first mention as the Rose and Crown public house was in 1822 when it was kept by the flatulently-named James Belch.

In 1838 the owner is declared to have been Edward Lucas, and it is therefore likely that ownership remained in the Lucas family, and that Belch paid them an annual rent. Repeatedly, one assumes.

The circumstances under which it became a part of Ebury's manor aren't known, but it may amuse today's publicans to know that in 1919, Salters brewery rented it for the sum of £25 per year.

The other public house on Ebury's books was The Coach and Horses Inn (Lot 46) at Batchworth, close to Batchworth House where Lady Ebury chose to live after the death of her husband. The Coach and Horses was a beer-house rather than a public house, and is believed to have been pulled down at the same time as Batchworth House. Like the Rose and Crown, it was rented from Ebury's estate by Salter's Brewery but, because it included provision for guest accomodation, and also the rights to an adjacent cottage, the annual rental was levied at a higher rate … a mere £40 per annum.

Its eventual demolition at least solved an identity problem, for it was frequently confused with the Coach and Horses in High Street, Rickmansworth, which is less than half a mile away and is now the town's oldest public house. Although it was first listed as a licensed premises in 1741, the building itself goes back to the late 16th century – much of the construction is of the narrow type of brick which was already becoming obsolete – and it is possible that it was used as an ale-house from the time it was built.

The legend that Cromwell's Roundheads used the Coach and Horses is palpably false since there is no record that Parliament's forces were stationed either in, or even close to, the town. However, it is true that the barn which stood at the rear of the pub was used as an unlikely, but regular, venue for local Baptist meetings...

In 1841, records show that the licensee was Elizabeth Ellingham, and ten years later it had passed to her son, Ephraim. It is possible that his love for

The oldest remaining pub in Rickmansworth is the 'Coach and Horses' once owned by Salters brewery. The original inglenook fireplace still remains. (*Drawings by R. J. Walsh*).

the national game prompted him to rename it 'The Cricketers' but the change was only temporary. By the time William Buyers held the licence in 1866, it had reverted to its original name.

The Coach and Horses is certainly one of the earliest public houses to come into the possession of Samuel Salter who is thought to have started brewing in Rickmansworth in 1721. (To bring the year into focus, it was just a few months after Moor Park had been purchased by Benjamin Styles, who was soon to convert the mansion into the graceful stone-clad edifice which is so familiar today.) By the mid-nineteenth century, Salter's brewery owned fourteen licensed premises in the town and dozens more within a ten-mile radius.

In 1750 the brewery passed from Samuel, the founder, to his son Stephen, who continued to expand the empire. On his demise in 1795, it passed to his nephew, also named Samuel, and still the brewery flourished. When Samuel died in 1829, there was no natural successor, so he appointed trustees, Thomas Fellowes and William Capell. He also endeared his memory to the beer-swilling section of the community by adding a clause in his will that a barrel of ale should be placed each day close to the brewery entrance for the refreshment of inhabitants and visitors to the town.

News of free beer spread rapidly, and the Illustrated London News dated October 11th, 1851, carried a short article bemoaning the fact that when the writer eventually reached Rickmansworth 'the barrel had been drained to its dregs'. Later, in 1896, a contributor to the Herts Advertiser recalled that the barrel still appeared daily in 1857 when he was a boy, 'and he had seen as many as a hundred roughs around it at one time. They would empty the barrel in an hour and then begin fighting.'

The company ceased brewing in the 1920s, when the business was sold to the Cannon Brewery in Watford, later becoming part of Ind Coop, who sold the Coach and Horses in November 1960 to Wells and Winch of Biggleswade. Greene-King, its current owners, took over Wells and Winch the following year.

The Skidmore family, whose name is perpetuated by the housing estate which now stands on the site of the old station, was also a formidable force among the victuallers of Rickmansworth. In addition to once owning the Swan Inn, the historic old coaching house which was tragically torn down in the name of progress in 1964, it appears that they also made their own beer. When the Skidmore brewhouse closed in 1820, the inn was seized by the Lord of the Manor (*not* Moor Park) and Joseph Skidmore was found guilty of 'failing to apply for a licence to alienate.' It is satisfying to note that the Swan Inn was judiciously returned to the Skidmore family upon the death of the Lord of the Manor thirteen years later!

The Evils of Drink...

With twenty-one pubs in the town, it would appear that Dr J. W. Henderson, of Basing House, had good reason to be perturbed by the drinking habits of the Rickmansworth community. Enforcing his power as a Justice of the Peace, he closed fourteen licensed premises for a limited period during a purge against 'the evils of alcohol' in 1912.

Northwood, Middlesex.

Particulars, Plan and Conditions of Sale

OF VALUABLE

Copyhold Properties

COMPRISING THE

OLD LICENSED BEER HOUSE

CALLED

"THE GATE,"

Situate on the Western Side of the Town of Northwood, on the Road to Rickmansworth, and near the Vicarage,

WITH ABOUT

Three Acres of Pasture Land

AT THE BACK, WHICH COULD BE DEVELOPED FOR

BUILDING PURPOSES,

AND

Two Pretty Semi-Detached Cottages

NEAR, WHICH MESSRS.

NORMAN & SON

WILL SUBMIT BY AUCTION,

At the "Essex Arms" Hotel, Watford,

ON TUESDAY, JULY 23RD, 1907

At Half-past Four o'clock precisely, in Lots.

May be Viewed on application to the Occupiers, and Particulars with Plan and Conditions of Sale obtained of WM. MERCER, ESQ., Solicitor, Uxbridge, Middlesex; and of

Messrs. NORMAN & SON, Land Agents and Surveyors,

UXBRIDGE, MIDDLESEX.

John King, Printer, Uxbridge.

The Skidmores also owned the Bell Inn which, in a photograph dated 1904, was selling Benskins beer. Immediately next door was the George Inn, where the Ales, Stout and 'Porter' were supplied by Sedgwick, a rival brewery also based in Watford. ('Porter' was a popular mixture of cheap ale, quality ale and stout).

In contrast to Rickmansworth, there were very few licensed premises in Northwood which was still a developing area. Old maps show Northwode or North Wood as part of the 'the Ancient Manor of Riselip' with its main activity on or around Batchworth Heath. It is here that legendary highwayman Dick Turpin is reputed to have slipped through a rear window of Ye Olde Greene Manne to evade the Bow Street Runners, but it is only fair to point out that many other road-houses have built a reputation on similar pretentions.

There has been a Greene Manne on 'Bacher Heath' since 1728, and the original True Lover's Knot in Northwood dates back to 1740. Although both were obviously frequented by Lord Ebury's tenants and estate workers, there is no record of either of them having been a part of the old Manor of The More.

It is perhaps mildly incongruous to find The Gate has closer associations with the Moor Park estate than other road houses. Although there was no mention of it as a public house before 1869, it is known to have sold alcohol long before that date. It was almost certainly a beer house (having taken its name from the Qu'ferry turnpike) and premises of this type were allowed to operate without a Justice's licence prior to 1869, although a nominal £2 was payable to the Customs and Excise authorities.

Records of a census conducted in 1851 show that The Gate was owned by Mary Anne Bourne, and 'Anne Bourne – beer retailer' was the registered owner in 1882. She retained the licence until 1907 when it was purchased by Gifford Grigg, then butler to the second Lord Ebury at Moor Park. Although Grigg chose to remain in his Lordship's service, The Gate continued to be run by his family for many years.

'The Gate' in Rickmansworth Road (formerly Qu'ferry Hill) during the early 1930s. It was a favourite haunt of Moor Park staff and in 1907 it was purchased at auction by Lord Ebury's butler, Gifford Grigg.

The mansion as it was in 1912, under Lord Ebury's ownership, long before the second window from the right was removed to provide an entrance for golfers. (*Copyright Country Life*).

On the next few pages are details of the Lots as published in the original auction document, produced by Knight, Frank and Rutley, in 1919. A copy of the original map pinpointing each location is included with this volume but, as stated earlier, no records appear to remain of the prices achieved by each Lot.

After the Park and mansion had been sold to Rickmansworth District Council in 1937, Lord Leverhulme's company, Moor Park Ltd., continued to own many sites on the Moor Park estate until 1957. Because of the location of the land, they also owned certain roads within the estate boundaries, and were therefore responsible for their upkeep. In 1957, a decision was made to sell off the land and liquidate the company, passing control to a board of directors drawn from the residents of the estate. The following year, with the help and guidance of what had now become the Unilever Group, Moor Park (1958) Ltd was formed and is still responsible for administering the estate, and safeguarding the interests of local residents.

In 1959, the remaining land was sold by auction by Bernard Thorpe and Partners and details of the thirty-seven lots, including a record of the prices they achieved, follow details of the earlier auction sale. A map showing locations of the Lots offered in the 1959 sale is also included.

CHAPTER EIGHT

1919 Auction

(Reproduction of the original Auction Document)

Particulars

LOT I

(Coloured Green on Plan)

In this Lot is comprised the principal Mansion House on the Estate

known as

Moor Park

"ONE OF THE STATELY HOMES OF ENGLAND"

rich in historical associations, with its

ANCIENT DEER PARK OF OVER 400 ACRES

many of the oaks being reminiscent of the centuries through which they have stood.

Seated on a plateau near where the ground attains its greatest altitude some 300ft above sea level, the Mansion stands facing South-West and North-East, almost in the centre of the Park.

ENTRANCE LODGES

guard the three Carriage Drives from the directions of Rickmansworth, Northwood and Watford, the distances to these Stations being about one-and-a-half miles, two miles, and four miles (to Watford Junction) respectively, the two former Stations being on the joint Metropolitan and Great Central line and the latter on the main London and North Western Railway. Sandy Lodge Station is less than a mile due East of the Mansion and a Right of Roadway thereto is provided for herein.

The Drives converge on the South-Western front of the Mansion, the routes by which they traverse the Park each exemplifying the diversity of its contours, and the beauty and wealth of its timbering.

The Lot in all extends to about

510 a. 2 r. 5 p.

nearly the whole being in hand.

The Entrance to the Mansion is beneath a massive and imposing stone Portico whose four circular pillars are equal in height, some 43 ft., to the top of the third floor storey. The columns are crowned with Corinthian capitals and carry a well-balanced pediment displaying the Coat of Arms of the present owner. The Portico is about 54 ft. long by 18 ft. deep, and from it a pair of oak glazed doors open into the

GRAND ENTRANCE HALL

an apartment of fine proportions, measuring about 38 ft. 6 in. by 38 ft. 6 in. and surrounded on its four sides at a height of about 21 ft. by a wide gallery supported on scroll-shaped trusses painted to represent carving, the full height of the Hall being about 36 ft. The four large mural panel paintings of mythological subjects and the painted ceiling are the work of Giacomo Leoni.

On the Gallery level the walls are painted with representations of statuary in niches of classical figures, while the ceiling is deftly painted to represent a coved dome with central opening rising to a second Gallery circular in form and surrounding a higher floor, and through the opening are seen a domed roof, with its supporting pilasters, and other niches and statuary.

The Hall has a polished white marble floor and dado, the doorways on the ground floor and gallery level being of greyish-white marble with marble pilasters having Corinthian capitals on either side and dentilled pediments on which recline finely-moulded plaster figures arranged in pairs

The marble doorways from the Hall open to a

SUITE OF SIX ENTERTAINING ROOMS

these being exclusive of three other Reception Rooms of less importance. They comprise, on the left

THE LITTLE DINING ROOM OR MORNING ROOM

(SOUTH-WEST), measuring about 21 ft., 9 in. by 18 ft. 3 in., and about 19 ft. 6 in. in height, having canvas-hung walls with painted margins and corners of floral design..

DINING ROOM

lighted by windows on three sides and measuring about 60 ft. by 22 ft. 6 in., inclusive of five narrow square bays on its North-West side. The floor is of oak, and the walls are hung in panels with hand paintings on canvas of birds and foliage by a Japanese artist. The polished white statuary marble chimneypiece is boldly carved with pilasters supporting half-length figures, and along the frieze on a background of lapis lazuli runs a row of little marble figures standing out in high relief. The ceiling is decorated with paintings from the brush of Cipriani, the elaborate geometrical and foliated design including two central groups of figures with marginal panels of cupids and medallions at the corners.

LIBRARY

(NORTH-EAST) measuring about 21 ft. 9 in. by 18 ft. 3 in. and 19 ft. 6 in. in height and having a variegated mauve marble chimneypiece and oak bookcase and cupboards.

SALOON

about 40 ft. by 22 ft. 6in. by 19 ft. 6 in. in height, having polished oak block floor and three casement windows overlooking the Italian Gardens and leading to the Terrace. The chimneypieces at either end of the apartment are of oak with bold carvings of figures and cupid frieze, the doorway to the Grand Hall being *en suite* and guarded by fluted pilasters having Corinthian capitals and dentilled pediment. The dado is also of oak, parcel gilt, and the walls and ceiling are decorated with hand paintings by Sir James Thornhill. The panels on the walls represent The Four Seasons, and the ceiling, Aurora and Boreas, Spirits of the Dawn and Wind, the artist's work occupying practically the full length and breadth of the room.

BLUE ROOM

(NORTH-EAST) measuring about 21 ft. 9 in. by 21 ft. 9 in., and 19 ft. 6 in. in height, its walls hung with an oriental hand painted paper and crowned by a coved frieze with central medallion and cupids in relievo. The Chimney-piece is of carved polished statuary Marble enclosing a dog-grate.

DRAWING ROOM OR WHITE ROOM

about 41 ft. 6 in. by 20 ft. 9 in., and 19 ft. 6 in. in height, an apartment of well balanced proportions having two pairs of fluted pillars at one end, the larger part of the room having a carved stone mantel and steel grate. Here also is a finely executed plaster ceiling of figures in high relief, and a deep coved frieze with cupids in relievo and festoons of flowers and fruit. The Telephone is installed in this Room

ANTE ROOM, about 12 ft. 9 in. by 12 ft. 3 in., and 11 ft. in height, and communicating with

STUDY, about 21 ft. 9 in. by 18 ft. and 19 ft. 6 in. in height, having massive variegated marble mantel and overmantel with bevelled plate glass mirror.

Near the Ante Room is a W.C., and up a winding stairway close by is a Valet's Bedroom, having fireplace and measuring about 12 ft. 9 in. by 12 ft. 3 in.

In the North-West wing of the Mansion and approached by a heated corridor from the Dining Room is the LONG ROOM or PLAY ROOM, measuring about 52 ft. 9 in. by 19 ft., by about 18 ft. in height, heated by a fireplace and well lighted.

THE PRINCIPAL STAIRCASE

rises from the central staircase Hall, measuring about 21 ft. 9 in. by 19 ft., and is lighted by a large lantern light in the roof. The floor is of white marble, and the staircase of solid polished oak with balusters and dado *en suite*. Hand paintings on canvas executed by Sleker, signed by the artist and dated 1732, adorn the walls and soffits of the Staircase and Hall. Monochromes by the same artist occupy the lower panels and the space above the dado.

THERE ARE TWELVE PRINCIPAL BEDCHAMBERS

on the First Floor, which level may also be reached by two secondary staircases. The Rooms are numbered from 1 to 12, and their respective dimensions are as follows:— No. 1, 18 ft. by 17 ft. 6 in.; No. 2, 20 ft. 3 in. by 13 ft.; No. 3, about 20 ft. 9 in. by 20 ft. 3in.; No. 4, 20 ft. 6 in. by 12 ft. 9 in., and heated by radiator; No. 5, 22 ft. 6 in. by 22 ft. 3 in.; No. 6, 16 ft. 6 in. by 13 ft. 6 in.; No. 7, 17 ft. 6 in. by 9 ft. 6 in.; No. 8, 23 ft. 3 in. by 19 ft.; No. 9, 22 ft. by 19 ft.; No. 10, 23 ft. 9 in. by 23 ft.; No. 11, 23 ft. 9 in. by 20 ft.; and No. 12, 22 ft. by 18 ft. 9 in.

The foregoing Bedrooms are each provided with marble and other appropriate fireplace appointments. A Corridor leading to some of them is heated by hot water pipes, and there are two W.C.'s in convenient positions.

ON THE SECOND FLOOR, approached by two staircases, are

TWELVE SECONDARY AND BACHELORS' BEDROOMS

numbered from 13 to 16, 18 to 23, and 27 and 28 respectively, a Dressing Room, four Maidservants' Bedrooms (one numbered 17), Bathroom, with bath (h. and c.), and two W.C's.

The respective dimensions of the Bedrooms are as follows :—No. 13, 24 ft. by 20 ft. 6 in. ; No. 14, 24 ft. 3 in. by 20 ft. 9 in. ; No. 15, 22 ft. 9 in. by 14 ft. 3 in. ; No. 16, 14 ft. 9 in. by 14 ft. 6 in. ; No. 17, 14 ft. 6 in. by 10 ft. ; No. 18, 14ft. 6in. square ; No. 19, 22 ft. 6 in. by 16 ft. ; No. 20, 20 ft. 6 in. by 13 ft. ; No. 21, 20 ft. 6 in. by 16 ft. 3 in. ; No. 22, 20 ft. 6 in. by 13 ft. ; No. 23, 18 ft. 6 in. by 14 ft. 3 in. ; No. 27, 14 ft. by 12 ft. 9 in. ; and No. 28, 19 ft. 3 in. by 9 ft. 3 in.

Each of these Bedrooms is about 10 ft. in height. There are also on this floor large Box Room, Store Cupboard ; and Housemaid's Cupboard with sink having hot and cold services. The Corridor to the Maidservants' Bedrooms is heated by hot water pipes.

ON THE THIRD FLOOR, reached by a stone stairway well lighted from the roof are :— A Chapel (consecrated), measuring about 17 ft. 3 in. by 12 ft. 3 in. ; Photographic Dark Room, having fireplace and water laid on ; Servants' Bedroom, having fireplace and measuring about 17 ft. by 15 ft., Tank and Lumber Rooms. The Corridor is lighted by gas.

THE DOMESTIC OFFICES

are commodious and well planned, the kitchen and its departments being situate in an annexe on the ground level and with its Bedroom accommodation on the floorabove. The remainder of the offices are in the basement of the main building, and these are airy and well lighted.

THE KITCHEN OFFICES

comprise :—Lofty Kitchen about 30 ft. by 24 ft. 9 in., fitted with two double oven ranges, gas stove, hot plate and sink (h. and c.) ; Scullery, with sink having hot, cold and soft water services, and stove for heating water for washing up purposes ; Larder, with slate shelving and walls hung with white-glazed tiles ; Pastry Larder ; having similar tiled walls and two refrigerators ; Cleaning Room with fireplace and, sink (h. and c.) ; Sitting Room for kitchen maids ; three Kitchenmaids' Bedrooms, and W.C.

THE BASEMENT OFFICES

include :—Valet's Bedroom with fireplace, and measuring about 12 ft. square ; W.C. another Manservant's Bedroom, having fireplace and sink (h. and c.); Bottle, Beer and Wood Cellars ; Butler's Pantry, fitted with sink and Telephone on the G.P.O. system ; Butler's Bedroom with sink and strong room ; Boot Hole ; Brushing Room with sink and cold water supply ; Scullery, similarly fitted ; Servants' Hall, about 24 ft. by 18 ft. 6 in. with fireplace and hot water supply ; Steward's Room, about 20 ft. 3 in. by 17 ft. 6 in. ; Mineral Water, Wood and Wine Cellars, the latter large and brick binned ; Housemaids' Sitting Room, about 20 ft. 6 in. by 20 ft. 3 in., having china and linen cupboards, and sink with cold water service ; Still Room with fireplace, sink and hot and cold services ; two W.C.'s ; Coal, Paraffin, and Anthracite Stores.

Here are also placed two furnace Rooms, the one heating the Grand Hall, Drawing Room and Saloon by means of hot air ; and the other heating the water for lavatory basins, the hot water pipes in Bedrooms Nos. 3 and 4, and on the third floor. The basement is lighted by gas.

Near the Kitchen Offices is a

WELL-FITTED LAUNDRY

consisting of :—Washhouse with two coppers, five wash-tubs (h. and c.) ; Ironing Room ; Laundry Maids' Sitting Room ; two good Bedrooms, and W.C.

The Water supply to the Laundry is from a spring near the Home Farm.

Near by are Carpenters' and Plumbers' Shops and Office.

SUMMARY OF ACCOMMODATION

Grand Hall.	Twelve Principal Bedrooms.
Morning Room.	Twelve Bachelors' Bedrooms.
Dining Room.	Dressing Room.
Library.	Eight Maidservants' Bedrooms.
Saloon.	Three Menservant's Bedrooms.
Blue Room.	Two Maids' Sitting Rooms.
Drawing Room.	Bath Room and Seven W.C.'s.
Ante Room.	Chapel (or Bedroom).
Study.	Laundry, with Sitting Room.
Long Room.	Two Bedrooms and W.C.

The Mansion is of massive stone construction, roofed with slate and in sound condition.

WATER.—There is a never failing supply of good drinking water by gravitation from a spring near the Home Farm. Fire hydrants are installed, the water for them also coming from the spring. The fountains in the Grounds are well served from a sheet of water in the Old Pleasure Grounds.

LIGHTING.—Gas is laid on to the Offices, Corridors, etc., from the Rickmansworth Company's Mains.

HEATING.—The Grand Hall, Drawing Room and Saloon are heated by hot air, and certain of the Corridors and Bedrooms are heated by hot water pipes.

SANITATION AND DRAINAGE.—The sanitary fittings are of a modern type, and the effluent is disposed of on the irrigation principle, the nature of the soil rendering this method of disposal at once simple, economical and efficient.

THE STABLING AND GARAGE

are arranged on four sides of an enclosed Stable Yard, the Buildings being situate on the North-West side of the Mansion and built of brick and slate. They are surmounted by a Clock Turret and Vane, and afford the following accommodation :—Garage with pit, two Loose Boxes, Cart House, five-stall Stable with Loose Box at end three-stall Stable, two large Loose Boxes, Harness Room, Mess Room, three Stall Stable (now loose box) with Loft above, two Coach or Motor Houses with stone flagged floor, Corn Room with fireplace, seven Men's Bedrooms, five of which have fireplaces, another Harness Room, Store Place, Messing Place, and two W.C's.

THE COACHMAN'S QUARTERS

form part of the above buildings and consist of Sitting Room, Kitchen, Scullery with sink (h. and c.), Bedroom, and W.C.

Company's Gas, and Water from the Spring in the Park are laid on.

THE PLEASURE GROUNDS

may be described as being laid out in three self-contained sections, and comprise THE ITALIAN GARDEN on the immediate North-East front of the Mansion, THE LAWNS and TERRACE, adjoining on the North-West, and THE OLD PLEASURE GROUND, lying detached from the others, some little way to the South.

The Italian Garden, to which a wide flight of stone steps leads down from the Mansion, is laid out with parterres, edged with box and planted with Pyramid Irish Yews and Junipers. A Fountain and Fish Pond occupy a central space, the whole producing an attractive and symmetrical effect and in character with the style of the Mansion. Near this Garden also are two fine old Cedar Trees.

Adjoining the Italian Garden wide-spreading lawns stretch away to the North to the Terrace, where the Parklands fall sharply to the Watford drive, and a fine avenue of trees on the opposite bank carries the eye to the brow of the hill and beyond.

The Lawns are adorned by timber trees of fine proportions, and here also thrive many trees of other climes, notable among them being Japanese Cedar, Ailanthus Glandulosis (Chinese Tree of Heaven), Hemlock Spruce, Abies Nobilis, Quercus Ilex, and Catalpa Syringæfolia. A Fountain playing near the shade of another large Cedar forms a delightful feature in a corner of these Gardens.

The Gardens known as THE OLD PLEASURE GROUNDS occupy a site of natural beauty where the Landscape Gardeners' art by planting in years gone by has brought about an effect of wonderful charm and restfulness. An Ornamental Sheet of Water in a dell, elliptical in form, is surrounded on three sides by banks, their slopes clothed by rhododendrons and other shrubs and the higher ground studded with specimen trees in full maturity. From the summit of the ellipse, where stands a Summerhouse known as the Temple of the Winds, the contour of the Garden takes a gentle slope towards the Mansion, glimpses of which are seen in the distance set as in a framing of foliage, with a fine old Cedar on the brow of a terrace and the lake in the foreground.

Amongst the Trees in this Garden are well-grown specimens of Spruce, Deodara, Larch, Douglas and Scots Fir, Wellingtonia and Araucaria.

THE PARK

in addition to providing good Pasturage as a whole, and in parts herbage of particular richness, has been laid out for Golf, and in other sections of it are a Rabbit Warren, and Withy Beds frequented by Wild Fowl. The latter are situated at the North-Eastern corner of the Park, and surrounded by them on three sides is a Pasture Enclosure numbered 151 on the Sale Plan and Let to Mr. R. T. Dickins, together with other Lands, under Yearly Michaelmas Tenancy, at an apportioned rent of £9 per annum.

THE FRUIT AND VEGETABLE GARDENS

are on the South Western boundary of the Park and occupy a sheltered position on a gentle slope facing the direction named. They are walled all round, with inner Gardens also walled, and in all they extend to about Five Acres.

The Gardens are fully stocked with all kinds of walled, Standard and Espalier Fruit Trees, and Bush Fruit, the soil and situation of the Gardens increasing their productiveness and ensuring early maturity. Herbaceous borders line the walks, and the Gardens are made further attractive by dwarf walls, clipped yew hedges, and edgings of box.

There is a FULL COMPLEMENT of GLASS HOUSES, and were some of the older ones removed, sufficient would remain for all ordinary needs. They comprise :—Lean-to Peach House, four Span-roof Pits and a six-light Pit ; Lean-to four division Peach House and Vinery, two Fern Houses, a three division House (two divisions with Vines and one used as a Cucumber House), a heated Pit of ten lights, three-quarter Span Greenhouse, lean-to two division Fig and Carnation House, three ranges of Cool Pits, Cucumber or Melon House, three other ranges of Cool Pits, lean-to Stove House Mushroom House, a long lean-to Peach and Nectarine Case, Fruit and Grape Rooms.

Water is available in or about the Houses from an underground tank at the back of the Buildings and from a large pond in the Park. The majority of the Houses are fitted for heating by hot water pipes.

There is a BOTHY, containing Sitting Room, Kitchen, Larder and two Bedrooms, other Buildings in these Gardens comprising Potting Shed, Fruit Room, Office, Packing Shed, Men's Mess Room, Potato Store and Paint Shop, etc.

Near the South Western Corner of the Gardens and on the opposite side of the Road is a

PAIR OF COTTAGES

for Gardeners, built of brick, and containing respectively three Rooms downstairs and four above, and two Rooms downstairs and two above. Each Cottage also has a Wash-house with Copper.

Company's Water is laid into the Front Garden.

The Cottages are Let under weekly tenancies to Mr. Frederick Horsenell and Mrs. Haines respectively, the landlord paying rates and water charges.

The Accommodation of the Entrance Lodges, already alluded to, is as follows :—

NORTHWOOD LODGE

this comprises two stone-built Houses, one on either side of a central stone Carriage Archway, that on the left having four rooms, and the one on the right seven rooms ; near by is a timber and slated, match-lined Room, suitable for village meetings, etc. There is a supply of Rain Water, and that for drinking is obtained from a stand pipe on Batchworth Heath ; one Lodge is occupied by a gardener, the other being vacant.

RICKMANSWORTH LODGE

a picturesque brick and thatched ivy-clad Building, with Pleasure Garden at the side, bounded by the River Colne and the Grand Junction Canal. In the Garden is an exceptionally fine Tulip Tree. This Lodge contains four rooms, and in addition there is an OCTAGONAL GOLF OR TEA ROOM about 20 ft. in diameter, and having stained glass windows and domed ceiling, the decorations of the Room being by Robert Adam. Gas and Water are laid on. This Lodge is in the occupation of a gardener.

THE WATFORD LODGE

is occupied by the Head Keeper. It is brick, slated and ivy-clad, and contains six rooms, with Kennels, Game Larder, Cart Shed and Corn Store at the back. Well Water.

THE HOME FARM

is situate on the Southern Boundary of the Park and adjoining the Fruit and Kitchen Gardens. The Homestead includes a commodious and pleasantly situated Farm House and a modern set of Buildings, well arranged and in good order.

THE HOUSE

is substantially built of brick with tiled roof, having terraced front Lawn planted with clipped yews and containing :—Small Hall, Dining Room with modern tiled fireplace, Drawing Room with similar grate, Kitchen with range, Scullery having water laid on, two Larders, Scullery with furnace, copper, and sink, also having water laid on ; well-fitted Dairy heated by hot water pipes, ventilated, and having slate shelving, and its walls hung with white glazed tiles ; and on the First Floor, approached by two Staircases, are five Bed Rooms. Beneath the House is a good Cellar.

THE FARMBUILDINGS

are for the most part built of timber on brick foundations, with tiled roofs, and comprise :—Cowshed for fourteen, having water laid on ; Chaff House, Root and Mixing Houses, Cake Store, Boiler House, Forage Barn, Granary with divisions for cake and corn, Calving Box, Tool Shed, four-bay open Cattle Shed with Yard in front, five-stall Cart Horse Stable with Loose Box at end and Harness Room adjoining, five Pigsties, corrugated iron two-bay Cart Shed with Implement Shed at end, Hen House, and two timber and felted Poultry Houses. There are also three timber and thatched Cattle Shelters in the Park.

Water is laid on into the Yard from a Pond in the Park, and the Drainage is taken into a Cesspool in Lot 27.

The Home Farm is held and farmed in conjunction with the Parklands (and other Lands not included in Lot 1) and the whole is in hand.

The Mansion, Gardens, and Lodges are also in hand, and vacant possession can be given on completion of the Purchase

INCLUDED IN THIS LOT ALSO IS THE MANOR OR REPUTED MANOR OF MOOR AND ITS APPURTENANT PRIVILEGES AND LIABILITIES, IF ANY.

There is a liability on the Vendor to keep in repair the two Bridges over the River Colne, and the Roadway for lengths of 100 yards on both sides of the same, the liability in respect of the upkeep of the Road lengths being at present arranged by a payment to the Hertfordshire County Council of £21 per annum. The Bridges and Roadway lengths are situate near the Keeper's or Watford Lodge, the former being indicated by the letters S and T on the Plan. The Bridges are of iron construction.

Lot 1 is sold and will be conveyed subject to the above liabilities, whether offered separately or in conjunction with other Lots.

SCHEDULE.

No. on Plan.	Tenant.	Description.	Quantity.	Total Quantity
	PARISH OF RICKMANSWORTH RURAL (Det. 3).			
17	In hand . . .	Gardens	6.257	
18		Home Farm, Buildings, etc. .	1.276	
19		Pond	.240	
20		Lodge and Woodlands . .	2.671	
80		Lodge	.455	
81		Park	423.180	
81A		Do.	.988	
81B		Do.	.625	
81C		Do.	.495	
81D		Pond	.150	
81E		Bathend Clump . . .	1.192	
144		Withy Bed	1.080	
145		Do.	1.097	
Pt. 146		Do.	3.403	
147		Do. . . .	.622	
148		Do.	1.316	
149		Do	1.065	
Pt. 150		Do.	12.118	
166		Old Pleasure Ground . .	13.184	
167		Lake	.825	
168		Reservoir	.460	
169		Spinney	1.108	
170		Arable	3.971	
175		Spinney	1.942	
176		Pond	.209	
188		Pasture	5.441	
189		Mansion and Grounds . .	8.302	
190		Keeper's Lodge . . .	.446	
191		Withy Bed	.091	
192		Do.	.265	
Pt. 194		River .	.513	
Pt. 199		Stream	1.150	
	PARISH OF RICKMANSWORTH URBAN.			
639		Lodge and Gardens . .	2.131	
Pt. 646		River	.300	
672A		Roadway	.500	
	PARISH OF WATFORD RURAL (Det.)			
Pt. 1038		River	.480	
1042		Tolpits Plantation . .	3.456	
				503.004
	PARISH OF RICKMANSWORTH RURAL (Det. 3)			
Pt. 146	Mr. R. T. Dickins .	Roadway	.160	
151		Pasture	7.098	
				7.258
171	Mr. F. Horsenell and Mrs. Haines .	Two Cottages and Gardens .		.269
			Total	A.510.531

LANDLORD'S OUTGOINGS.

Commuted Tithe Rent Charge £74 8 1

The Timber on this Lot will be included in the Sale.

A purchaser of this Lot will be required to take and pay for by valuation in addition to his purchase money, the tenant's fixtures and fittings, planned and fitted furniture, etc., on the premises according to Inventories to be prepared or approved by the Auctioneers in accordance with General Remark No. 4.

This Lot is Sold with the benefit of and is sold and will be conveyed subject to the following provisions :—

(*a*)—A right in conjunction with or without Lot 12 to make and use a Footway not more than 7 ft. wide or a Roadway not more than 42 ft. wide immediately to the South of and adjoining and following the line of the Northern boundary fence or ditch of Enclosures, Nos. 131 and 132 on Plan, Lot 16. Lot 12 is to have a Right to use the Footway or Roadway if and when made by Lots 1 and 16 or either of them without payment. Should Lot 16 make the footway or roadway mentioned one half the cost of same is to be borne by and paid to Lot 16 by Lot 1 as soon as any use is made of either by Lot 1. Should Lot 12 make the Footway or Roadway one-third the cost of the same is to be borne by and paid to Lot 12 by each of Lots 1 and 16 as soon as any use is made by either of the Path or Road. (See footnotes to Lots 12 and 16.)

(*b*)—A right to the continued existence and use by this Lot as at present of the Cesspool and overflow therefrom serving the Home Farm, the Cesspool mentioned being on Lot 27, and the piped overflow discharging into a ditch on Lot 26, with a further right to enter Lots 26 and 27 for the purpose of inspecting, cleansing, emptying, repairing and reinstating the Cesspool and line of pipes making compensation for any damage in so doing. (See footnotes to Lots 26 and 27.)

(*c*)—An Agreement with the Rickmansworth Urban District Council dated February 19th, 1912, for diverting the Roadway on Batchworth Hill so far as it relates to this Lot.

(*d*)—As to the Spring or Well at the corner of the Park near Batchworth Mill and the water supply therefrom and the pipes to Batchworth Mill, subject to the rights in favour of the owners of the Mill and of certain cottages and the public reserved by a deed of May 23rd, 1828, and an agreement of September 7th, 1899.

(*e*)—As to Nos. 1042 and Pt. 1038, subject to and with the benefit of the Agreement of May 20th, 1823 mentioned in the Conditions.

LOT 2

(Coloured Pink on Plan)

Hampton Hall Farm

a rich Dairying Holding, situate within half-a-mile of the Town of Rickmansworth and bounded on the South and East by the Road to Watford and on the North by the Grand Junction Canal and the River Colne.

The Lot includes a small brick and tiled Farm House, a useful set of Buildings, several enclosures of excellent Pasture and Orchard Land and a Withy Bed.

The whole extends to an area of about

70A. 0R. 13P.

and underlying same are believed to be valuable deposits of gravel.

Let as to part to Mr. Samuel King under Yearly Michaelmas Tenancy, rent £178 10s. the remainder together with the Shooting over the Farm and the Fishing from one bank in the River Colne being in hand.

THE FARMHOUSE

contains Sitting Room, Kitchen, Dairy, having Company's water laid on to the sink, Wash House, with copper and fireplace and a large dry Granary above; and two Bed Rooms.

THE FARMBUILDINGS

comprise timber and tiled Cow House for sixteen with Root House at end, two Grain Pits, two bay timber and slated open Barn on brick foundation with Cow Shed for five at one end and a two-stall Stable at the other, and in No. 193 on Plan is a timber and tiled three-bay Cattle Shed.

SCHEDULE.

No. on Plan	Tenant	Description.	Quantity.	Total Quantity.
	PARISH OF RICKMANSWORTH RURAL (Det. 3).			
193	Mr. S King . .	Pasture	12.887	
195		Watercress Bed .	.262	
Pt. 199		Stream	1.699	
200		Pasture	7.686	
201		Do.	11.550	
206		Do. . .	4.882	
209		Do.	6.750	
211		Do.	1.250	
212		Do	1.886	
213		Do	5.196	
	PARISH OF RICKMANSWORTH URBAN.			
637		Pasture	8.979	
638		House, Buildings and Orchard	3.229	
				66.256
	PARISH OF RICKMANSWORTH RURAL (Det. 3).			
Pt. 194	In hand . .	River	1.500	
208		The Alders	2.326	3.826
			Total	A.70.082

LANDLORD'S OUTGOINGS.

Commuted Tithe Rent Charge £10 5 6

The Timber on this Lot has an estimated valued of £45 and is included in the Sale.

N.B.—It is believed that the tenant of the farm would be willing to give vacant possession at Michaelmas, 1919, on terms to be arranged with the purchaser.

The part of this Lot in the Parish of Rickmansworth Rural is sold subject to and with the benefit of the agreement dated May 20th, 1823 mentioned in the Conditions.

LOT 3

(Coloured Brown on Plan)

A USEFUL SMALL HOLDING

comprising four enclosures of ACCOMMODATION PASTURE LAND with two pieces of Woodland and rough Pasture adjoining, situate on the road from Rickmansworth to Watford, and being about one-and-a-quarter miles from the former and two miles from the latter.

In No. 1043 on plan is a SMALL SET OF BUILDINGS constructed of timber with tiled roofs and comprising a Cowhouse for three, another Cowhouse for eight, three Loose Boxes, and Brick Built Furnace.

The Lot embraces an area of about

33A. 3R. 39P.

and is let as to part to Mr. James Saunders under yearly Michaelmas tenancy, rent £52 10s., the remainder, together with the shooting and the fishing from one bank in the River Colne, being in hand.

SCHEDULE.

No. on Plan.	Tenant.	Description.	Quantity.	Total Quantity.
	PARISH OF WATFORD RURAL (Det.).			
Pt. 1032	Mr. J. Saunders .	Pasture	.600	
Pt. 1035		Do.	4.500	
1037		Do.	13.544	
1043		Do.	4.030	
				22.674
1033	In hand . .	Rough Pasture	8.907	
Pt. 1038		River	.830	
1039		Plantation . . .	1.215	
1040		Do.	.370	
				11.322
			Total A.	33.996

LANDLORD'S OUTGOINGS.

Commuted Tithe Rent Charge £4 2 3

The Timber on this Lot has an estimated value of £25 and is included in the Sale.

The Lot will be Sold and conveyed subject to a Right of Cart Way over enclosures Nos. 1037 and Pt. 1035 on Sale plan in favour of Lot 4 (see footnote to that Lot).

The overflow from the cesspool serving the Cottages on Lot 15 discharges into the Eastern extremity of No. 1033 on Sale plan, and this Lot is Sold and conveyed subject to this easement, and with a right for Lot 15 to enter enclosure No. 1033 for the purpose of inspecting, cleansing, and reinstating the outlet on making proper compensation for any damage done.
Nos. 1039 and 1040 are sold subject to and with the benefit of the agreement of May 20th, 1823 mentioned in the Conditions.

LOT 4

(Coloured Blue on Plan)

A SMALL SPORTING PROPERTY

situate to the North of the foregoing Lot, and comprising a

LAKE OF ABOUT FOUR ACRES

and Parcels of Grazing Land adjoining, the whole extending to an area of about

9A. 3R. 4P.

Let as to the Lake and Fishing to Mr. Frederick Ivatt under lease for fourteen years, from 29th September, 1915, determinable by Tenant at 7th year, rent £20, and as to the remainder to Mr. W. L. Watson under Yearly Michaelmas Tenancy.

SCHEDULE.

No. on Plan.	Tenant.	Description.	Quantity.	Total Quantity.
		PARISH OF WATFORD RURAL (Det.).		
Pt. 1032	Mr. F. Ivatt	Rough Pasture . . .	.906	
1032A		Tolpits Lake . . .	4.244	5.150
Pt. 1028	Mr. W. L. Watson	Pasture . . .	.412	
Pt. 1030		Do. . . .	1.542	
Pt. 1031		Do. . . .	2.673	4.627
			Total	A.9.777

LANDLORD'S OUTGOINGS.

Commuted Tithe Rent Charge £1 13 4

Any Timber on this Lot will be included in the Sale

The Lot is Sold with a Right of Cart Way approach over enclosures Nos. 1037 and Pt. 1035, Lot 3 (see footnote to that Lot).

Nos. 1028, 1031 and 1032A are Sold subject to and with the benefit of the Agreement of May 20th, 1823 and the Conveyance of October 3rd, 1867, mentioned in the Conditions.

LOT 5

(Coloured Pink on Plan)

Tolpits House

a compact and PRETTILY SITUATED RESIDENTIAL PROPERTY abutting the roadway, known as Tolpits Lane, from Rickmansworth to Watford, which towns are both about two miles distant. The House stands about 182 ft. above sea level, commands extensive views in a South-Easterly direction, and the grounds and adjoining paddocks slope down to the River Colne which forms the Southern boundary of the property, and is at a level of some 20 ft. below that of the House.
The Lot extends to an area of about **14A. 3R. 10P.**

and together with the Fishing is in hand. Vacant possession will be given on Completion of the Purchase.

THE HOUSE

is substantially built of red brick, partly ivy clad, with slated roof, approached by a short Carriage Drive with LODGE AT ENTRANCE and contains :—

ON THE GROUND FLOOR : PORCH ; HALL, with tiled floor, about 18 ft. by 8 ft. ; DINING ROOM (East), about 18 ft. by 15 ft. 3 in., with Slate Mantel ; DRAWING ROOM (South and East), about 22 ft. by 18 ft. including a bay from which a casement leads to a Verandah and the Grounds ; MORNING ROOM (South), about 18 ft., including a bay and having a similar Verandah to the Drawing Room, by 13 ft. 9 in. ; W.C. with modern pedestal fitting ; KITCHEN having double-oven range and measuring about 19 ft. by 15 ft. 6 in. by 11 ft. in height ; SERVING LOBBY to Dining Room ; BUTLER'S PANTRY with Fireplace, Dresser and Cupboards, and hot and cold water services to sink ; SCULLERY with sink having hot and soft water services and drinking water supply by pump ; Larder, and Store Room.

ON THE FIRST FLOOR, reached by principal and secondary staircases are FOUR BEST BEDROOMS, their respective dimensions being about 17 ft. 6in. by 15 ft. 3 in. ; 18 ft. 3 in. by 13 ft. 9 in. ; 15 ft. 6 in. by 14 ft. 6 in. ; and 14 ft. 3 in. by 13 ft. 9 in ; BATH ROOM with metal bath having h. and c. services ; and W.C. with modern pedestal fitting ; and

ON THE SECOND FLOOR are THREE BEST AND TWO SECONDARY BEDROOMS, measuring respectively about 18 ft. 3 in. by 15 ft. ; 19 ft. 6 in. by 13 ft. 6 in .; 15 ft. by 14 ft. 3 in. ; 14 ft. 6 in. by 13 ft. 9 in. ; and 11 ft. by 7 ft. 6in. ;

There are THREE MAIDSERVANTS' BEDROOMS, two situate on the half landing between the Ground and First Floors, and measuring respectively about 15 ft. by 10 ft. 9 in. ; and 14 ft. 6 in. by 10 ft. 3 in. ; where there is also a Housemaid's Closet with Sink having h. and c. services ; the other Bedroom being reached by a separate staircase from the Kitchen.

Beneath the House is UNDERGROUND CELLARAGE comprising Dairy, Wine and large Storage Cellars, and Dark Room. Outside are timber and tiled Boot Hole and Coal Shed, W.C. and Wood Shed.

SUMMARY OF ACCOMMODATION

Hall.	Seven Best Bedrooms.
Dining Room.	Two Secondary Bedrooms.
Drawing Room.	Three Maidservants' Bedrooms.
Morning Room.	Bath Room, and Two W.C's.
Ground Floor Offices.	Underground Cellarage.

TOLPIT'S HOUSE. (LOT 5.)

BRIGHTWELL'S FARM. (LOT 8.)

The House is in good order, structurally and decoratively.

The principal aspects of the House are South and East.

The Rooms are of good height, and there is ample Cupboard accommodation.

Gravel subsoil ; Water supply from a well on the premises ; cesspool drainage.

THE ENTRANCE LODGE

is of similar construction to the Residence and contains Sitting Room, Kitchen, Scullery and two Bedrooms with W.C. and Coal House outside.

THE GARAGE AND STABLING

adjoins the Lodge, and is built of like materials, the accommodation being : Motor House with two pairs of double doors, two Loose Boxes, two Stalls, Harness Room and Corn Chamber.

Water is obtained by force pump from a well, and the drainage is into a cesspool in the Stable Yard.

Near the Stabling is a small SET OF OUTBUILDINGS consisting of Timber and Tiled Cowshed for three, with Hayshed adjoining and loft over ; Pigsty, two Loose Boxes with Loft over, Coke Shed, Timber and Slated Granary, two Kennels and Fowl House.

THE PLEASURE GROUNDS

are laid out on a terrace overlooking the front Paddock and River ; they are well Timbered and particularly noticeable is a large thriving Araucaria. There are also a Tennis, Lawn, Rock Garden, Rose and Herbaceous Walks.

The KITCHEN GARDENS are well stocked, partially walled in, and include a lean-to two-division Greenhouse (heated), and two ranges of brick pits. The Garden Walls and the Walls of some of the Buildings are trained with Peach, Nectarine and other Fruit Trees ; there is also a small Orchard and three Grass Paddocks.

SCHEDULE.

No. on Plan.	Tenant.	Description.	Quantity.
	PARISH OF WATFORD RURAL (Det.).		
Pt. 1048	In hand . .	River	.342
1049		Pasture	4.235
1050		Do.	2.185
1051		House and Garden . .	3.380
1055		Pasture . . .	.924
1056		Trees	.217
1057		Pasture	1.296
1058		Old Roadway . . .	.454
Pt. 1060		River	.433
Pt. 1061		Trees, etc. . . .	.329
	PARISH OF RICKMANSWORTH RURAL (Det. 3)		
Pt. 153		River	.560
Pt. 165		Do.	.460
		Total .	A14.815

LANDLORD'S OUTGOINGS.

Commuted Tithe Rent Charge £3 0 0

The Timber on this Lot is included in the Sale. The Sale also includes the whole width of the River where it abuts land forming part of this Lot.

LOT 6

(Coloured Purple on Plan)

LITTLE TOLPITS COTTAGE

situate immediately to the West of the foregoing Lot and eminently suitable for a small week-end Residence. The surroundings are finely Timbered and the Gardens slope down to the River Colne.

The Lot extends to an area of about

1 A. 3 R. 20 P.

and is Let as to Part to Mr. Alfred Evans under Yearly Tenancy, determinable by six months' notice at either Lady day or Michaelmas, the remainder together with Fishing in the river being in hand.

THE COTTAGE

is constructed for the most part of brick with tiled roof, half timber work at the back, timbered gable end and cement faced front. It stands a short distance back from the road and contains :—Large Sitting Room (about 19 ft. by 11 ft.), Kitchen, Scullery with Copper and Sink, Pantry, Larder, Cellar and three Bedrooms, the largest of a similar size to the Sitting Room. Outside are a Brick, Timber and Tiled Shed adjoining the Cottage, and Timber and Tiled three-bay open Cart Shed, and two Pigsties.

Water is obtained from an artesian well on the premises.

SCHEDULE.

No. on Plan.	Tenant.	Description.	Quantity.	Total Quantity.
	PARISH OF WATFORD RURAL (Det.)			
1046A	Mr. A. Evans .	Cottage and Garden . .	.496	
1046B		Trees	.461	
				.957
1046	In hand . .	Trees	.106	
Pt. 1048		River	.330	
	PARISH OF RICKMANSWORTH RURAL (Det. 3)			
Pt. 153		River	.185	.921
			Total	A.1.878

LANDLORD'S OUTGOINGS.

Commuted Tithe Rent Charge £0 12 0

The Timber on this Lot has an estimated value of £35 and is included in the Sale.

The whole width of the River where it abuts land forming part of this Lot is included in the Sale.

The lot will be Sold and conveyed subject to a right for a strip of Land on the Eastern boundary of this lot to be converted into a roadway by Lot 12. The width of the strip alluded to will be such as is requisite to make the present roadway and bridge 40 ft. wide, measuring from the Western boundary of Lot 5 (see footnote to Lot 12).

The Lot is sold subject to and with the benefit of the Agreement of May 20th, 1823 mentioned in the conditions.

LOT 7

(Coloured Blue on Plan)

THREE ENCLOSURES OF ACCOMMODATION ARABLE LAND

abutting on and having a long frontage to Tolpits Lane The Lot extends to an area of about

41A. 0R. 13P.

and is Let to the Hertford County Council under lease for 21 years, expiring 29th September, 1930, power being reserved to the Landlord to resume possession of any part of the land required for building purposes at three months' notice. Rent £61 10s.

SCHEDULE.

No. on Plan.	Description.	Quantity.
	PARISH OF WATFORD RURAL (Det.)	
1052	Arable	12.360
1059	Do.	16.260
Pt. 1062	Do.	12.462
	Total	A.41.082

LANDLORD'S OUTGOINGS.

Commuted Tithe Rent Charge £9 10 9

The Timber on this Lot has an estimated value of £26 and is included in the Sale.

The Cesspool and line of overflow pipes and drains serving the three Cottages on Lot 15 are situate in enclosure No. 1052, and this Lot is Sold and will be conveyed subject to the continued existence of the same with a right in favour of Lot 15 to enter this Lot for the purpose of inspecting, repairing, renewing, emptying and cleansing the Cesspool, pipes and drains on making proper compensation for any damage done (see footnote to Lot 15).

LOT 8

(Coloured Pink on Plan)

A Valuable Agricultural Property known as

Brightwells Farm

abutting on Tolpits Lane, bounded on two sides in part by the River Colne, and being only a little over a mile from Watford.

The Lot includes a SUPERIOR FARMHOUSE, A COMPACT SET OF BUILDINGS, two COTTAGES, rich Pastures bordering the River Colne, and Fertile Arable Lands at present provided with means of irrigation by the effluent from the Holywell Sewage Works which are situate a little distance to the North of the London and North Western Railway line.

The Property, which also comprises Brightwell's Spring, an enclosure of Woodland placed in the centre of the Lot, has a gentle slope to the South and East, and in all extends to an area of about

147A. 2R. 20P.

Let as to part to Mr. Thomas J. Simmons under Yearly Michaelmas Tenancy, rent £284, the remainder together with the Shooting over the Lot and Fishing in the River Colne being in hand.

THE FARMHOUSE

occupies a pleasant situation, is well built of brick with tiled roof and contains :—Hall, Dining and Drawing Rooms, each with bay window ; Kitchen, now used as a Sitting Room or office and having Telephone laid on ; Scullery with hand pump from a drinking water well ; Dairy and Larder, each having slate shelving ; Wash-house and Underground Cellar. On the First Floor reached by front and back staircases are a large Landing, five Bedrooms, and another Bedroom (fitted up by the present tenant as a Bath Room with Lavatory and W.C.), and another W.C.

The House is wired for and lighted by Electricity.

Outside is a Wood Shed, and there is a nice Garden with Tennis Lawn, Kitchen Garden and small Orchard.

THE FARMBUILDINGS

include timber and tiled Granary on stone supports, Root House or Cart Shed, and a three-bay open Cart Shed adjoining; brick, timber and tiled Cart Horse Stable for five with Loose Box at end and Hen House adjoining ; a four-bay open Shed ; timber and slated two-bay Barn ; Brick, timber and iron roofed Cattle Shed with yard adjoining ; brick, timber and tiled Cattle Shed or Cow House for eight with lean-to box at rear ; brick, timber and slated Cow Shed for fourteen with large Loose Box at end ; and on the opposite side of the road are a three-bay open Implement Shed and a four-bay open Cart Shed built of timber with slated or tiled roofs.

At a little distance to the North of the Homestead is a

PAIR OF BRICK AND SLATED COTTAGES

each containing Front Room, Kitchen, Scullery, Pantry, Coal Cellar, and three Bedrooms.

The installation of electric light to the House and some of the Farmbuildings, and the carrying of water pipes into the latter, and the conversion of certain of the Buildings into Boxes and Stalls were carried out at the present tenant's expense.

SCHEDULE.

No. on Plan.	Tenant.	Description.	Quantity.	Total Quantity.
	PARISH OF WATFORD RURAL (Det.)			
Pt. 1006	Mr. T. J. Simmons .	Roadway	1.034	
1007		Cottages and Gardens . .	.228	
1008		Arable	4.187	
1013		House, Buildings, etc. . .	1.850	
1014		Buildings and Rickyard .	.820	
1015		Copse	.269	
Pt. 1016		Arable	18.000	
1018		Do.	16.047	
Pt. 1063		Waste	.075	
1067		Pasture	7.627	
1068		Do.	16.855	
1069		Do.	8.791	
1070		Do.	2.887	
1072		Arable	10.206	
1073		Do.	20.954	
1074		Grass	7.436	
1075		Pasture	3.225	
1075A		Do.	2.486	
1093		Do.	2.609	
1094		Do.	16.705	142.291
Pt. 1009	In hand. . . .	River	.795	
Pt. 1060		Do.	.205	
1071		Brightwells Spring . .	2.881	
Pt. 1095		River	1.115	
Pt. 1095		Do.	.335	5.331
			Total	A.147.622

LANDLORD'S OUTGOINGS.

Commuted Tithe Rent Charge £36 16 6

The Timber on this Lot has an estimated value of £260 and is included in the Sale.

The Lot is Sold and will be conveyed subject to a right of way over the portions of the accommodation roadway to the North and East of Lot 76, and to the South of Lot 77, in favour of Lots 76 and 77 respectively (see footnotes to Lots 76 and 77).

It will also be Sold and conveyed subject to a right in favour of Lot 76 to lay one line of 6 in. pipes beneath any part of the length of the accommodation roadway above referred to for the purpose of a conduit from the Holywell Sewage Works to that Lot making proper compensation for any damage so caused (see footnote to Lot 76).

LOT 9

(Coloured Green on Plan)

A USEFUL OSIER BED

a small PASTURE ENCLOSURE and TWO COPPICES, situate abutting on Tolpits Lane and lying between it and the River Colne. The Lot has a pleasant South-Eastern aspect and in all extends to an acrea of about

9A. 3R. 0P.

Let as to part to Mr. John Lantaff under Yearly Michaelmas Tenancy, Rent £15, the remainder being in hand

SCHEDULE.

No. on Plan.	Tenant.	Description.	Quantity.	Total Quantity.
		PARISH OF WATFORD RURAL (Det.)		
1064	Mr. J. Lantaff .	Pasture	1.159	
1065		Osier Bed	5.432	
				6.591
Pt. 1060	In hand. . .	River	.480	
Pt. 1061		Spinney	1.990	
Pt. 1063		Trees	.656	
Pt. 1063		Do.	.033	3.159
			Total	A. 9.750

LANDLORD'S OUTGOINGS.

Commuted Tithe Rent Charge £0 19 0

The Timber on this Lot has an estimated value of £55 and is included in the Sale.

SANDY LODGE CLUB HOUSE. (LOT 10.)

ON SANDY LODGE GOLF COURSE. (LOT 11.)

SCHEDULE.

No. on Plan.	Description.	Quantity.
	PARISH OF RICKMANSWORTH RURAL (Det. 3).	
122	Golf Course	.032
123	Farmbuildings, etc.	.453
Pt. 126	Golf Course	69.105
128	Plantation	5.444
Pt. 136	Do	1.960
	PARISH OF WATFORD RURAL (Det.)	
1122	Orchard	.353
1123	Cottages and Gardens	.428
1124	Golf Course	64.115
1139A	Plantation	1.969
	Total	A.143.859

LANDLORD'S OUTGOINGS.

Commuted Tithe Rent Charge £26 4 8

The Timber on this Lot has an estimated value of £140 and will be included in the Sale.

LOT 10

(Coloured Brown on Plan)

Comprised in this Lot is the well-known

Sandy Lodge Golf Course

with its MODERN GOLF HOUSE, and Sandy Lodge Farmsteading, the whole extending to an area of about

143A. 3R. 17P.

Let to the Sandy Lodge Golf Club, Ltd., under lease for 21 years, from 29th September, 1909, at a rental of £400 per annum.

There are TWO GOLF COURSES, of eighteen holes and nine holes respectively, and the GOLF HOUSE, which is a substantial Building of brick with rough-cast exterior and tiled roof, affords adequate accommodation for a membership of five or six hundred. The Courses are of an undulating nature, they occupy a high and health-giving position some 250 feet above sea level with extensive views of the surrounding country, and the sub-soil is of gravel interspersed with pockets of sand. Sandy Lodge Station on the Joint Metropolitan and Great Central Railway is contiguous to the North Western Corner of the Property with a public roadway thereto from the direction of Watford, running along the Northern boundary of the Lot.

The Courses are screened from the Railway and Sandy Lane by a Plantation of Larch and other Conifers, and a strip of woodland.

THE FARMSTEAD

includes TWO BRICK, STUCCO AND TILED COTTAGES, each containing five Rooms, and the following timber and tiled buildings :—Barn, six bay open Cattle Shed, four-bay open Cart Shed, five-stall Cart Horse Stable with Granary adjoining, and Loft over both, and another open Shed.

By the terms of the lease to the Golf Club a right of cart way is reserved in its favour from the Course over Eastbury Farm (Lot 17) into Claypit Lane, the right of Shooting over the Course is reserved to the Lessor, and the felling, lopping and topping of the timber is prohibited except with the permission in writing of the Lessor. The Lot is Sold with the benefit of such right of cart way during the term of the Lease (see footnote to Lot 17).

LOT 11

(Coloured Blue on Plan)

A VALUABLE
BLOCK OF BUILDING AND ACCOMMODATION LAND

situate immediately to the North of and facing the Sandy Lodge Golf Course and abutting on Sandy Lodge Lane, a public thoroughfare to be 40 ft. in breadth and when made to be maintained under the terms of and for the duration of their lease, by the Sandy Lodge Golf Club, Ltd.

The Lot has a frontage to Sandy Lodge Lane of about 3,200 ft., a public footpath at its northern boundary affords direct access to Tolpits Lane and the road to Rickmansworth, while Sandy Lodge Station is situate at its South Western corner, and Hampermill Lane on the East leads direct to Bushey Station about one-and-a-half miles distant. The Lot extends to an area of about

64A. 3R. 5P.

and is Let as to part, together with other Lands, to Mr. Reginald T. Dickins, under Yearly Michaelmas Tenancy at an apportioned rent of £90, with power to the landlord to resume possession of any part for building purposes, the remainder of the Lot with the Shooting over the Lot being in hand.

SCHEDULE.

No. on Plan.	Tenant.	Description.	Quantity.	Total Quantity.
	PARISH OF RICKMANSWORTH RURAL. (Det. 3)			
124	Mr. R. T. Dickins .	Arable	.012	
Pt. 138		Do	13.330	
138A		Do.	13.568	
	PARISH OF WATFORD RURAL. (Det.)			
Pt. 1096		Pasture	1.320	
Pt. 1100		Arable	17.878	
Pt. 1120		Do.	16.839	
				62.947
	PARISH OF RICKMANSWORTH RURAL. (Det. 3)			
Pt. 136	In hand. . . .	Plantation	1.652	
Pt. 138		Gravel Pit . .	.183	1.835
			Total	A.64.782

LANDLORD'S OUTGOINGS.

Commuted Tithe Rent Charge £17 11 0

The Timber on this Lot has an estimated value of £50 and will be included in the Sale.

LOT 12

(Coloured Yellow on Plan)

AN IMPORTANT AGRICULTURAL HOLDING

known as

Moor Farm

situate about one-and-three-quarter miles from Rickmansworth and two miles from Watford, while the South-Eastern extremity of the Lot abuts on the Sandy Lodge Station.

The property extends to an area of about

193A. 0R. 30P.

and is Let as to part together with other Lands to Mr. Reginald T. Dickins under Yearly Michaelmas Tenancy, at an apportioned rent of £241 2s., the remainder, with the Shooting and Fishing in the part of the River Colne included in the Lot, being in hand.

THE FARMHOUSE

is a substantial and commodious brick and tiled structure with Gardens and Orchard on two sides and containing square Hall, Dining Room, Drawing Room, Morning Room, Kitchen with range and cupboards, Scullery, Men's Mess Room with fireplace and having Men's Bedroom or Store Room above, three dry underground Cellars, five Bedrooms on the first floor, and another Bedroom (fitted up by the tenant as a Bathroom and having lavatory basin and W.C.), and two small Attic Rooms on the second floor. Drinking water is obtained by pump from a well sunk by the present Tenant. The drains discharge into a cesspool in the yard.

THE FARMBUILDINGS

are compactly and conveniently arranged on all sides of a large yard, built of timber on brick foundations and having tiled roofs, and comprise :—Two-stall Nag Stable with Loose Box adjoining ; Cart Horse Stables for four, three and two respectively, a Loose Box adjoining the latter, and Chaff Bin ; two-bay Straw Barn, with two Calves' or Cattle Sheds and Manure Shed under the same roof ; eight-bay open Cart Shed, Trap House with Granary over, Coach-house ; two-bay Barn, the bays fitted with mangers for cattle ; Hay House, Cowshed for 30 or more, Mixing House, Workshop with Loft above ; another two-bay Barn, six Pigsties, Cow House for six, with Calf Pen at end ; concrete built Granary fitted with two large bins and four smaller ones ; five Hen Houses and Coal Store.

Water is available at a point adjoining the large yard.

The Lands have been well farmed and include some useful arable enclosures and capital Pastures bordering the River Colne. Half of the width of the River is included in the Sale of the Lot except where it abuts Lots 5 and 6. The boundary on the North-East side of Pt. 1096 from the river to the footpath is the centre of the ditch, and from the footpath to the Hamper Mill is the North-East side of the ditch.

Enclosures No. 133 and 141 have a pleasant aspect and possess a high prospective value for building purposes.

SCHEDULE.

No. on Plan.	Tenant.	Description.	Quantity	Total Quantity.
	PARISH OF RICKMANSWORTH RURAL (Det. 3).			
133	Mr. R. T. Dickins.	Arable	16.099	
139		Do.	26.041	
Pt. 140		Pasture	5.188	
141		Do.	7.776	
142		House, Buildings, etc. . .	3.548	
143		Pasture	1.037	
152		Do.	1.871	
154		Do.	2.843	
Pt. 155		Roadway	1.170	
156		Pasture	1.906	
Pt. 157		Do.	4.500	
Pt. 158		Do.	2.884	
Pt. 159		Roadway	.400	
160		Pasture	5.715	
161		Do.	3.939	
162		Arable	19.199	
163		Pasture	6.823	
164		Do.	13.876	
	PARISH OF WATFORD RURAL (Det.)			
1047		Roadway	.098	
1066		Pasture	9.505	
Pt. 1096		Do.	5.415	
1097		Arable	10.230	
1098		Do.	5.321	
1099		Do.	22.789	
Pt. 1100		Do.	9.680	
				187.836
Pt. 1060	In hand. . . .	River	.435	
Pt. 1095		Do.	1.115	
	PARISH OF RICKMANSWORTH RURAL (Det. 3).			
134		Plantation	2.882	
141A		Do.	.695	
Pt. 165		River	.222	5.349
			Total	A.193.185

LANDLORD'S OUTGOINGS.

Commuted Tithe Rent Charge £40 5 10

The Timber on this Lot has an estimated value of £350 and is included in the Sale.

This Lot is sold with the benefit of the provision made in the Sale of Lot 16 for this Lot (Lot 12) in conjunction with or without Lot 1 to use, or make and use a footway or roadway immediately to the South of and adjoining and following the line of the Northern boundary fence or ditch of enclosures, Nos. 131 and 132 on Lot 16 (for terms of user or making the road, see footnote to Lot 16 and the provision made in the Sale of Lot 6 for the owner or purchaser of this Lot to widen the roadway and bridge on the East side of Lot 6 (see footnote to Lot 6).

LOT 13

(Coloured Yellow on Plan)

A PAIR OF BRICK AND TILED COTTAGES

and a SMALL AREA OF WOODLAND fronting the road from Rickmansworth to Tolpits and together extending to an area of about

2A. 1R. 23P.

Let as to part, together with other Lands, to Mr. Reginald T. Dickins under Yearly Michaelmas Tenancy, at an apportioned rent of £15 12s., the remainder being in hand.

THE COTTAGES

contain respectively Front Room, Kitchen, back Kitchen with Copper, and three Bedrooms ; and Front Room, Kitchen and two Bedrooms. Each has a Wood Shed and good Garden.

Drinking Water is obtained by pump.

SCHEDULE.

No. on Plan.	Tenant.	Description.	Quantity.
	PARISH OF RICK	MANSWORTH RURAL (Det. 3).	
196	Mr. R. T. Dickins . .	Two Cottages and Gardens . .	.420
197	In hand	Green Knoll	1.973
		Total	A.2.393

LANDLORD'S OUTGOINGS.

Commuted Tithe Rent Charge	£0	2	6
Land Tax	0	10	0
Total	£0	12	6

The Timber on this Lot has an estimated value of £70 and is included in the Sale.

LOT 14

(Coloured Blue on Plan)

This Lot, lying a short distance to the West of Lot 13, comprises

A ROW OF THREE COTTAGES

and ANOTHER COTTAGE, situate detached on the Eastern side of the above, the four, together with the Gardens, embracing an area of about

0A. 3R. 16P.

Let respectively under weekly Tenancies to Mrs. Baldwin, Mr. Henry Coster, Miss Saunders, and Mr. W. James Gould.

The rates are paid by the Landlord.

THE COTTAGES IN THE ROW are well built of brick with tiled gabled roofs, the two end houses containing front Room, Kitchen with Copper and Sink, and three Bedrooms, and the centre one having front Room, Kitchen and two Bedrooms.

Each Cottage has a brick and tiled Shed at the rear, and there is a well of drinking Water for the three.

THE SINGLE COTTAGE is of brick with half timber work and tiled roof and contains large living Room, Scullery with Copper and two Bedrooms. Good Garden, Water from a Well.

LANDLORD'S OUTGOINGS.

Commuted Tithe Rent Charge	£0	2	0
Land Tax	0	15	0
TOTAL	£0	17	0

LOT 15

(Coloured Green on Plan)

A ROW OF THREE BRICK AND TILED COTTAGES

situate near Moor Park Crossing, and together with their Gardens extending to an area of about

0A. 1R. 30P.

Two of the Cottages are Let respectively, under Weekly Tenancies, to Mr. Henry Hornsby and Mr. A. Stapleton, and the other, together with other Lands to Mr. Reginald T. Dickins, under Yearly Michaelmas Tenancy, at an apportioned Rent of £7 16s.

The rates on two of the Cottages are paid by the Landlord.

THE COTTAGES

are faced with cement, the two end ones each containing Sitting Room, Kitchen, Pantry and three Bedrooms, and the centre one Front Room, Kitchen and two Bedrooms.

At the rear there is a brick and tiled Barn and Pigsty for each Cottage, and a Wash House with Copper for the use of the three.

Drinking Water is obtained by pump from a well, and there is Storage for Rain Water.

LANDLORD'S OUTGOINGS.

Commuted Tithe Rent Charge £0 1 3

The drainage from the Cottages discharges into a cesspool in Lot 7 with a line of overflow pipes passing through the same Lot and discharging into a ditch at the Eastern extremity of Lot 3, and this Lot (Lot 15) is Sold with the benefit of the continuance of this method of sewage disposal, and with a right to enter Lots 7 and 3 for the purpose of inspecting, repairing, renewing, emptying and cleansing the cesspool and lines of pipes and their outlet in Lot 3 on making proper compensation for any damage done (see footnotes to Lots 7 and 3).

LOT 16

(Coloured Pink on Plan)

Grove Farm

A valuable DAIRYING FARM situate about three-quarters of a mile from Northwood Station, the Lands stretching Northwards, and at their North-Eastern extremity being practically contiguous to Sandy Lodge Station.

Bounded on the West as to the greater part by the Parklands of Lot 1, and varying in altitude from about 300 ft. to 250 ft. above sea level, with South-East aspect and extensive views, the Western fringe of the Lot offers some of the best sites in the district for high class Residences. The lower Lands are only less advantageously situated, and the proximity to Sandy Lodge and Northwood Stations, and the gravelly nature of the soil renders this block of Land, about 172 acres in extent, eminently suitable for development as a BUILDING ESTATE.

The Lot in all embraces an area of about

181A. 2R. 30P.

and is Let as to part, together with other Lands, to Mr. Alfred H. Churchill, at an apportioned Rent of £229 10s., as to a further part together with other Lands, to Mr. Reginald T. Dickins, at an apportioned rent of £65, both Tenancies being Yearly Michaelmas, the remainder comprising the Plantations and Shooting over the Lot being in hand.

Power is reserved to the Landlord to resume possession for building purposes of any part of the fields Let.

THE FARMHOUSE

is a comparatively modern building of red brick with tiled roof and weather tiled upper part, and contains Porch, small Hall, Dining Room with modern tiled Grate, Kitchen with Range and Dresser, Scullery having Company's Water laid on, Dairy with slate shelving, two Pantries, and four Bedrooms.

Outside is a newly erected brick built Milk Cooling House and Churn Washing Place fitted with Copper and two Sinks, and having Water laid on.

THE FARMBUILDINGS

are situate close by. They are built of brick with tiled roofs and include a two-stall Cart Horse Stable with Meal Shed adjoining, two Cowhouses each for nine, three-bay open Cattle Shed, two-bay Barn and Root Shed, Cart Horse Stable for two, another Cowhouse for eight, and two timber and Iron Roofed Pigsties.

In Enclosure No. 112 on plan is a timber and slated Cattle Shed, having concrete floor and manger, and shown as No. 113 on plan is a brick and tiled Dwelling House known as

ASTON'S LODGE

at present occupied as two Cottages. Each Cottage contains large Sitting Room, back Kitchen, Pantry and two Bedrooms, with Coal House outside and good Garden.

Drinking Water is obtained from a spring near the Park boundary fence.

SCHEDULE.

No. on Plan.	Tenant.	Description.	Quantity.	Total Quantity.
		PARISH OF RICKMANSWORTH RURAL (Det. 3).		
82	Mr. A. H. Churchill.	Pasture	10.619	
83		Do.	17.035	
85		Do.	5.604	
86		House, Buildings and Orchard	.605	
89		Pasture	4.084	
89A		Rickyard . . .	.494	
110		Pasture . . .	26.381	
111		Do.	13.316	
111A		Do.	15.115	
112		Do.	13.682	
113		Aston's Lodge . . .	.300	
114		Arable	9.925	
				117.160
115	Mr. R. T. Dickins .	Pasture	16.373	
116		Arable	16.638	
132		Pasture	19.493	
				52.504
93	In hand. . .	Pond	.351	
94		Plantation	1.708	
117		Do.	4.180	
118		Do.	2.015	
129		Do.	.713	
131		Do.	3.058	12.025
			Total	A.181.689

LANDLORD'S OUTGOINGS.

Commuted Tithe Rent Charge £36 12 11

The Timber on this Lot has an estimated value of £600 and is included in the Sale.

The Lot is Sold and will be conveyed subject to a right in favour of Lots 1 and 12 or one of them to make and use a footway not more than 7 ft. wide or a roadway not more than 42 ft. wide immediately to the South of and adjoining and following the line of the Northern boundary fence or ditch of enclosures, Nos. 131 and 132 on plan. Lot 12 is to have a right to use the footway or roadway as and when made by Lots 1 and or either of them without payment. Should Lot 16 make the footway or roadway mentioned, one half the cost of the same is to be borne by and paid to Lot 16 by Lot 1 as soon as any use is made of either by Lot 1. Should Lot 12 make the footway or roadway one third the cost of the same is to be borne by and paid to Lot 12 by each of Lots 1 and 16 as soon as any use is made by either of the path or road (see footnotes to Lots 1 and 12).

GROVE GREEN FARM. (LOT 16.)

EASTBURY FARM. (LOT 17.)

LOT 17

(Coloured Yellow on Plan)

Eastbury Farm

a compact Grazing and Dairying Holding, conveniently situate abutting on Claypit Lane and only one mile from Northwood Station.

The Lot, which is bounded on the North by the Sandy Lodge Golf Club, has a frontage of about 2,200 ft. to Claypit Lane, and in all embraces an area of about

87A. 3R. 23P.

Let together with other Land to Mr. A. W. Wild under Yearly Michaelmas Tenancy at an apportioned rent of £176 the Shooting over the Property being in hand.

The Land has a high prospective value for building and accommodation purposes.

THE FARMHOUSE

is a comfortable double-fronted red brick and tiled Building, standing some little distance back from the road with Garden and Orchard in front and contains small Hall, Dining Room, and Drawing Room, each of good size, Kitchen with range, Sink having Water laid on and soft Water service by pump, Dairy, Larder, Cellar and five Bedrooms, two of which (each with fireplace) are now occupied as one room. There is a Closet outside drained into a cesspool.

THE FARMBUILDINGS

are of a commodious character and include a brick and tiled Cowshed for eight, with Calves' Pen at end and Loft over; timber and tiled lean-to Building of two Loose Boxes, two bay Barn with Meal or Root House adjoining, four Pigsties, two-bay open Cattle Shed, another five-bay Shed with Trap House at end ; detached four-bay open implement Shed on brick foundation, and another, detached, substantially built range of brick and slate comprising Stable for five with louvre ventilation in the roof, Harness Room, Corn Barn with Granary or Hay Loft over, large half-open Loose Box for horses or cattle, four-bay open Cattle Shed with Yard in front and Granary over, and two large Loose Boxes at the end. And forming part of this range and under the same roof is

A COTTAGE

containing Sitting Room, Kitchen, Scullery, Larder and two Bedrooms.

Water is available outside the last mentioned range of Buildings from a spring.

SCHEDULE.

No on Plan.	Description.	Quantity.
	PARISH OF RICKMANSWORTH RURAL (Det. 3).	
105	Pasture	1.727
106	House, Buildings, etc.	1.637
107	Orchard	.967
108	Pasture	42.504
109	Do.	21.119
Pt. 119	Do.	16.844
	PARISH OF WATFORD RURAL (Det.)	
1143	Pasture	1.218
1144	Do.	1.878
	Total	A.87.894

LANDLORD'S OUTGOINGS.

Commuted Tithe Rent Charge £14 15 0

The Timber on this Lot has an estimated value of £260 and is included in the Sale.

The Lot is sold and will be conveyed during the term of the lease of Lot 10 to the Sandy Lodge Golf Club, Ltd., to a right of cartway granted to the Lessees of that Lot from the Course over this Lot, the cartway passing along the line of the footpath over No. 119 and thence into Claypit Lane over a direct line to the accommodation road between the Farm House and Buildings (see footnote to Lot 10).

Nos. 105 to 109 inclusive and 1143 are sold subject to a restriction prohibiting thereon the trade of an innkeeper, victualler or retailer of wines, spirits or beer.

LOT 18

(Coloured Green on Plan)

Two Enclosures of

ACCOMMODATION PASTURE LAND

and a well situated area of WOODLAND, bounded on the North by the Sandy Lodge Golf Course and having a frontage of about 850 ft. to Sandy Lane. At its highest point the Wood attains an altitude of over 300 ft. above sea level and is well suited as a SITE FOR ONE OR MORE RESIDENCES.

The Lot extends to an area of about **25A. 1R. 32P.**

and is Let as to part, together with other Lands, to Mr. A. W. Wild under Yearly Michaelmas Tenancy at an apportioned rent of £10, the remainder comprising the Woodland with the Shooting over the Lot being in hand.

SCHEDULE.

No. on Plan.	Tenant.	Description.	Quantity.	Total Quantity.
	PARISH OF	WATFORD RURAL (Det.)		
1126	Mr. A. W. Wild	Pasture	2.103	
1138		Do.	3.462	
				5.565
1139	In hand.	The Roughs		19.885
			Total	A.25.450

LANDLORD'S OUTGOINGS.

Commuted Tithe Rent Charge £0 18 7

The Timber on this Lot has an estimated value of £430 and is included in the Sale.

LOT 19

(Coloured Pink on Plan)

TWO VALUABLE ENCLOSURES OF ACCOMMODATION PASTURE LAND

situate adjacent to the foregoing Lot and extending to an area of about **11A. 3R. 28P.**

Let to G. A. Sanford, Esq., under Yearly Michaelmas Tenancy, the Shooting over the Lot being in hand.

The Lot has a frontage of about 400 ft. to Sandy Lane, at its higher part is about 330 ft. above sea level and commands extensive views to the East and West.

It forms an EXCELLENT SITE FOR ONE OR MORE RESIDENCES, and is only about one-and-a-half miles from Northwood Station.

SCHEDULE.

No. on Plan.	Description.	Quantity.
	PARISH OF WATFORD RURAL (Det.)	
1140	Pasture	5.527
1142	Do.	6.395
	Total	A. 11.922

LANDLORD'S OUTGOINGS.

Commuted Tithe Rent Charge £2 1 5

The Timber on this Lot has an estimated value of £25 and is included in the Sale.

This Lot is sold subject to a restriction prohibiting thereon the trade of an innkeeper, victualler or retailer of wines, spirits or beer.

LOT 20

(*Coloured Blue on Plan*)

AN ENCLOSURE OF ACCOMMODATION PASTURE LAND

abutting on Claypit Lane, situate just over a mile from Northwood Station and extending to an area of about

3 A. 2 R. 2 P.

Let together with other Lands to Mr. A. W. Wild under Yearly Michaelmas Tenancy, at a rent of £7.

The Lot stands in prettily timbered surroundings, and attains an altitude of about 300 ft. above sea level. It has a frontage of about 300 ft., and forms a CAPITAL BUILDING SITE.

SCHEDULE.

No. on Plan.	Description.	Quantity.
	PARISH OF WATFORD RURAL (Det.)	
1145	Pasture	2.542
1145D	Do.	.968
	Total	A. 3.510

LANDLORD'S OUTGOINGS.

Commuted Tithe Rent Charge £0 10 10

The Timber on this Lot has an estimated value of £4 10s., and is included in the Sale.

No. 1145 is sold subject to a restriction prohibiting thereon the trade of an innkeeper, victualler or retailer of wines, spirits or beer.

LOT 21

(*Coloured Yellow on Plan*)

AN ENCLOSURE OF ACCOMMODATION AND BUILDING LAND

situate at the corner of Kewferry Road and Claypit Lane, the frontages to these roads being about 300 ft. and 350 ft. respectively. The Lot has an area of about

4 A. 0 R. 24 P.

and is Let, together with other lands, to Mr. Alfred H. Churchill under Yearly Michaelmas Tenancy.

The Field is under Pasture and watered from a Pond.

LANDLORD'S OUTGOINGS.

Commuted Tithe Rent Charge £0 17 2

Any Timber on this Lot will be included in the Sale.

LOT 22

(Coloured Green on Plan)

ANOTHER ENCLOSURE OF ACCOMMODATION LAND

situate at the rear of Kewferry Road having an Approach roadway 40 ft. in width therefrom and adjoining Lot 21. It has an important bearing in connection with the scheme of development of the adjacent lands and in area extends to about

5 A. 0 R. 27 P.

Let as to Nos. 30 and Pt. 31 (Footpath) together with other lands, to Mr. Alfred H. Churchill under Yearly Michaelmas Tenancy, at an apportioned rent of £8 15s., the remainder being in hand.

The Field is under Pasture and watered by a Pond.

SCHEDULE.

No. on Plan.	Tenant.	Description.	Quantity	Total Quantity.
	PARISH	OF RUISLIP (Middlesex).		
30	Mr. A. H. Churchill	Pasture	4.879	
Pt. 31		Footpath	.115	4.994
Pt. 31	In hand . .	Roadway		.174
			Total	A.5.168

LANDLORD'S OUTGOINGS.

Corn Rents £0 16 0

Any Timber on this Lot is included in the Sale.

LOT 23

(Coloured Blue on Plan)

A VALUABLE AND COMPACT BLOCK OF BUILDING LAND

extending to an area of about

60 A. 1 R. 8 P.

and known as KEWFERRY FARM.

The Land is prettily timbered, has a very pleasant South-East aspect and varies in altitude from about 350 ft. to 250 ft. above sea level. On the North-West it is adjacent to Batchworth Heath and on the South Northwood Station is only about two-thirds of a mile distant. It is bounded on three sides by public roads the frontages to same being as under.

Rickmansworth Road	about	1,650 ft.
Claypit Lane	about	1,600 ft.
Kewferry Road	about	300 ft.

The latter is exclusive of two 40 ft. roadway outlets.

Kewferry Road is sewered and partially paved, and the Rickmansworth Road, an old-established thoroughfare, has a sewer laid in for a part of its length.

The Land is Let as to the greater part, with other lands, to Mr. Arthur Nichols under Yearly Michaelmas Tenancy, at an apportioned rent of £102 15s., as to a small part, together with other Lands, to Mr. Alfred H. Churchill under Yearly Michaelmas Tenancy, at an apportioned rent of £5 10s., and as to No. Pt. to Mr. A. Nichols at an apportioned rent of £4, the Shooting over the Lot being in hand.

Power is reserved to the Landlord to resume possession of any part of the Land for building purposes.

A Deed of Covenant dated June 15th, 1910, provides *inter alia* that (*a*) the present Vendor shall at his convenience make the 40 ft. Roadway shown on the Plan and thereon marked A, in consideration of a reimbursement of £100 towards the cost of the same, (*b*) that no licensed premises shall be erected nor existing premises used as such on Land owned by the present Vendor within 500 yards of the "Gate Inn" (shown on the Plan), and (*c*) that on the Land crossbarred black no buildings shall be erected other than good-class Cottage Property to be built either singly or in pairs 15 ft. apart (but not in terraces). This Lot is sold and will be conveyed subject to and with the benefit of the said Deed of Covenant so far as it affects this Lot.

SCHEDULE.

No. on Plan.	Tenant.	Description.	Quantity.	Total Quantity.
	PARISH OF RUISLIP (Middlesex).			
Pt. 35	Mr. Arthur Nichols	Pasture		2.187
Pt. 32	Do.	Do.	2.727	
Pt. 32A		Roadway	.180	
Pt. 32A		Do.	.180	
Pt. 32A		Footpath	.090	
Pt. 33		Arable	4.924	
34		Do.	10.781	
Pt. 134		Pond	.031	
Pt. 135		Pasture	13.387	
136		Do.	15.503	
137		Do.	5.240	
	PARISH OF RICKMANSWORTH RURAL (Det. 3).			
Pt. 78		Pasture	2.028	
				55.701
84	Mr. A. H. Churchill.	Arable		3.040
			Total	A.60.298

LANDLORD'S OUTGOINGS.

Commuted Tithe Rent Charge	£1	1	0
Corn Rent	10	13	7
Total	£11	14	7

The Timber on this Lot has an estimated value of £325 and is included in the Sale. Nos. Pt. 32 and Pt. 32A are subject to the reservations as to mines and minerals contained in section 48 of the Copyhold Act 1852.

LOT 24

(Coloured Yellow on Plan)

THREE COTTAGES, GARDENS AND PASTURE LAND

occupying a commanding and healthy position facing Batchworth Heath, standing 350 ft. above sea level and enjoying extensive views in an Easterly direction over Oxhey woods. The Lot extends to an area of about

2A. 0R. 13P.

and is Let as to part to Mr. Henry Kirby under Weekly Tenancy, as to further part, together with other Lands, to Mr. Alfred Nichols under Yearly Michaelmas Tenancy, at an apportioned rent of £7 16s., as to a further part to Mrs. Douglas under Weekly Tenancy, and as to a further part, together with other Lands, to Mr. Arthur Nichols under Yearly Michaelmas Tenancy, at an apportioned rent of 5s.

The Parochial and Water Rates appurtenant to two of the Cottages are discharged by the Landlord.

THE COTTAGES

are under one roof, brick and tiled, gabled and partially ivy clad. They contain respectively Front Room, Kitchen Scullery, and two Bedrooms, with Coal House outside ; Kitchen, Scullery and two Bedrooms, with Wood Shed at the rear ; and Front Room with another small Sitting Room adjoining, Back Kitchen, Pantry and two Bedrooms, Wood Shed outside. Two of the Cottages have coppers, each has a large Garden, and drinking water (from Company's main) is obtained from a standpipe, used in common by the tenants of other Lots, on Batchworth Heath. Company's Water is available for laying on direct to the Lot if desired.

SCHEDULE.

No. on Plan.	Tenant.	Description.	Quantity.	Total Quantity
	PARISH OF RICKMANSWORTH RURAL (Det. 3).			
Pt. 75	Mr. H. Kirby	Cottage and Garden	.179	
Pt. 78		Pasture	1.400	
				1.579
Pt 75	Mr. Alfred Nichols.	Cottage and Garden		.225
Pt. 75	Mrs. Douglas	Do.		.179
Pt. 76	Mr. Arthur Nichols.	Pasture		.100
			Total	A.2.083

LANDLORD'S OUTGOINGS.

Commuted Tithe Rent Charge	£0 8 9
Land Tax	0 15 0
Total	£1 3 9

Any Timber on this Lot is included in the Sale.

LOT 25

(Coloured Brown on Plan)

A healthily positioned area ot

ACCOMMODATION LAND.

screened from the North-West by a BELT OF WOODLAND the whole extending to an area of about

19A. 3R. 36P.

The Lot stands at an altitude of about 340 ft. above sea level, is nicely timbered and having a frontage of 1,150 ft. to the Rickmansworth Road is well adapted for Building Development. On the North-West the Woodland has a frontage to White Hill and Common Land adjoining.

Let as to part, together with other Lands, to Mr. Alfred Nichols under Yearly Michaelmas Tenancy, at an apportioned rent of £30 the remainder comprising the Woodland being in hand. The Shooting over the Lot is Let until February 2nd, 1920, to Donald A. Stewart, Esq.

SCHEDULE.

No. on Plan.	Tenant.	Description.	Quantity.	Total Quantity.
	PARISH OF RUISLIP (Middlesex).			
138	Mr. Alfred Nichols.	Pasture	8.191	
140		Arable	6.777	14.968
141	In hand. . .	Woodland		5.008
			Total	A.19.976

LANDLORD'S OUTGOINGS.

Corn Rent	£2	1	7
Land Tax	0	15	4
Total	£2	16	11

The Timber on this Lot has an estimated value of £160 and is included in the Sale.

Under a Deed of Covenant dated June 15th, 1910, it is provided *inter alia* that no licensed premises shall be erected nor existing premises used as such on land owned by the present Vendor within 500 yards of the "Gate Inn," Northwood (shown on the Plan) and such parts of this Lot as fall within the distance named are Sold and will be conveyed subject to this restriction.

The Ditch on the Northern side of the Hedge forming the Northern Boundary of Enclosure No. 138 on Plan is, so far as it abuts on other Land the property of the Vendor, excluded from the Sale of this Lot (see footnote to Lots 31 and 32).

The lot is sold and will be conveyed subject to an easement in favour of Lots 31 and 32 in respect of the line of pipes taking the drainage from these Lots into Enclosure No. 141 on Plan (see footnote to Lots 31 and 32).

LOTS 26 to 30

INCLUSIVE WILL FIRST BE OFFERED TOGETHER.

As a whole these Lots form a capital Residential and Sporting Property that must rapidly increase in value.

SUMMARY OF LOTS 26 to 30.

Lot.	Description.	Tenant.	Quantity.
26	Batchworth Heath House and Farm	W. J. Morton, Esq., others, and in hand . . .	117.714
27	Accommodation Pasture . .	In hand	5.432
28	Bishops Wood, etc. . . .	D. A. Stewart, Esq., and in hand	113.201
29	Accommodation and Woodland .	Mr. H. C. Hayter and in hand .	37.303
30	Pasture and Orchard . . .	F. Nash, Esq.	1.536
		Total . .	A.275.186

LANDLORD'S OUTGOINGS.

Commuted Tithe Rent Charge £34 16 2

The Timber on these five Lots has an estimated value of £2,430 and is included in the Sale.

LOT 26

(Coloured Pink on Plan)

A Valuable Residential and Agricultural Property known as

Batchworth Heath House

situate on the Western side of Batchworth Heath and being about one-and-a-half miles from Northwood Station and Rickmansworth.

This Property, together with the Lands comprised in BATCHWORTH HEATH FARM, the adjacent small Woods and two Cottages, in all extends to an area of about

117A. 2R. 34P.

BATCHWORTH HEATH HOUSE. (LOT 26.)

The Lot lies compactly together, is well timbered, and forms as pretty a little Residential Property as any within a like distance of London.

Let as to part to William J. Morton, Esq., under Tenancy, terminating by notice at Christmas 1919, the Tenant being responsible for repairs, as to a further part, together with other Lands to Mr. Alfred Nichols under Yearly Michaelmas Tenancy at an apportioned rent of £202 12s., as to a further part (Cottage) to Mr. Walter Parker under Weekly Tenancy, the remainder, comprising the Woodland and Enclosure No. 14, being in hand. The Shooting over the Lot is Let until February 2nd, 1920, to Donald A. Stewart, Esq.

BATCHWORTH HEATH HOUSE.

is a comfortable old-fashioned well-appointed Residence, substantially built of brick, partly ivy clad, and with tiled and slated roof, standing about 340 ft. above sea level, and commanding extensive views. It has principal aspects of East and South, is entered from a carriage sweep overspread by a fine old Chestnut Tree, and contains : —

ON THE GROUND FLOOR : Hall or Lounge (East), having fireplace and measuring about 17 ft. 9 in. square ; Dining Room (East), about 22 ft. by 13 ft. 9 in., and having register grate and marble surround ; Drawing Room (East), with marble mantel " Well " pattern fireplace, and measuring about 17 ft. 9 in, (inclusive of a bay) by 14 ft. ; small Lobby having Telephone laid on ; Smoking Room or Maids' Sitting Room (South), measuring about 11 ft. by 9 ft. 9 in. and having modern tiled fireplace ; Kitchen about 15 ft. by 14 ft. 3 in. with double-oven range ; Butler's Pantry with sink having h. and c. services ; Scullery with glazed stoneware sink (h. and c.) and copper, and Company's Water laid on ; two Larders, Dairy with slate shelving, and fitted for heating, and two outside W.C.'s. Underground are Wine and Storage Cellars.

ON THE FIRST FLOOR, reached by principal and secondary staircases, are

FIVE BEST BEDROOMS

one of which facing South is now used as a Sitting Room, its dimensions being about 16 ft. 6 in. by 15 ft. 6 in. exclusive of bay. The other four Rooms measure respectively about 18 ft. 9 in. (including bay) by 18 ft. ; 18 ft. (including bay) by 14 ft. 3 in. ; 14 ft. 6 in. by 13 ft. 9 in., and 11 ft. by 10 ft. Also on this floor are Bathroom with glazed ware lavatory basin (h. and c.), and W.C.

ON THE SECOND FLOOR, are two good Attic Bedrooms, each having fireplace and measuring about 14 ft. 6 in. by 14 ft. 3 in., and two smaller Attic Bedrooms.

SUMMARY OF ACCOMMODATION.

Lounge Hall.	Five Principal Bedrooms.
Dining Room.	Bath Room and W.C.
Drawing Room.	Four Attic Bedrooms.
Smoking Room.	Ground Floor Offices and two W.C.'s.

Underground Cellarage.

The Principal Rooms on the Ground and First Floors are about 10 ft. in height.

The Radiators and Furnace in connection with same and the Bath are the property of the tenant.

Water is laid on from the local Company's mains.

The Drainage system is on modern principles, the disposal being by means of a cesspool.

THE STABLING AND GARAGE.

are of timber, with tiled roof and dormer windows, and include Motor House for two cars, two good Stalls and a Loose Box, Harness Room, Workshop and Oil Store.

Water by pump from a well. Other Outbuildings comprise Coal House, two Fowl Houses, Fruit House, Potting and Store Sheds.

Adjacent to the Stabling is

A PAIR OF BRICK AND TILED COTTAGES

partly ivy clad, one containing living Room, Scullery with Copper, Pantry and three Bedrooms, and a lean-to Wood Shed outside, and the other having Living Room, back Kitchen, and two Bedrooms, and lean-to Coal House, and Pigsty. Underground Rain Water Tank. Good Gardens.

Drinking Water (Company's) is obtained from a stand-pipe on Batchworth Heath, and used in common with other Lots.

The Parochial and Water Rates in respect of one of the Cottages are discharged by the Landlord.

THE PLEASURE GROUNDS

are walled in and include Rose Garden, shrubbed Front Lawn, Tennis and Croquet Lawns, with Greenhouse (heated) in two divisions. The walls are planted with Fruit Trees and Trained Bushes. Adjoining is a Kitchen Garden and Apple Orchard with a four-light brick Pit in the former.

THE FARMBUILDINGS

used in connection with Batchworth Heath Farm are chiefly of timber with tiled or galvanized iron roofs and include Cowhouse for 20, with Cooling House having water laid on at side, four Pigsties, two-bay Cart Shed, Loose Box, Cart Horse Stable for four, Root House, Grain Pit, four Loose Boxes, three-bay open Cart Shed, two Loose Boxes for cattle, Mixing House with water laid on and boiler outside, Cowhouse for ten, and Fowl House ; in No. 31 on Plan are two Sick Boxes with Loft over, and in No. Part 73 on Plan are a brick and tiled Granary, timber and tiled two-bay Barn with loose place for cattle, and Fowl House, and in No. 72 on Plan is a brick and tiled Workshop or Corn Store.

THE AGRICULTURAL LANDS

include a large proportion of good well-watered Pastures and two Enclosures of fertile arable

SCHEDULE.

No. on Plan.	Tenant.	Description.	Quantity.	Total Quantity.
	PARISH OF RICKMANSWORTH RURAL (Det. 3).			
23	W. J. Morton, Esq..	House and Garden . .	1.022	
24		Orchard	1.080	
Pt. 73		Cottage and Garden . .	.120	
				2.222
Pt. 15	Mr. Alfred Nichols .	Pasture	18.103	
25		Do.	.554	
26		Arable	4.216	
27		Building and Yard . .	.540	
28		Arable	4.397	
30		Pasture	7.649	
31		Arable	3.235	
33		Pasture	5.694	
35		Arable	6.683	
35A		Pasture	4.454	
63		Do.	17.643	
69		Arable	6.598	
70		Pasture	13.149	
71		Do.	11.262	
72		Roadway	.252	
Pt. 73		Buildings	.120	
				104.549
Pt. 73	Mr. W. Parker .	Cottage and Garden . .		120
14	In hand. . .	Pasture	8.061	
29		Howard Spring . . .	1.217	
32		Whipping Spring . . .	1.166	
34		Copse	.249	
174		Roadway	.130	10.823
			Total	A.117.714

LANDLORD'S OUTGOINGS.

Commuted Tithe Rent Charge	£22	2	8
Land Tax	2	17	6
Total . . .	£25	0	2

The Timber on this Lot has an estimated value of £490 and is included in the Sale.

The overflow pipe from the Cesspool on Lot 27, which serves the Home Farmbuildings on Lot 1, discharges into a ditch on this Lot, and this Lot is sold and will be conveyed subject to the continuance of this easement in favour of Lots 27 and 1 (see footnotes to Lots 27 and 1). The Lot is also Sold and will be conveyed subject to a Right of Way over the Roadway numbered 174 on Plan to Enclosure numbered Pt. 15 on Plan, Lot 30, in favour of that Lot (see footnote to Lot 30).

LOT 27

(*Coloured Blue on Plan*)

An enclosure of rich

ACCOMMODATION PASTURE LAND

situate abutting Batchworth Heath Hill on the Northern side of Lot 26. The higher part of the Field, which is some 350 ft. above sea level and has South-West aspect, with extensive views, forms a capital Building Site. The Lot extends to an area of about

5A. 1R. 29P.

and is at present in hand. The Shooting is Let until February 2nd, 1920, to Donald A. Stewart, Esq.

LANDLORD'S OUTGOINGS.

Commuted Tithe Rent Charge £0 15 11

An Timber on this Lot will be included in the Sale.

There is a Cesspool on the Lot with pipes thereto, serving the Home Farmbuildings on Lot 1 and with piped overflow into a ditch on Lot 26, and this Lot is sold and will be conveyed subject to the continued existence and user of the same, and to the right in favour of Lot 1 to enter this Lot for the purpose of inspecting, cleansing, emptying, repairing and reinstating the Cesspool and the pipes thereto and the piped overflow, making compensation for any damage in so doing, and with a right for this Lot to enter Lot 26 to inspect and repair such overflow (see footnote to Lots 1 and 26).

LOT 28

(*Coloured Green on Plan*)

A KEEPER'S COTTAGE AND A VALUABLE AND COMPACT AREA OF WOODLAND

situate to the South of Lot 26 and having Building Frontages to the Harefield Road of some 3,100 ft. in length. These frontage Lands have an altitude of over 300 ft. above sea level, and Company's Water is available. In the Woods is an abundance of Oak and Beech Timber of fine growth. The Lot extends to an area of about

113A. 0R. 32P.

the Woodlands being in hand and the Cottage and Sporting Rights over the Lot being Let to Donald A. Stewart, Esq., until February 2nd, 1920.

THE COTTAGE

is well built of brick with tiled roof, and contains Sitting Room, Kitchen, Scullery with copper, fireplace and sink ; Pantry, and three Bedrooms each having a fireplace. At rear are two timber and tiled Sheds, Garden, Drinking Water Well, and Soft Water Storage.

SCHEDULE.

No. on Plan.	Tenant.	Description.	Quantity.	Total Quantity.
	PARISH OF RICKMANSWORTH RURAL (Det. 3).			
Pt. 54	In hand . .	Bishops Wood	61.709	
62		Park Wood	9.209	
63A		Waste	.302	
64		Poorfield	4.472	
Pt. 65		Lockwell Wood . . .	37.339	
				113.031
55A	D A. Stewart, Esq..	Keeper's Cottage . . .		.170
			Total	A.113.201

LANDLORD'S OUTGOINGS.

Commuted Tithe Rent Charge £7 13 1

The Timber on this Lot has an estimated value of £1,490 and is included in the Sale. The Tithe stated is exclusive of an apportioned amount of Rectorial Tithe of 5d. charged on No. 55A, which is owned by the Vendor. This latter Tithe will be included in the Sale of the Lot.

LOT 29

(Coloured Blue on Plan)

A USEFUL ACCOMMODATION PROPERTY

situate to the West of the foregoing Lot, and comprising a Double-fronted COTTAGE, three Enclosures of Pasture and Arable Land, screened from the North by two Pieces of Woodland, the whole extending to an area of about

37A 1R. 8P.

Let as to part to Mr. Henry C. Hayter under Yearly Michaelmas Tenancy at the yearly rent of £40, the remainder comprising the Woodland being in hand. The Shooting over the Lot is Let until February 2nd, 1920, to Donald A. Stewart, Esq.

THE COTTAGE

is of brick and tile with cement faced front and contains Sitting Room, Kitchen, Back Kitchen with Glazed Ware Sink, Copper and Fireplace, and two Bedrooms. Front and side Gardens and small Apple Orchard. Well Water.

Near the Cottage are a brick timber and tiled Fowl House, Barn and two Loose Boxes with galvanized iron roof.

SCHEDULE.

No. on Plan.	Tenant.	Description.	Quantity	Total Quantity.
	PARISH OF RICKMANSWORTH (Det. 3).			
55	Mr. H. C. Hayter	Pasture	8.470	
56		Cottage and Garden	.811	
60		Arable	4.342	
61		Do.	8.107	21.730
58	In hand.	Square Spring	2.361	
59		Long Spring	13.212	15.573
			Total	A 37.303

LANDLORD'S OUTGOINGS.

Commuted Tithe Rent Charge £1 2 2

The Timber on this Lot has an estimated value of £450 and is included in the Sale.

The Tithe stated is exclusive of an apportioned amount of Rectorial Tithe of £3 2 2 charged on Nos. 55, 56, 60 and 61, which are owned by the Vendor. This latter Tithe will be included in the Sale of the Lot.

LOT 30

(Coloured Y?llow on Plan)

Two Small Plots of

PASTURE AND ORCHARD LAND

situate at the Northern extremity of Lot 26 and having a frontage of about 150 ft. to the roadway from Rickmansworth to Batchworth Heath.

The Lot extends to an area of about

1A. 2R. 6P.

and is Let to Fitzgerald Nash, Esq., under Lease for fourteen years from 29th September, 1914, at the Yearly Rent of £5. The Lease is determinable in the event of the exercise of an option to purchase the adjoining House, the property of the Lessee, which was given to the Lessor previous to the granting of the Lease. The benefit of this option if and so far as it can be assigned by the Vendor is included in the Sale of this Lot.

SCHEDULE.

No. on Plan.	Description.	Quantity.
	PARISH OF RICKMANSWORTH RURAL (Det. 3).	
Pt. 15	Pasture	1.000
172	Orchard	.536
	Total	A.1.536

LANDLORD'S OUTGOINGS.

Commuted Tithe Rent Charge £0 4 10

Any Timber on this Lot will be included in the Sale.

The Lot is Sold with the benefit of a Right of Way to the Pasture Enclosure, No. Pt. 15 on Plan, over the roadway numbered 174 (Lot 26) on Plan (see footnote to Lot 26).

BATCHWORTH HEATH.
(For Lots see above.)

LOT 31

(Coloured Blue on Plan)

A PAIR OF MODERN COTTAGES

situate on the South side of Batchworth Heath and, together with the Gardens adjoining, extending to an area of about

0A. 1R. 30P.

Let as to part, together with other lands, to Mr. Alfred Nichols under yearly Michaelmas tenancy, at an apportioned Rent of £7 16s., as to a further part to Mr. Mark Reakes under Weekly Tenancy, the remainder (a plot of garden land) being in hand.

THE COTTAGES

are well built of brick with tile-hung upper storey and tiled roof, and each contains Front Room, Kitchen, and three Bedrooms, with timber and slated Wash-house outsides The Sink drainage is taken into a cesspool.

Drinking Water is obtained from a standpipe (Company's supply) used in common with others on Batchworth Heath.

The Rates on one of the Cottages, and the Water charges appurtenant to both are discharged by the Landlord.

SCHEDULE

No on Plan.	Tenant.	Description.	Quantity.
Pt. 74	Mr. Alfred Nichols .	Cottage and Garden	.128
	Mr. M. Reakes .	Do. . .	.128
	In hand. . .	Garden	.181
		Total	A. .437

LANDLORD'S OUTGOINGS

Commuted Tithe Rent Charge	£0	2	2
Land Tax	1	2	0
Total	£1	4	2

The Ditch, where it abuts the Southern end of the Gardens, is included in the Sale of this Lot (see footnote to Lot 25).

The Lot will be sold with the benefit of the present method of drainage disposal into Lot 25 (see footnote to Lot 25).

LOT 32

(Coloured Pink on Plan)

THREE BRICK AND SLATED COTTAGES

situate on the South side of Batchworth Heath and together with their Gardens, extending to an area of about

0A. 0R. 31P.

Let as to part to Mrs. Wood under Weekly Tenancy, as to a further part together with other Land to Mr. Alfred Nichols under Yearly Michaelmas Tenancy, at an apportioned Rent of £7 16s., and as to the remaining part to Mr. George Taylor under Weekly Tenancy.

THE COTTAGES

contain respectively :—Living Room and Bedroom with lean-to Shed having Copper outside ; Living Room, Scullery with Copper and Sink, Coal Shed and two Bedrooms ; the third Cottage being similar to the last mentioned.

Drinking Water is obtained from a stand pipe (Company's supply), used in common with others on Batchworth Heath.

SCHEDULE

No. on Plan.	Tenant.	Description.	Quantity.
	PARISH OF RICKMANSWORTH RURAL (Det. 3).		
Pt. 74	Mrs. Wood . .	Cottage and Garden . .	.060
	Mr. Alfred Nichols .	Do. . .	.060
	Mr. G. Taylor .	Do. . .	.071
		Total	A. .191

LANDLORD'S OUTGOINGS.

Commuted Tithe Rent Charge	£0	1	1
Land Tax	0	12	0
Total	£0	13	1

The Rates on two of the Cottages and the Water charges appurtenant to all three are discharged by the Landlord.

The Ditch, where it abuts the Southern end of the Gardens, is included in the Sale of this Lot (see footnote to Lot 25).

The Lot will be sold with the benefit of the present method of drainage disposal into Lot 25 (see footnote to Lot 25).

LOT 33

(Coloured Yellow on Plan)

A ROW OF THREE RED BRICK AND TILED COTTAGES

situate facing White Hill and about a quarter of a mile South of Batchworth Heath. The Lot covers an area of about

0 A. 1 R. 25 P.

Two of the Cottages are Let under Weekly Tenancies to Mr. George W. Cooley and Mr. Joseph Smith respectively, the remaining Cottage being in hand.

THE COTTAGES

are of substantial construction, the two end ones contain Sitting Room, Kitchen Pantry and three Bedrooms, and the middle one having Sitting Room, Kitchen and two Bedrooms.

At the rear is a brick and tiled Building containing a Shed and Copper for each Cottage, and Garden Ground.

Drinking Water is obtained from a stand-pipe (Company's supply), situate on the opposite side of the road. There is also Rain Water storage.

SCHEDULE.

No. on Plan.	Tenant.	Description.	Quantity.
	PARISH OF RICKMANSWORTH RURAL (Det. 3).		
67	Mr. G. W. Cooley .	Cottage and Garden . .	.136
	Mr. J. Smith . .	Do. . .	.136
	In hand. . .	Do. . .	.137
		Total	A. .409

LANDLORD'S OUTGOINGS.

Commuted Tithe Rent Charge	£0	2	6
Land Tax	1	10	0
Total	£1	12	6

The Rates and Company's charges for Drinking Water are paid by the Landlord.

LOT 34

(Coloured Pink on Plan)

A Valuable Residential and Agricultural Property

known as

Moor Park Farm

situate within half-a-mile of Rickmansworth and possessing main road frontages, and great possibilities for

BUILDING DEVELOPMENT.

The Lot extends to an area of about

112A. 3R. 10P.

and is Let as to part to Major the Hon. Francis E. Grosvenor at a nominal rent, under tenancy, terminating at Michaelmas, 1920, as to a further part, together with other Lands, to Mr. Henry C. Hayter under Yearly Michaelmas Tenancy, at an apportioned Rent of £147 13s. 4d., the remainder being in hand. The Shooting over the Lot is Let until February 2nd, 1920, to Donald A. Stewart, Esq.

MOOR PARK FARMHOUSE

a comfortable old fashioned Residence, otherwise known as

BATCHWORTH HILL HOUSE

occupies a healthy and commanding position about 320 ft. above sea level, facing Moor Park and standing at a convenient distance back from the road with Lawns in front. It is built of brick with tiled roof and square central Portico and contains

ON THE GROUND FLOOR: Hall, with fireplace and tiled floor, and measuring about 14 ft. 6 in. by 11 ft. 6 in.; Dining Room about 23 ft. 9 in. (inclusive of bay) by 13 ft.; Drawing Room, about 19 ft. by 14 ft. 3 in.; Study having Telephone laid on; Cloak Lobby, Kitchen with range, dresser, and cupboard and speaking tube to the first floor; Scullery with glazed-ware sink (h. and c.), and copper; Dairy having cupboards and slate shelves; and underground is good commodious Cellarage.

ON THE FIRST FLOOR, reached by two staircases are six Bedrooms, Bathroom with bath (h. and c.), W.C. with modern fitting, and Linen Cupboard. The dimensions of the larger Bedrooms are about 19 ft. by 13 ft. 3 in., 18 ft. 6 in. by 13 ft., and 14 ft. 6 in. by 13 ft. 6 in.

Outside is a Wash-house with copper and fireplace, Coal House, and Closet.

Water is laid on from the local Company's mains. The drainage is on modern principles and discharges into a Cesspool at the back of the house.

There is brick and tiled STABLING affording the following accommodation:—Two-stall Stable with Loose Box adjoining and loft over (Water laid on), Coach or Motor House with cement floor, Harness Room, two Rooms for chauffeur, Box Room, Coal House, Fowl House, and Store.

THE FLOWER AND KITCHEN GARDENS are partially walled in, the walls being planted with Pears, Greengages and Plums. In the front of the House are a Rock Walk and a Weeping Ash.

THE FARMBUILDINGS

are compactly arranged on three sides of an Enclosed Yard and substantially built of brick with tiled roofs. They are of a modern character and include Cart Horse Stable for five with loft over, Cowhouse for ten with Hay Shed at end, Cowhouse for eighteen, having Company's Water laid on, another Cowhouse for seven with root and mixing houses adjoining ; Mixing House, Engine House, and two timber and tiled Cowhouses, each for four with three Loose Boxes adjoining.

At the back of the Farm Buildings is a

BRICK AND TILED COTTAGE

containing Front Room, Kitchen, two Bedrooms, each having fireplace, and another Room at the top of the stairs.

Also adjacent to the Farmbuildings is a SMALL ESTATE TIMBER YARD with the undermentioned timber built erections in connection with same :—Paint Shop, Ironmongery Store, Lime, Wood and Store Sheds, Carpenter's Shop, Office, Store Place, and a Cart Shed.

Also comprised in the Lot are a useful Gravel Pit at Juniper Hill, and a piece of Woodland.

The Property lends itself to BUILDING DEVELOPMENT by means of a roadway that might be formed across the Lot from Batchworth Hill to Juniper Hill, and provision is made for the Lot to have an outlet from such new roadway to the lower part of the Harefield Road.

SCHEDULE

No. on Plan.	Tenant.	Description.	Quantity.	Total Quantity.
	PARISH OF RICKMANSWORTH URBAN.			
669	Mr. H. C. Hayter .	Arable	15.566	
Pt. 675		Do.	15.858	
Pt. 676		Buildings, Yard and Garden .	1.219	
677		Pond	.056	
678		Pasture	7.143	
679		Arable	24.208	
680		Arable and Pasture ($2\frac{1}{4}$ acres)	9.016	
Pt. 683		Rough Pasture . . .	4.080	
Pt. 684		Pasture	1.837	
	PARISH OF RICKMANSWORTH RURAL (Det. 3).			
185		Arable	21.122	
186		Pasture	8.122	108.227
	PARISH OF RICKMANSWORTH URBAN.			
Pt. 676	Major the Hon. Francis E. Grosvenor	Batchworth Hill House . .		.582
668	In hand. . . .	Roadway	.328	
670		The Grove	2.730	
673A		Bank (New Cutting) . .	.600	
Pt. 676		Timber Yard . . .	.345	4.003
			Total	A.112.812

LANDLORD'S OUTGOINGS.

Commuted Tithe Rent Charge £17 12 8

The Timber on this Lot has an estimated value of £135 and is included in the Sale.

The Lot is Sold with a right in conjunction with or without Lot 45 to form and make a roadway 40 ft. wide, measured eastward from the line of the Eastern boundaries of Lots 40, 41, and 45 respectively, as indicated on the Sale plan, such line cutting the corner of the lane where the common boundary of Lots 40 and 45 meets the lane, the cost of making the road and of fencing the Eastern boundary of same to be borne when the full length of the roadway is completed as to two-thirds by this Lot and as to one-sixth by each of Lots 44 and 45 (see footnote to Lots 44 and 45).

The Lot is Sold and will be conveyed with the benefit of and subject to the provisions of an agreement with the Rickmansworth Urban District Council dated February 19th 1912, for diverting the roadway on Batchworth Hill, so far as it relates to this Lot.

BATCHWORTH HILL HOUSE OR MOOR PARK FARM, (LOT 34.)

PIPER'S FARM. (LOT 35.)

LOT 35

(*Coloured Yellow on Plan,*

Piper's Farm,

a capital, moderate-sized Agricultural Holding with a GOOD HOUSE and AMPLE BUILDINGS occupying a central position on the Lot, the Homestead being only about a mile from Rickmansworth. Together with a PLANTATION OF LARCH and other timber and a small piece of Woodland, the Lot extends to an area of about

82A. 2R. 12P.

and is Let as to part, together with other Lands, to Mr. Henry C. Hayter, under Yearly Michaelmas Tenancy, at an appointed rent of £100, the remainder comprising the Woodlands being in hand. The Shooting over the Lot is Let to Donald A. Stewart, Esq., until February 2nd, 1920.

THE FARMHOUSE

is a comparatively modern, double-fronted structure of brick with tiled roof, and contains Porch, Dining Room with bay window, Drawing Room also having bay, Kitchen with range, Scullery with fireplace and copper and Company's Water laid on to the sink, Pantry, and Coal Cellar underground ;

ON THE FIRST FLOOR, reached by two staircases, are three Bedrooms, each having fireplace and cupboard ; Bathroom with fireplace and cold Water service (the bath is the Property of the Tenant), and W.C., and on the Floor above are two good Attic Bedrooms. Cesspool Drainage.

There are small front and side Gardens and Kitchen Garden at the back. There is also a productive Orchard of Apple, Pear and Walnut Trees.

THE FARMBUILDINGS

are mainly constructed of timber and roofed with tiles and comprise Cowshed for twelve, another Cowshed for ten having loft over ; two-Stall Stable, Implement Shed, two-bay Barn, Cowshed for eight with loft over, Granary, two Loose Boxes, Trap House, Cowsheds for five and two respectively, two Pigsties, four-bay open Cart Shed, and brick and tiled Loose Box, Fowl House and Wood House.

Company's Water is laid into the farmyard.

The Pastures are well watered and the Arable Lands are in good heart.

SCHEDULE.

No. on Plan.	Tenant.	Description.	Quantity.	Total Quantity.
	PARISH OF RICKMANSWORTH RURAL (Det. 3).			
7	Mr. H. C. Hayter .	Pasture	8.636	
8		Do.	3.201	
9		House, Buildings, etc. . .	1.512	
10		Orchard	1.417	
11		Pasture	14.595	
12		Arable	13.654	
37		Pasture	9.456	
178		Arable	5.003	
179		Arable and Pasture (3 acres) .	9.935	
183		Arable	5.367	72.776
36	In hand. . . .	Bush Spring	1.077	
184		Sandfield Spring	4.989	
	PARISH OF RICKMANSWORTH URBAN.			
681		Greenbroom Spring . .	2.629	
682		Juniper Dell. . . .	1.101	9.796
			Total	A.82.572

LANDLORD'S OUTGOINGS.

Commuted Tithe Rent Charge £16 8 9

The Timber on this Lot has an estimated value of £175 and is included in the Sale.

The Tithe above stated is exclusive of an apportioned amount of Rectorial Tithe of £1 3s. 3d. charged on part of No. 37 which is owned by the Vendor. The latter Tithe is included in the Sale of the Lot.

LOT 36

(*Coloured Blue on Plan*)

A valuable Enclosure of

ACCOMMODATION PASTURE LAND

occupying a commanding position and fronting Moor Park and the main road between Rickmansworth and Batchworth Heath. It varies in altitude from about 250 ft. to 350 ft. above sea level, enjoys views of a wide stretch of country and in extent is about

26A. 1R. 15P.

Let together with other Land to Mr. Henry C. Hayter under Yearly Michaelmas Tenancy, at an apportioned rent of £30, the Shooting being Let to Donald A. Stewart, Esq. until February 2nd, 1920.

The field provides excellent Pasturage, and Company's Water is available. It also lends itself to BUILDING DEVELOPMENT.

LANDLORD'S OUTGOINGS.

Commuted Tithe Rent Charge £3 13 5

The Timber on this Lot has an estimated value of £35 and is included in the Sale.

LOT 37

(Coloured Brown on Plan)

Another

ACCOMMODATION PASTURE FIELD

situate immediately to the South of the foregoing Lot and enjoying like advantages of position and soil. It extends to an area of about

15A. 3R. 10P.

and is Let together with other Lands to Mr. Henry C. Hayter under Yearly Michaelmas Tenancy, at an apportioned rent of £17 10s., the Shooting being Let to Donald A. Stewart, Esq., until February 2nd, 1920.

LANDLORD'S OUTGOINGS.

Commuted Tithe Rent Charge £2 6 11

The Timber on this Lot has an estimated value of £45 and is included in the Sale.

LOT 38

(Coloured Pink on Plan)

A Parcel of

ACCOMMODATION PASTURE LAND

situate fronting Woodcock Hill, a little under one-and-a-half miles from Rickmansworth and extending to an area of about

6A. 0R. 10P.

Let together with other Lands to Mr. Henry C. Hayter under Yearly Michaelmas Tenancy, at an apportioned rent of £7, the Shooting being Let to Donald A. Stewart, Esq., until February 2nd, 1920.

The field has a frontage of about 550 ft. to the high road, with an altitude of between 300 and 325 ft. above sea level, and forms a good site for one or more Houses.

Company's Water is available in the road.

LANDLORD'S OUTGOINGS.

Commuted Tithe Rent Charge £0 6 5

The Timber on this Lot has an estimated value of £12 and is included in the Sale.

The fencing of the Northern boundary of this Lot is an obligation of the adjoining owner James Whittle, Esq.

The Tithe above stated is exclusive of an apportioned amount of Rectorial Tithe of £0 18 2 which is owned by the Vendor. This latter Tithe is included in the Sale of the Lot.

LOT 39

(Coloured Pink on Plan)

Batchworth House

a commodious, old fashioned Residence, situate at Batchworth, near the North Western corner of Moor Park and about half a mile from Rickmansworth Station. The House, together with its pleasure grounds, two Cottages and Stabling, extends to an area of about

2 A. 0 R. 34 P.

and is held by the Dowager Lady Ebury, by assignment from Madame Alderton, under three years' agreement from 29th September, 1918, during which term an option is granted in favour of the Tenant to take a Lease of the Premises for fourteen years from 29th September, 1921. The option to take the Lease referred to has been exercised.

THE RESIDENCE is of brick faced with cement, and having tiled gabled roof. It contains on the upper and lower ground Floor levels glazed Portico with tiled floor, small Hall, Dining Room with walls panelled in dark oak and measuring about 17 ft. 3 in. by 16 ft. 9 in. and about 11 ft. in height; Drawing Room, about 21 ft. 9 in. by 21 ft. 3 in. inclusive of a bay, with casement to the Garden and having a "Well" fire with blue tiled surround; Smoking Room about 28 ft. 9 in. by 14 ft., with tiled fireplace; Servants' Hall about 16 ft. 6 in. by 12 ft. 6 in.; Butler's Pantry with sink (h. and c.), Kitchen about 20 ft. 6 in. by 18 ft. by about 13 ft. high, and having double oven range; Scullery, having sink (h. and c.); Study or Maids' Sitting Room, two Pantries, Housemaid's Cupboard with sink and cold water supply; China Cupboard, Lobby having the Telephone installed, Boot Hole with water supply, and two W.C.'s, one apartment being fitted also with lavatory Basin having cold water supply; and beneath the House are three Storage Cellars, one having Water laid on, and Wine Cellar.

ON THE FIRST FLOOR, and Half Landing to same, and reached by principal and secondary staircases, the former having heavy oak handrail and dado, are Boudoir or Morning Room measuring about 21 ft. 6 in. square, one dimension being inclusive of a bay, and about 11 ft. in height; four Principal Bedrooms, the three larger ones measuring about 20 ft. 3 in. by 18 ft. 6 in., 17 ft. by 16 ft. 9 in. and 17 ft. by 14 ft. 9 in. respectively; Bathroom with bath (h. and c.), drip sink (h. and c.), and W.C.; and

ON THE SECOND FLOOR, and Half Landing below, are three other Best Bedrooms, the dimensions of the two larger apartments being about 17 ft. by 15 ft. 3 in., and 16 ft. 9 in. by 14 ft. respectively; Bathroom with bath and lavatory basin (h. and c.), W.C., and drip sink (h. and c.), and four Attic Bedrooms, the largest measuring about 18 ft. by 14 ft. 3 in., and having a fireplace.

SUMMARY OF ACCOMMODATION.

Hall.	Boudoir.
Dining Room.	Seven best Bedrooms.
Drawing Room.	Two Bath Rooms and two W.C.'s.
Smoking Room.	Four Attic Bedrooms.
Study	Commodious Domestic Offices.
Two W.C.'s.	Underground Cellarage.

Company's Water. Gas. Main Drainage.

THE STABLING is brick and tiled, and consists of two Stalls and Loose Box with Hay Loft over, Coach House or Garage with loft over, and adjoining is

A COTTAGE, brick and tiled and containing large Living Room, Kitchen, three Bedrooms, and W.C.

THE SECOND COTTAGE is also of brick with tiled roof and contains Sitting Room with marble mantel, Kitchen with portable range and sink with cold water service, three Bedrooms, another Bedroom or Box Room, and Bathroom. Outside is a Coal Shed and W.C.

THE PLEASURE GROUNDS

are fully matured with ornamental timber including a Weeping Wych Elm and a Mulberry. The inner Garden is enclosed by a high brick wall planted with various kinds of Fruit Trees and verged by Herbaceous borders, and in the centre is a Croquet Lawn and Rose Garden.

The outer or Fruit Garden is productive and well stocked with tree and bush fruit and adjoining it at the end of a herbaceous walk is a levelled Tennis Lawn, and another small Lawn with Rose Parterres.

The GLASSHOUSES include a good lean-to Greenhouse (heated), lean-to Peach House, also heated, Forcing House, a five light lean-to pit, and two other pits, and stoke hole.

Other buildings on the Lot comprise timber and iron roofed Pigsty, Vegetable and Fruit Store, and Wood House. There are also two Rain Water Tanks.

SCHEDULE.

No on Plan.	Description	Quantity
	PARISH OF RICKMANSWORTH URBAN.	
Pt. 643	Cottage	.060
649	House and Garden	2.015
Pt. 651	Buildings and Yard	.139
	Total	A.2.214

LANDLORD'S OUTGOINGS.

Commuted Tithe Rent Charge	£0	8	3
Land Tax	4	8	0
Total	£4	16	3

The Carriage entrance to the Stabling is over land at the North-Eastern corner of Lot 44 and is used in common as an entrance to the stabling on this Lot and to the farm buildings on Lot 44; the lot is sold with the benefit of such way and user (see footnote to Lot 44).

BATCHWORTH HOUSE. (LOT 39.)

FROGMOOR COTTAGE. (LOT 40.)

LOT 40

(Coloured Purple on Plan)

A small Residential Property known as

FROGMOOR COTTAGE

situate a little over half a mile from Rickmansworth Station and abutting the Harefield Road. Together with its Gardens, Stabling, Paddock, and an adjacent Cottage, it extends to an area of about

3A. 1R. 17P.

and is Let as to part to Colonel S. D. Gordon under Yearly Michaelmas Tenancy, at an annual rent of £80, and as to a further part to Mrs. Hall under Weekly Tenancy.

THE HOUSE

is a comfortable, old fashioned structure of brick with slated roof, partly ivy clad, and contains

ON THE GROUND FLOOR: Hall, Dining Room (South and West), about 20 ft. by 13 ft. 6 in., Drawing Room (North and West), having modern tiled grate and measuring about 20 ft. by 14 ft. 9 in.; Morning Room about 15 ft. 6 in. (inclusive of a bay) by 14 ft. Each of the three foregoing Rooms is about 10 ft. in height. Kitchen with double-oven range and measuring about 15 ft. square; Butler's Pantry, fitted with lavatory basin having (h. and c.) services; Scullery with sink (h. and c.), and Larder.

ON THE FIRST FLOOR, reached by two staircases are Five Best Bed and Dressing Rooms, the largest of the Bedrooms measuring respectively about 19 ft. by 14 ft., 15 ft. 3 in. by 14 ft. 3 in., and 15 ft. by 14 ft. Bathroom with porcelain lined Bath and lavatory Basin each with h. and c. services, W.C., Maidservants' Bedroom, Box Room and Loft.

Outside are Wood and Coal Houses and W.C.

Company's Water and Gas are laid on, the Telephone is installed in the Morning Room, and the Drains are on modern principles and discharge into the public sewer.

The Stabling is of brick and timber roofed with slate, and consists of two Loose Boxes, Motor House with cement floor and covered Washing Place outside, a two Stall Stable with Harness Room, having fireplace, adjoining and Loft over.

The Gardens are screened from the road by fully matured timber, the side Lawn is overspread by a fine Horse Chestnut Tree, and there are Tennis and Croquet Lawns, nicely laid out Flower Garden, and a large Kitchen Garden planted with Fruit Trees and Bushes. There is also a small span-roofed Greenhouse and Tool and Potting Shed.

A useful Paddock of about two acres adjoins the Gardens on the West.

THE COTTAGE

is built of brick and timber with tiled roof and contains Sitting Room, Living Room, Wash House with copper and sink, having Water laid on and two Bedrooms. It has a small Garden with a timber and tiled Shed at the rear.

The Parochial and Water Rates in respect of the Cottage are discharged by the Landlord.

SCHEDULE.

No. on Plan.	Tenant.	Description.	Quantity.	Total Quantity.
	PARISH OF RICKMANSWORTH URBAN.			
Pt. 655	Col. S. D. Gordon .	Frogmoor Cottage . . .	1.041	
667		Garden and Paddock . .	2.265	3.306
Pt. 655	Mrs. Hall . .	Cottage and Garden . .		.050
			Total .	A.3.356

LANDLORD'S OUTGOINGS.

Commuted Tithe Rent Charge	£0 17 5
Land Tax	1 18 6
Total	£2 15 11

The boundary on the Western side of No. 667 where it abuts on other property is 4 ft. from the centre of the hedge.

LOT 41

(Coloured Yellow on Plan)

FOUR COTTAGES AND GARDENS

(being at the Eastern end of a row of five) situate to the East of the foregoing Lot, fronting the Harefield Road and bounded on one side by an accommodation roadway leading towards Juniper Hill. The Lot has an area of about

0A. 0R. 27P.

and the Cottages are Let under Weekly Tenancies to the following tenants respectively :— Mr. Charles Pratt, Mr. William Hill, Mr. Walter Moss, and Mr. John Atkins.

Two of the Cottages are of brick with slated roof, the other two being brick and tiled, and each contains two Rooms upstairs and two below.

Company's Water is laid on, and there is a Wood Shed for each at the end of the Garden. The Sinks are drained into the public sewer.

LANDLORD'S OUTGOINGS.—Nil

The Parochial Rates and Water Rates are discharged by the Landlord.

LOT 42

(Coloured Brown on Plan)

FROGMOOR WHARF HOUSE

A comfortably arranged old fashioned RESIDENCE, built of brick with slated roof, and together with its Gardens, Garage and an adjacent WHARF extending to an area of about

0A. 3R. 31P.

Let as to part to John Sandy, Esq., under repairing lease for fourteen years from 24th June, 1917 at a rent of £50 per annum, with lessee's option to terminate the lease at the end of the third or seventh year, the remainder, comprising the Wharf, being in hand.

THE HOUSE, which is slightly over half-a-mile from Rickmansworth Station and fronts the Harefield Road, has a short carriage approach and contains :—

ON THE GROUND FLOOR : Hall, about 20 ft. by 7 ft. 9 in., Dining Room, about 17 ft. 6 in. by 16 ft. 6 in., inclusive of a bay and having veined Marble Mantel ; Drawing Room, measuring about 23 ft. by 15 ft. 3 in., and fitted with modern tiled register grate ; Breakfast Room, about 15 ft. 9 in. by 12 ft. 3 in., also with Marble Mantel ; Conservatory, heated ; Lobby with lavatory basin, having cold water supply ; W.C. ; Kitchen, about 19 ft. 6 in. by 12 ft. 6 in., and having double-oven range ; Scullery with sink (h. and c.) ; Larder and Servants' W.C. outside.

ON THE FIRST FLOOR, reached by two staircases are

FIVE BEST BEDROOMS

measuring respectively about 20 ft. 3 in. by 14 ft. 6 in., 23 ft. 6 in. by 12 ft., 16 ft. 3 in. by 11 ft. 9 in., 15 ft. by 10 ft. 9 in., and 12 ft. by 10 ft. 9 in. Bath Room with bath and lavatory basin, each having hot and cold supplies, and W.C. ; and

ON THE SECOND FLOOR are two Secondary Bedrooms, their respective dimensions being 14 ft. by 11 ft. 9 in., and 12 ft. by 8 ft. 9 in.

The Reception Rooms are between 10 ft. and 11 ft. in height, and the principal Bedrooms about 10 ft.

Company's Water and Gas are laid on, and the Drains discharge into the Public Sewer.

FROGMOOR WHARF HOUSE. (LOT 42.)

FROGMOOR HOUSE. (LOT 43.)

THE OUTBUILDINGS are of brick with tiled or slated roofs and include Garage with cement floor, Loose Box, Knife, Wood and Coal Houses.

THE GARDENS are surrounded by a wall and high hedge, and comprise a capital Tennis or Croquet Lawn, Flower and Kitchen Gardens, the latter walled on one side and planted with standard and walled Fruit Trees.

THE WHARF has a frontage to the Grand Junction Canal of about 200 ft.

SCHEDULE.

No. on Plan.	Tenant.	Description.	Quantity.
	PARISH OF RICKMANSWORTH URBAN.		
657	J. Sandy, Esq. . .	House and Garden	.726
Pt. 656	In hand . . .	Wharf	.220
		Total . .	A. .946

LANDLORD'S OUTGOINGS.

Commuted Tithe Rent Charge	£0	3	6
Land Tax	1	5	0
Total	£1	8	6

The mines mentioned under General Remark 11 are excepted from this Lot.

The sale of this Lot does not include any right to use the roadway on the South-West of the Lot and numbered Pt. 658a on Plan, or any part of the Grand Junction Canal.

The Lot is sold and will be conveyed subject to a restriction for the benefit of Lots 40 and 43 that no part of the premises now leased to Mr. J. Sandy shall at any future time be used for any other purpose than for a Private Residence and the appurtenances thereof, and that no buildings, structure, works or machinery shall be erected or used on the Wharf, nor the Wharf be used for any other purpose than the loading or unloading of goods, and that nothing of a noxious or offensive nature shall be stored or be allowed to remain thereon.

LOT 43

(Coloured Blue on Plan)

A moderate sized Residential Property known as

FROGMOOR HOUSE

situate on the Harefield Road, about half-a-mile from Rickmansworth Station and together with its Grounds, Stabling and Paddock, extending to an area of about

5 A. 2 R. 37 P.

The Property is at present in the occupation of and held rent free until Lady-day, 1920, by Henry B. Couchman, Esq., the Resident Agent for the Moor Park Estate. Vacant possession can be given at Lady-day, 1920, and the lot is sold and will be conveyed subject to such occupation.

THE HOUSE

stands at a convenient distance back from the road, and has a short carriage approach, its principal aspects being East and West.

It is an old fashioned structure of brick, faced with cement and part tiled and part slated roof, and contains :—

ON THE GROUND FLOOR : Portico, Hall with tiled " low-fire " grate and hearth, and measuring about 16 ft. by 15 ft. 6 in. ; Dining Room, about 17 ft. 6 in. (exclusive of a square bay) by 13 ft. 9 in. and having chimney corner with brick fireplace and hearth ; Drawing Room with modern tiled grate and hearth, and casement opening to the grounds, its dimensions being about 23 ft. by 15 ft. ; Smoking Room having tiled fireplace and telephone laid on ; Kitchen about 19 ft. 3 in. by 10 ft. 6 in. exclusive of a bay and having a double oven " Herald " range ; Scullery, with sink (h. and c.) ; China Pantry, Larder with slate shelving ; Pantry with sink (h. and c.), Cloak Cupboard, and Lavatory with basin (h. and c.), and W.C. Outside are Servants' W.C., and Coal House.

ON THE FIRST FLOOR and half landing to same, reached by a principal staircase rising from a square inner Hall are :—

FOUR BEST BEDROOMS

measuring respectively about 17 ft. 9 in. by 14 ft. 6 in., 16 ft. 6 in. by 14 ft., 16 ft. by 15 ft., and 16 ft. by 15 ft. Three of these Rooms have modern tiled register grates, and are about 10 ft. in height. Another Bedroom, Dressing Room, Bathroom with porcelain lined bath (h. and c.), and W.C. with modern fitting ; and

ON THE SECOND FLOOR are two Attic Bedrooms, the larger measuring about 15 ft. 3 in. by 14 ft. 3 in.

Company's Water and Gas are laid on, the Drainage is on modern principles, and is connected with the Public Sewer.

THE GARAGE AND STABLING are brick and slated, and include two Loose Boxes and one Stall, and Motor House with cemented floor.

THE GARDENS

are well timbered and fully matured, a feature in them being a sheet of Ornamental Water dividing the Paddock from the Western Lawn and skirting a wilderness walk on the Northern boundary of the Property.

The Kitchen Garden is walled on one side, and very productive.

The Paddock is about three-and-a-half acres in extent.

SCHEDULE.

No. on Plan.	Description.	Quantity.
	PARISH OF RICKMANSWORTH URBAN.	
Pt. 658	House and Garden	1.689
659	Pond	.352
660	Paddock	3.692
	Total .	A. 5.733

LANDLORD'S OUTGOINGS.

Commuted Tithe Rent Charge £1 8 10

Any Timber on this Lot will be included in the Sale.

The sale of this Lot does not include any right to use the roadway on the North-East of the Lot and numbered 658A on the plan or any part of the Grand Junction Canal. The mines mentioned in General Remark No. 11 are excepted from this Lot.

LOT 44
(Coloured Blue on Plan)

Three Valuable Enclosures of

ACCOMMODATION PASTURE LAND

TWO COTTAGES and a USEFUL SET OF BUILDINGS, situate fronting the Harefield Road and Batchworth Hill, and less than half-a-mile from the centre of the Town of Rickmansworth. The Lot extends to an area of about

13A. 2R. 0P.

and is ripe for BUILDING DEVELOPMENT.

Let as to part to Mr. Frederick Barton under Yearly Michaelmas Tenancy, as to further part (Cottage and Gardens) to Mr. George Leaper under Weekly Tenancy, the remaining part (vacant Cottage) being in hand.

THE COTTAGES

are of brick with tiled roof and each contains Living Room, Kitchen having gas and water laid on, and two Bedrooms. At the rear is a timber and tiled Shed. The Drainage is taken into the Public Sewer.

The Rates on the Cottages are paid by the Landlord.

THE BUILDINGS

constructed of brick with tiled roof consist of Barn, two Loose Boxes, Grain Pit and Cowhouse for twelve.

SCHEDULE.

No. on Plan.	Tenant.	Description.	Quantity	Total Quantity.
	PARISH OF RICKMANSWORTH URBAN.			
650	Mr. F. Barton .	Pasture	1.237	
Pt. 651		Building and Yard . .	.210	
654		Pasture . . .	3.581	
Pt. 671		Do.	8.324	
				13.352
Pt. 651	Mr. G. Leaper .	Cottage and Gardens . .		.140
Pt. 651	In hand. . .	Cottage		.010
			Total .	A.13.502

LANDLORD'S OUTGOINGS.

Commuted Tithe Rent Charge £3 11 8

The Timber on this Lot has an estimated value of £75 and is included in the Sale.

The Carriage Entrance at the North-Eastern corner of this Lot to the Buildings is used in common with the Entrance to the Stabling, etc., on Lot 39 and this Lot is sold and will be conveyed subject to such right of way and user over the same (see footnote to Lot 39).

The Lot is Sold and will be conveyed subject to a right for Lots 34 and 45 or either of them to form and make a Roadway 40ft. wide, measured Eastward from the line of Eastern Boundaries of Lots 40, 41 and 45 respectively, as indicated on the Sale Plan, such line cutting the corner of the lane where the common boundary of Lots 40 and 45 meets the lane, the cost of making the Road and of fencing the Eastern Boundary of same to be borne, when the full length of the Roadway is completed, as to one-sixth by this Lot and Lot 45 and as to two-thirds by Lot 34 (see footnote to Lots 34 and 45).

LOT 45

(Coloured Green on Plan)

TWO ENCLOSURES OF
ACCOMMODATION PASTURE LAND

occupying a pleasant situation facing the Harefield Road, to which they have a frontage of about 280 ft., and about three-quarters of a mile from Rickmansworth Station.

The Lot is suitable for the erection of one or more good-class Residences, or for development in greater detail. It extends to an area of about

7A. 2R. 12P.

and is Let to Mr. George Jones under Yearly Michaelmas Tenancy.

The Buildings on the Lot are the property of the Tenant.

The Harefield Road is sewered, Company's water is laid along it, and provision is made for a Road Outlet on the Eastern side of the Lot.

The Western boundary of No. Pt. 666 where it abuts on property not belonging to the Vendor is 4 ft. from the centre of the hedge.

The Shooting over the Lot is let to Donald A. Stewart, Esq., until February 2nd, 1920.

SCHEDULE.

No. on Plan.	Description.	Quantity.
	PARISH OF RICKMANSWORTH URBAN.	
Pt. 664	Pasture	3.210
Pt. 666	Do.	4.363
	Total .	A. 7.573

LANDLORD'S OUTGOINGS.

Commuted Tithe Rent Charge £1 15 9

The Timber on this Lot has an estimated value of £16 and is included in the Sale.

The Lot is Sold with a right in conjunction with or without Lot 34 to form and make a Roadway 40 ft. wide, measured Eastward from the line of the Eastern Boundaries of Lots 40, 41 and 45 respectively, as indicated on the Sale Plan, such line cutting the corner of the lane where the common boundary of Lots 40 and 45 meets the lane, the cost of making the Road and of fencing the Eastern Boundary of same to be borne when the full length of Roadway is completed, as to one-sixth by this Lot and Lot 44 and as to two-thirds by Lot 34 (see footnote to Lots 34 and 44).

LOT 46

(*Coloured brown on Plan*)

" THE COACH AND HORSES " INN,

BATCHWORTH.

a Beer House, licensed for seven days a week, occupying an open position near Batchworth Corner where converge the Main Roads to London, Watford, and Rickmansworth, and being only about a third of a mile from the Rickmansworth High Street.

THE INN, with a COTTAGE adjoining and its Garden extends to an area of about

0A. 2R. 29P.

and is Let to Salter & Co., Limited, under Repairing Lease for fourteen years from September 29th, 1915, rent £45, determinable by the Lessees at the end of the seventh year if the licences should be terminated or refused renewal.

THE INN

is an old-fashioned structure of brick with tiled roof having a large open space in front and containing Bar, Taproom, Parlour, Kitchen, Cellar, Pantry, Wash House with copper, Scullery with copper and sink having water laid on, and four Bedrooms.

Outside are two W.C.'s. Facing the front open space is

TIMBER AND TILED STABLING for three horses, with Loft over, and Trap House.

THE COTTAGE

is built of similar materials to the Inn, and contains small Sitting Room, Living Room, Back Kitchen with copper and sink having water laid on, and two Bedrooms. At the back of the premises is a LARGE GARDEN planted with Fruit Trees.

The Buildings are drained into the Public sewer.

LANDLORD'S OUTGOINGS.

Commuted Tithe Rent Charge	£0	3	6
Land Tax	1	0	0
Total .	£1	3	6

On the Eastern side of the Lot is a Passage Way forming part of Lot 47, used in common with this Lot and Lot 47, and this Lot is Sold with the benefit of such way and user (see footnote to Lot 47).

In the existing lease is a covenant by the lessor to erect a boundary fence on the North-West side if such fence is required by the licensing authority, the purchaser shall covenant to perform this obligation and indemnify the Vendor and the Estate of the Lessor against it.

LOT 47

(Coloured Purple on Plan)

A ROW OF FOUR COTTAGES

situate at Batchworth and adjoining the foregoing Lot. Together with a detached PLOT OF GARDEN GROUND, the Property extends to an area of about

0A. 1R. 9P.

the Cottages being Let under Weekly Tenancies with a useful piece of Garden Ground each, to Mr. Alfred Swan, Mr. Ernest Smith, Mr. Arthur Kibbles, and Mr. Thomas Gander, respectively.

THE COTTAGES

are substantially built of brick with slate roofs and each contains Living Room, Scullery and two Bedrooms. At the rear, each has a brick and tiled Shed with copper and sink having water laid on and W.C. Company's Water, Main Drainage.

The Rates and Water Charges are paid by the Landlord.

SCHEDULE.

No. on Plan.	Tenant.	Description.	Quantity.
	PARISH	OF RICKMANSWORTH URBAN.	
Pt. 642	As above . .	Four Gardens	.187
Pt. 643	Do. . .	Four Cottages	.120
		Total	A. .307

LANDLORD'S OUTGOINGS.

Commuted Tithe Rent Charge £0 0 4

At the rear of the Cottages is a Passage Way forming part of this Lot used in common with this Lot and Lot 46, and this Lot is Sold and will be conveyed subject to such way and user (see footnote to Lot 46).

The Lot is sold with the benefit of a right of way to the gardens in this Lot over enclosure No. Pt. 642 Lot 48 (see footnote to Lot 48).

LOT 48

(Coloured Yellow on Plan)

A ROW OF

SIX BRICK AND SLATED COTTAGES

situate immediately to the South of the foregoing Lot. Together with a PLOT OF GARDEN GROUND adjoining, they extend to an area of about

0A. 2R. 2P.

Each Cottage is Let together with a piece of Garden Ground under Weekly Tenancy, the respective Tenants being Mr. Frederick Collier, Mr. Henry Williamson, Mr. Herbert Caffall, Mr. Thomas Waller, Mr. Edmund King and Mr. Charles Armstrong; and there is one Plot of the Garden Ground Let separately to Mr. Joseph Paddick.

The Cottages contain Living Room, Back Kitchen and two Bedrooms, and each has a timber and tiled Shed with copper and sink, and W.C. ; Company's Water, Main Drainage. The Landlord pays all Rates.

SCHEDULE.

O. ON PLAN.	TENANT.	DESCRIPTION.	QUANTITY.
	PARISH OF RICKMANSWORTH URBAN.		
Pt. 642	As above .	Seven Gardens	.344
Pt. 643	Do. .	Six Cottages	.170
		TOTAL .	A. .514

LANDLORD'S OUTGOINGS.

Commuted Tithe Rent Charge £0 0 8

The Lot is sold and will be conveyed subject to a right of way in favourof Lot 47 over enclosure No. Pt. 642 in this Lot to the gardens shewn as No. Pt. 642, Lot 47 (see footnote to Lot 47).

LOT 49

(Coloured Brown on Plan)

THE VALUABLE GRAVEL BEDS

as now being worked by the Rickmansworth Gravel Company, Limited, under a Lease of a right to dredge for gravel, &c., the Lands included in the Lot forming parts of Bury Farm and Stockers Farm, and in all extending to an area of about

23A. 3R. 12P.

The Lease to the Rickmansworth Gravel Company Limited is for a term of fourteen years from March 1st, 1914, and includes a parcel of Land, about 3½ acres in extent, which is now worked out and forms part of Lot 50.

The Lease provides for the payment by the Company of Rent at the rate of £250 per acre for every acre worked, until a total of £5,000 has been paid in Rent, the payment in any one quarter of a year to be not less than £100. The total of the payments made by the Company up to March 1st, 1919, was £2,237 2s. 6d., and the acreage remaining unworked under the Lease at the same date was about ten acres.

Other provisions of the Lease include *inter alia*

(*a*) The erection and maintenance of a swing or other sufficient Bridge across the Accommodation Roadway in Enclosure No. 250 on Plan and the formation of a Waterway leading from the Grand Junction Canal to the Gravel Workings (both the Bridge and Waterway have been formed by the Gravel Company).

(*b*) The right to use the land on the South side of the Canal included in the Lot for the purpose of widening the Canal to allow barges to enter the Lot, such right to be subject to the consent of the Canal Company. (This has not yet been done.)

(*c*) That the Lessees shall only take possession of and fence off so much of the Land as is actually required for working purposes, the Land not fenced off remaining in the sole control of the Lessor.

(*d*) That the Lessees shall compensate the Lessor's Tenants for giving up possession of the Land in respect of which a right is demised to them.

(*e*) That the Lessor shall not during the continuance of the Lease permit any other person to Dredge on his Estate at Rickmansworth for Washed Ballast.

(*f*) That the Lessees will not during the continuance of the Lease Dredge for Washed Ballast elsewhere (with one exception) than on Land Leased or Sold to them by the Lessor, except that so long as the rent was paid and the covenants performed, they should have liberty to dredge for washed ballast on No. 224 (Lot 50).

(*g*) The area Leased for Dredging purposes was limited to 20 acres.

The approach to the Gravel Company's workings is by way of the Grand Junction Canal and the Waterway leading therefrom.

The Washed Ballast as dredged from the Workings is in great demand, hard, and free from the softest fine siftings ; and the adjoining Lands up to very many acres in extent are believed to contain equally valuable deposits of gravel.

The Lands forming part of the Workings of the Lot that are not fenced in are Let to and held respectively with their other Farm Lands by Mr. W. Aves and Mr. Henry Giles, the Tenants of Bury Farm, Lot 51, and Stockers Farm, Lot 53, the rents apportioned to this Lot being respectively £35 and £4 5s.

The Shooting over the Lot is let to Donald A. Stewart, Esq., until February 2nd, 1920.

SCHEDULE.

No. on Plan.	Tenant.	Description.	Quantity.	Total Quantity.
	PARISH OF RICKMANSWORTH RURAL (Det. 3).			
Pt. 244	Rickmansworth Gravel Co., Ltd.	Waterway	.126	
Pt. 250		Do.	.164	
Pt. 250		Gravel Pit	1.450	
Pt. 251		Waterway	.036	
Pt. 252		Do.	.252	
Pt. 253		Do.	.018	
Pt. 271		Gravel Pit	1.680	
Pt. 272		Do.	3.090	
				6.816
Pt. 236	Mr. H Giles . .	Canal Bank	.015	
Pt. 250		Pasture	.020	
Pt. 257		Canal Bank	.072	
Pt. 272		Pasture	2.660	
Pt. 272		Do.	1.070	3.837
Pt. 225	Mr. W. Aves . .	Marsh	.272	
Pt. 259		Pasture	.580	
Pt. 264		Do.	6.728	
Pt. 271		Do.	5.590	13.170
			Total .	A.23.823

LANDLORD'S OUTGOINGS.

Commuted Tithe Rent Charge	£4	10	10
Land Tax		14	0
Total .	£5	4	10

Any Timber on this Lot will be included in the Sale.

The Lot is Sold and will be conveyed subject to a Right of Way with horses and carts and for all necessary purposes in favour of Lot 53 over the Accommodation Roadway and Bridge leading from Stockers Farm towards Mill End and subject to the obligation to maintain the bridge and such fences on either side thereof as are necessary for driving cattle and other animals over it, but with a right to enter upon Lot 53 for the purpose of effecting such maintenance (see footnote to Lot 53).

It is also sold and will be conveyed subject to a right of way over enclosure No. Pt. 264 shown on the Plan for the duration of the term of the Lease of the Lake, etc. (Lot 50) to W. H. Walker, Esq., with horses and carts for the purpose of farming enclosures, Nos. 266 and 267 on Plan, Lot 50 (see footnote to Lot 50).

No. Pt. 225 is sold subject to and with the benefit of an arrangement dated August 10th, 1832, mentioned in the Conditions.

LOT 50

(Coloured Blue on Plan)

THIS LOT COMPRISES

BATCHWORTH LAKE

having an area of about 23 ACRES, a stretch of the River Colne of nearly a mile in length together with the valuable and exclusive Right of Fishing, and if and so far as the Vendor can grant the same, the right of Boating and Bathing therein, and about five-and-a-half acres of Accommodation Land adjoining the Lake and River; included also are such rights of access to the Lake from the Ebury Pleasure Ground as may be vested in the Vendor. The Lot in all extends to an area of about

38A. 2R. 25P.

land is held as to the greater portion by William H. Walker, Esq., under Lease for a term of nineteen years from September 29th, 1914, terminable at the Lessee's option at the end of the fifth or fourteenth year at a rent of £80 10s., the remainder being in hand.

THE LAKE is a

FINE SHEET OF WATER

lying practically contiguous to the Town of Rickmansworth, dotted with Islands and secluded on two sides by strips of Plantation threaded by shady Walks and in parts laid-out as Gardens. The Lake also lies contiguous to the River Colne whence as well as from the River Chess it derives an abundant and continuous flow of fresh water rendering the Boating, Fishing and Bathing, and the adjacent River Walks of a most enjoyable description.

Under the terms of the Lease provision is made *inter alia* for

(*a*) A right for the Lessee to pass over the Bridge at W on the Sale Plan and such Rights of Way as the Lessor has power to delegate between the points Z and W on Plan ; and a Right of Way for all purposes between the points marked U and V on the Sale Plan (see footnote to Lot 74).

(*b*) The exclusive right of fishing in conjunction with the Vendor in the River Colne between the Footbridge carrying the canal towing path over the River near Batchworth to the point marked L on the Sale Plan, the fishing including that from the whole of the Southern bank and parts of the Northern bank of the River ; and the right of boating and bathing from the said Footbridge to the point marked X on Plan, and the right to pass on the Southern bank and parts of the Northern bank for the purpose of exercising such rights of fishing and bathing.

(*c*) A right for the Lessee to the whole of the moneys received for skating permits on the Lake for the first two days of a period of frost, the moneys so received for the third and subsequent days of the period of skating being divided, after the deduction of expenses, between the Lessor and Lessee equally.

(*d*) No other grant being made by the Lessor for Boating purposes within five miles of this Lot without the Lessee being given the first option of carrying on the same.

(*e*) For the Lessee to keep the Lake and River properly stocked with fish, and to maintain the banks of the Lake and River.

In addition to the Fishing and other rights granted under the Lease to Mr. Walker, a length of about 650 ft. of the River Colne at the Eastern end of the Lot with the Fishing and other rights therein, together with a strip of Land about 10 ft. in width fronting the River and situate at the back of the Pumping Station, is included in the Sale of this Lot.

SCHEDULE.

No. on Plan.	Tenant.	Description.	Quantity.	Total Quantity.
	PARISH OF RICKMANSWORTH RURAL (Det. 3).			
216	W. H. Walker, Esq.	Lake	3.500	
216A		Bank	.668	
217		Waste	.344	
220		Bank	.257	
221		Do.	.273	
222		River	.938	
223		River Bank	1.476	
224		Lake	19.588	
265		Bank	.494	
266		Pasture	2.263	
267		Do.	3.153	
Pt. 276		River	2.620	
	PARISH OF RICKMANSWORTH URBAN.			
601		River	.923	
Pt. 606		Island	.050	
608		River	1.083	37.630
646A	In hand. . .	River	1.000	
Pt. 652		Wharf	.025	1.025
			Total .	A.38.655

LANDLORD'S OUTGOINGS.

Commuted Tithe Rent Charge £5 18 6

Any Timber on this Lot will be included in the Sale.

The Lot is Sold with the benefit, during the term of the Lease to Mr. W. H. Walker (Lot 50), of a Right of Way with horses and carts for the purposes of farming enclosures numbered 266 and 267 on Plan over the accommodation Roadway passing from the Canal Bridge near Frogmoor House towards Bury Farm Homestead and thence direct to Enclosure No. 266 on Plan (see footnote to Lots 49 and 51).

It will also be Sold with a right of way over the Roadway No. Pt. 658A on Plan Lot 51 (see footnote to Lot 51).

It will also be Sold with a right for all time to enter enclosures Nos. Pt. 264, 269, 270 and 273 of Lot 51 and with a right until the termination of the Lease of the Lake to enter enclosures Nos. Pt. 606 and Pt. 615 of Lot 74 for the purpose of fishing there from along the River Bank (see footnotes to Lots 51 and 74).

A Public Sewer runs beneath the river numbered 646A on Plan and the Lot is sold and will be conveyed subject to the rights of the Rickmansworth Urban District Council in connection therewith.

This Lot is sold subject as to parts thereof to the Agreements of May 20, 1823, and August 10th, 1832, referred to in the Conditions. It is also sold with the benefit of a right of footway, in common with the Rickmansworth Urban District Council, over the footpath WZ from the Uxbridge Road to and as far as the River Colne during such hours as the Ebury Pleasure Ground shall be open to the public.

LOT 51

(Coloured Pink on Plan)

A VALUABLE PROPERTY

known as

BURY FARM,

consisting of a RICH DAIRYING HOLDING situate only about half-a-mile from Rickmansworth and comprising a superior Farmhouse, a capital set of Farmbuildings, a Cottage and excellent Pasture Lands, the whole extending to an area of about

40A. 3R. 28P.

and underlying same, are believed to be Beds of Gravel of very considerable value and depth.

The Farm is Let, together with other Lands, to Mr. W. Aves under Yearly Michaelmas Tenancy, at an apportioned rent of £190. The Gravel is as yet unworked. The Shooting over the Lot is Let to Donald A. Stewart, Esq., until February 2nd, 1920.

THE HOUSE

is a comparatively modern double-fronted Structure of brick, partly ivy clad, with tiled roof, and contains

ON THE GROUND FLOOR: Small Hall; Dining Room; Drawing Room with bay; Kitchen with range; Scullery having fireplace and copper, Rain Water supply, and Drinking Water by pump from a Well; W.C. with pedestal fitting; Dairy having slate shelving, Store Place and large Coal and Wood House.

ON THE FIRST FLOOR are five good Bedrooms, each having fireplace; Maids' Bedroom, and Bathroom with bath and lavatory basin (each having h. and c. services) and W.C.

There is a pretty Flower Garden with Lawn in front, two plots of Kitchen Garden, and a small Apple and Pear Orchard.

THE COTTAGE

is brick and tiled and contains two Rooms upstairs and two below, with Wash-house having copper and sink, and a lean-to Shed.

THE FARMBUILDINGS

are very compactly and conveniently arranged, chiefly built of brick with tiled roofs and comprise four-bay open Cattle Shed with yard in front; good Cowhouse for twenty-four, with Hay, Root and Chop Shed adjoining; Chicken House, two Loose Boxes, Granary, Galvanised Iron Cart and Implement Shed, and Trap House.

There is a Well with Pump near the Cottage.

BURY FARM. (LOT 51.)

STOCKER'S FARM. (LOT 53.)

SCHEDULE.

No. on Plan.	Description.	Quantity.
	PARISH OF RICKMANSWORTH RURAL (Det. 3).	
Pt. 225	Marsh	2.099
Pt. 225	Do.	.227
Pt. 226	Pasture	5.008
Pt. 259	Do.	4.592
Pt. 260	Do.	2.626
261	House, Buildings etc.	1.339
262	Pasture	1.432
263	Orchard	.789
Pt. 264	Pasture	1.000
Pt. 264	Do.	4.736
Pt. 264	Do.	.433
269	Do.	3.275
270	Do.	2.261
Pt. 271	Do.	4.365
Pt. 271	Do.	.540
273	Arable and Watercress Beds	6.046
	PARISH OF RICKMANSWORTH URBAN	
Pt. 658A	Roadway	.160
	Total	A.40.928

LANDLORD'S OUTGOINGS.

Commuted Tithe Rent Charge	£9	4	0
Land Tax	7	0	0
Total .	£16	4	0

The Timber on this Lot has an estimated value of £55, and is included in the Sale.

The Lot is Sold and will be conveyed subject to a Right of Way for the duration of the term of the Lease of the Lake, etc (Lot 50), to W. H. Walker, Esq., with Horses and Carts for the purpose of Farming Enclosures, Nos. 266 and 267 on Plan, Lot 50, over the accommodation roadway passing from the Canal Bridge near Frogmoor House towards Bury Farm Homestead, and thence direct to Enclosure No. 266 on Plan (see footnote to Lot 50).

It is also Sold and will be conveyed subject to a right of way in favour of Lot 50 over the Roadway No. Pt. 658A on Plan (see footnote to Lot 50).

It is sold and will be conveyed subject to all rights of fishing in the Colne bordering the Lot, including a right in favour of Lot 50, to enter enclosures Nos. Pt. 264, 269, 270 and 273, for the purpose of fishing therefrom along the River Bank. (see footnote to Lot 50). No part of the River is included in the Sale of this Lot (51).

A portion of this Lot near to the Canal is sold subject to and with the benefit of the Agreement of May 20th, 1823, and August 10th, 1832, mentioned in the Conditions.

LOT 52

(*Coloured Pink on Plan*)

An Enclosure of

ACCOMMODATION ARABLE LAND

situate off the Harefield Road, near Woodcock Hill, and now occupied as THE RICKMANSWORTH SEWAGE FARM, the enclosure together with a Right of Way thereto, and a STRIP OF WOODLAND on its North-Western boundary extending to an area of about

19 A. 0 R. 35 P.

Let as to the Arable Land to the Rickmansworth Urban District Council under Lease for a term of 32 years from 29th September, 1901, at rents amounting to £82 13s. per annum, the remainder comprising the Woodland being in hand. The Shooting over the Lot is Let to Donald A. Stewart, Esq., until February 2nd, 1920.

Under the terms of the Lease provision is made *inter alia* for :—

(*a*) The Lessees to have a Right of Way for all purposes to the field from the Harefield Road over a roadway 20 ft. wide on Enclosure No. 4, as indicated on the Sale plan, and the right to lay a sewage main under this roadway and at any time to open the road to repair the main.

(*b*) The right of Sporting and the Timber and Gravel being reserved to the Lessor.

(*c*) The Lessees to have a right to lay an effluent outfall Sewer between the points marked E^1 and D^1 on the plan, the sewer being laid so as to discharge into the dyke at D^1. (This right has not yet been exercised.)

(*d*) The Lessees to have a right in the event of their being unable to carry out the outfall scheme between B^1 and D^1 under (*c*) above, to lay an alternate outfall sewer between the points marked B^1 and C^1 on the plan, on terms to be subsequently arranged between themselves and the Lessor. (This right has not yet been exercised or arranged for.)

(*e*) That the Lessees shall at the end of the Lease, if so required to do, remove the Works, Buildings, etc., on the demised Premises and make good all damage occasioned by such removal.

(*f*) That in the event of the Lessees purchasing the demised Premises, they shall not be called upon to remove their Works or to pay any consideration for the Works or improvements carried out by them.

(*g*) That the Lessees shall not be entitled at the end of the Lease to any payment in consideration for unexhausted improvement by reason of sewage having been applied to the Land.

(*h*) That the Lessees shall distribute the sewage over the Land in such a manner as not to be an annoyance, nuisance, danger or disturbance to the Lessor or his Tenants of adjoining Lands, and that no crude or untreated sewage shall be allowed to run, flow into, or in any way pollute the rivers, canals, water courses, ditches and ponds, upon the adjoining Lands of the Vendor, or upon adjoining Properties.

Until the present time, not only have the powers of the Lessees to lay an effluent outfall sewer not been exercised, and the expense of so doing been spared, but an appreciable income has been derived from payments made to the Lessees by the Tenant of adjoining Lands in connection with the irrigation of some of the fields adjacent to this Lot.

SCHEDULE.

No. on Plan.	Tenant.	Description.	Quantity.
	PARISH OF RICKMANSWORTH RURAL (Det. 3).		
2	Rickmansworth U.D.C.	Sewage Farm	18.147
1	In hand . . .	Sixteen-Acre Spring	1.073
		Total .	A.19.220

LANDLORD'S OUTGOINGS.

Commuted Tithe Rent Charge £4 1 5

The Timber on this Lot has an estimated value of £20 and is included in the Sale.

This Lot is Sold with the benefit of the provisions contained in the Lease for rights and easements and other matters affecting Stockers Farm (Lot 53) and is sold and will be conveyed subject to a restriction in the terms of the Lease mentioned in (*h*) above for the benefit of all other Lots, the property of the Vendor and otherwise.

It is also Sold with the benefit of a Right of Way for all purposes of the Sewage Farm over a roadway 20 ft. in width running along the Northern boundary of Enclosure No. 4 on plan, Lot 57 (see footnote to Lot 57).

LOT 53

(Coloured Yellow on Plan)

Stockers Farm

A CAPITAL AGRICULTURAL AND SMALL SPORTING PROPERTY, situate about one mile from Rickmansworth, and together with the superior Farmhouse, Homesteading, two Cottages, and Woodlands, extending to an area of about

197A. 3R. 14P.

Underlying the Lands between the River Colne and the Grand Junction Canal are believed to exist Valuable and Extensive Beds of Gravel, the Canal affording most economical facilities for working the same and transit.

Let as to part, together with other Lands, to Mr. Henry Giles under Yearly Michaelmas Tenancy at an apportioned rent of £213 5s., the remainder comprising the Woodlands and Enclosure No. 242 on Plan being in hand. The Shooting over the Lot is Let to Donald A. Stewart, Esq., until February 2nd, 1920. The Gravel is as yet unworked.

THE FARMHOUSE

is a commodious, well-planned Building of brick with tiled gabled roof, partly ivy clad, and occupies a pleasant position in the centre of the holding. It is surrounded on three sides by well laid out Gardens and contains :—

ON THE GROUND FLOOR: Square Hall, large Dining and Drawing Rooms, each with bay, and marble and slate mantels respectively ; Side Hall and small Conservatory, Kitchen with double-oven Range, Dairy, having slate shelving ; Scullery with copper and force pump from Drinking Water well ; Wash-house, having open fireplace and stone sink ; China Closet, Pantry, W.C., and Lavatory Basin with Water supply pumped up from the well ; and Men's Bedroom with separate entrance from the Kitchen : underground is a Cellar.

ON THE FIRST FLOOR, to which there are principal and secondary staircases are four large Bedrooms, two smaller Bedrooms, (Bathroom with h. and c. services), and Box Cupboard.

THE FARMBUILDINGS

are for the most part timber and tiled and arranged around two Enclosed Yards, they comprise Fowl House, brick built Granary, three-bay open Cattle Shed, Cowshed for eleven with Calf Pen at end, two-bay Barn, four-bay open Cattle Shed with Loose Box at end, Cowshed for ten with Calf Pen adjoining and Loft over both, two-bay Barn, Root and Mixing House, three-stall Stable, three bay open Cattle Shed, two-bay open Implement Shed, timber and slated Trap House, and timber and galvanised two-bay open Cart Shed. On the opposite side of the roadway are a four-bay open Cattle Shed, two-bay Corn and Straw Barn, Chaff House, Cart Horse Stable for nine or eleven, with Chaff House adjoining, and Workshop. And in the Orchard No. 235 on Plan, are a three-bay open Implement Shed, an enclosed ditto, and Forge with hearth. In number 605 on Plan is a timber and tiled three-stall Stable.

Shown as No. 661A on Plan is a PAIR OF BRICK and TILED COTTAGES, of comparatively modern construction and each containing Sitting Room, large Kitchen, Wash-house with copper, Pantry and three Bedrooms.

Drinking Water is obtained by pump, and there is Rain Water storage underground.

THE FARM LANDS

are in excellent condition, and very conveniently situated around the Homestead. The Arable fields lie on the Southern side of the lot, and enjoy the advantage of being able to be irrigated by gravitation by the effluent from the Rickmansworth Sewage Farm (Lot 52), and the Pasture Lands are rich and well watered. There is also a capital Apple, Pear and Cherry Orchard.

The Lot is interspersed and partially bounded by convenient areas of Woodland and Plantations, affording good sporting.

SCHEDULE

No. on Plan.	Tenant.	Description.	Quantity.	Total Quantity.
	PARISH OF RICKMANSWORTH RURAL (Det 3).			
227	Mr. H. Giles . .	Arable	33.454	
Pt. 232		Do.	20.436	
233		Do.	7.939	
234		Old Gravel Pit . .	.567	
235		Orchard	3.989	
Pt. 236		Arable . . .	26.649	
240		Pasture	9.416	
Pt. 244		Do.	17.024	
Pt. 244		Waste	.118	
246		Pasture . .	2.307	
249		Do.	1.836	
Pt. 250		Do. . . .	4.237	
Pt. 250		Do. etc.	.560	
Pt. 251		Do.	1.458	
Pt. 252		Do.	1.089	
Pt. 252		Do.	.200	
Pt. 253		Do. . . .	2.503	
Pt. 254		Roadway	.050	
Pt. 257		House, Buildings, etc. . .	1.694	
258		Pasture	16.056	
Pt. 272		Do.	5.203	
277		Do.	3.602	
284		Do.	7.092	
	PARISH OF RICKMANSWORTH URBAN.			
Pt. 605		Pasture	7.357	
661A		Cottages and Gardens . .	.128	
				174.964
	PARISH OF RICKMANSWORTH RURAL (Det. 3).			
181	In hand.	Shepherds Close Dell . .	.519	
182		Spinney	.191	
228		Plantation	1.317	
229		Do.	1.103	
Pt. 232		Do.	.091	
237		High Wood	9.618	
241		Springhead Spinney . .	2.839	
242		Arable	2.537	
243		Spinney	.666	
245		Do.	.285	
247		Do.	.446	
248		Big Alders	3.262	22.874
			Total	A.197.838

LANDLORD'S OUTGOINGS.

Commuted Tithe Rent Charge	£42	3	1
Land Tax	9	0	0
TOTAL .	£51	3	1

The Timber on this Lot has an estimated value of £275 and is included in the Sale.

This Lot is Sold and will be conveyed subject to a Right of Way for all purposes in favour of Lot 60 over the accommodation roadway leading from the Harefield Road through Enclosures, Nos. 258 and Pt. 605 on Plan, and thence over the road-way through the Homestead to Lot 60 (see footnote to Lot 60).

It is also Sold with a Right of Way with horses and carts and for all purposes over the accommodation roadway and Bridge on Lot 49, leading from the farmstead towards Mill End and with the benefit of the obligation on the owner of Lot 49 to maintain the bridge and such fences on either side as are necessary for driving cattle and other animals over it subject to the right of the owner of Lot 49 to enter on this Lot for the purpose of effecting such maintenance (see footnote to Lot 49).

It is also Sold and will be conveyed subject to a right in favour of Lot 52 to enter this Lot with or without horses, men, and all necessary appliances for the purposes of laying and thereafter maintaining for all time an effluent outfall sewer with all necessary means of ventilation, inspection or otherwise following the courses indicated on the Sale Plan, and thereon lettered E^1 and D^1, B^1 and C^1 on making proper compensation for all damage done (see footnote to Lot 52).

The Southern boundary of No. Pt. 244 (17.024 ac.) is 4 ft. from the centre of the hedge. The mines mentioned in General Remark 11 are excepted from Pt. 605.

LOT 54

(Coloured Blue on Plan)

A CAPITAL SMALL HOLDING

known as

ANDREW'S FARM

occupying a convenient situation within a mile of Rickmansworth and having a long frontage to the Harefield Road. The Lot comprises a double-fronted Cottage, a small set of Farmbuildings, an Apple Orchard and useful Pasture and Arable Lands, the whole extending to an area of about

34A. 1R. 13P.

Let, together with other Lands, to Mr. Henry Giles under Yearly Michaelmas Tenancy at an apportioned rent of £45. The Shooting over the Lot is Let to Donald A. Stewart, Esq., until February 2nd, 1920.

THE COTTAGE

is built of brick with tiled roof and contains Sitting Room, Kitchen, Wash House with copper, and two Bedrooms. Well Water; Company's water mains are laid in the Road.

THE FARMBUILDINGS

are built of timber with tiled roofs and include Cart or Implement Shed, one-bay Barn, open Shed, two-stall Stable, two-bay open Shed, and Fowl House.

The Arable Lands possess the advantage of being able to be irrigated by gravitation by the effluent from the Rickmansworth Sewage Farm (Lot 52).

SCHEDULE.

No. on Plan.	Description	Quantity.
	PARISH OF RICKMANSWORTH URBAN.	
685	Pasture	4.414
686	Cottage, Buildings, etc.	.522
687	Orchard	.734
	PARISH OF RICKMANSWORTH RURAL (Det. 3).	
2A	Arable	7.570
230	Do.	11.665
231	Do.	9.426
	Total	A.34.331

LANDLORD'S OUTGOINGS.

Commuted Tithe Rent Charge	£8	2	0
Land Tax	1	15	0
Total	£9	17	0

The Timber on this Lot has an estimated value of £15 and is included in the Sale.

The mines mentioned in General Remark 11 are excepted from Nos. 686, 687, 230 and 231.

LOT 55

(Coloured Brown on Plan)

THE JUNIPER HILL ALLOTMENT GARDENS

situate abutting the Harefield Road and only a little over half-a-mile from Rickmansworth. The Lot extends to an area of about

10A. 0R. 27P.

and the Gardens are Let to some ninety-six tenants at the low rate of 3d. per pole per annum, under Yearly Christmas Tenancies, the total income so derived from the Lot amounting to about £19 per annum. The Lot has a frontage of about 800ft. to the Harefield Road, nearly the whole of which is sewered. Company's Water Mains are laid throughout the length of the Road.

The Shooting over the Lot is let to Donald A. Stewart, Esq., until February 2nd, 1920.

LANDLORD'S OUTGOINGS.

Commuted Tithe Rent Charge	£2	2	11
Land Tax		11	0
TOTAL .	£2	13	11

The Rates are also discharged by the Landlord.

Any Timber on this Lot will be included in the Sale.

LOT 56

(Coloured Yellow on Plan)

THE FULLY LICENSED INN

known as

"THE ROSE AND CROWN"

situate at Woodcock Hill, at the corner of the public roads leading from Rickmansworth to Harefield and Northwood respectively. The premises occupy a high and healthy position over 300 ft. above sea level, and could advantageously be extended and improved with every chance of success. Together with a large Garden they cover an area of about

0A. 0R. 39P.

and are Let to Salter and Co., Limited, under Yearly Midsummer Tenancy, determinable at Midsummer or Christmas, at a rent of £25, the Tenants being responsible for repairs.

The Inn is an old-fashioned brick and tiled double-fronted structure with gable ends, and front trained with a large wistaria, and contains Bar with fireplace, Tap Room with modern tiled grate, Sitting Room, Kitchen, Beer Cellar, Scullery with copper and sink and pump from drinking water well, and four Bedrooms.

The Out Premises include timber and tiled Stable or Wood Shed, Trap House, Fowl House and covered Booth. There is a good Garden.

LANDLORD'S OUTGOINGS.

Commuted Tithe Rent Charge	£0	1	2
Land Tax	1	0	0
Total .	£1	1	2

LOT 57

(Coloured Green on Plan)

FOUR VALUABLE ENCLOSURES OF

ACCOMMODATION, PASTURE AND ARABLE LAND

situate at Woodcock Hill and having long frontages to the roads leading from Rickmansworth to Harefield and Northwood. The higher parts of the Land are over 300 ft. above sea level, and the Lot in all extends to an area of about

36A. 3R. 32P.

Let, together with other Lands, to Mr. Henry Giles under Yearly Michaelmas Tenancy; the Shooting over the Lot is Let to Donald A. Stewart, Esq., until February 2nd, 1920. Parts of the Lot are suitable for the erection of medium-sized Houses.

SCHEDULE.

No. on Plan.	Description.	Quantity.
	PARISH OF RICKMANSWORTH RURAL (Det. 3).	
3	Arable	9.389
4	Do.	11.260
41	Pasture	9.088
43	Trees, etc.	.381
44	Pasture	6.831
	Total . .	A.36.949

LANDLORD'S OUTGOINGS.

Commuted Tithe Rent Charge	£8	8	5
Land Tax	1	7	6
Total .	£9	15	11

The Timber on this Lot has an estimated value of £80 and is included in the Sale.

The Lot is Sold and will be conveyed subject to a Right of Way for all purposes of the Sewage Farm (Lot 52) over a Roadway 20 ft. in width running along the Northern Boundary of enclosure No. 4 on Plan and the right to lay and maintain a sewage main under such roadway and the Northern corner of such enclosure (see footnote to Lot 52).

The mines mentioned in General Remark No. 11 are excepted from No. 4.

LOT 58

(Coloured Pink on Plan)

A PAIR OF COTTAGES AND GARDENS

situate on the Harefield Road and adjoining the foregoing Lot. They are well built of brick with tiled roof, and together with their Gardens cover an area of about

0A. 1R. 8P.

Let under Weekly Tenancies to Mr. Leopold John Janaway and Mrs. Griffin respectively, the Landlord discharging the Rates.

Each Cottage contains Living Room, Kitchen, Cellar, and two Bedrooms. There is a lean-to Wash House with copper for the use of both Cottages. Underground is Rain-water Storage. Company's Water laid on.

LANDLORD'S OUTGOINGS—*NIL.*

LOT 59

(Coloured Pink on Plan)

FOUR COTTAGES AND GARDENS

situate near the foot of Woodcock Hill and fronting the Harefield Road.

The Cottages are built in two pairs, one pair being brick and slated, and the other pair brick and tiled, and together with their Gardens they extend to an area of about

0A. 1R. 11P.

The Cottages are Let under Weekly Tenancies, the first pair being occupied by Mr. Stephen Walker and Mr. William Pavey respectively, and the second pair by Mr. John Browning.

The first mentioned Cottages each contain Living Room, Kitchen, and two Bedrooms, the latter pair being occupied as one tenement, and containing Sitting Room, Kitchen, Scullery, Wash House, and four Bedrooms. There is also a Wash House, used in common by all the Tenants, having copper and Company's Water laid on.

The Rates and Water Charges are paid by the Landlord.

LANDLORD'S OUTGOINGS—*NIL.*

LOT 60

(Coloured Green on Plan)

STOCKER'S LOCK HOUSE.

A comfortable small Residence, situate at Stocker's Lock, near the centre of Lot 53, and being about one mile from Rickmansworth. The Lot extends to an area of about

0 A. 2 R. 0 P.

and is Let to A. C. Pemberton, Esq., under Quarterly Tenancy, at a Rent of £35 per annum.

THE HOUSE

is substantially built of brick with slated roof, is partially ivy clad and contains

ON THE UPPER GROUND FLOOR: Small Hall, Dining Room measuring about 18 ft. by 13 ft. 6 in. and about 10 ft. in height, and having veined marble mantelpiece, Drawing Room of similar size to the Dining Room.

ON THE FIRST FLOOR: Four Bedrooms, each having fireplace and measuring about 13 ft. 9 in. by 10 ft. and about 9 ft. 6 in. in height; Lobby and Boxroom, and

ON THE LOWER GROUND FLOOR: Kitchen with range, Scullery with copper and sink and pump from drinking water supply, and Larder.

In a detached brick and slated Building close by are Loose Box with room over, Coal House and Store House, and an underground Rain-water Tank.

The Garden is walled on three sides, part being laid-out for flowers and part planted with fruit trees and bushes.

LANDLORD'S OUTGOINGS.

Commuted Tithe Rent Charge £0 2 4

The Lot is Sold with a Right of Way for all necessary purposes over the accommodation roadway on Lot 53 leading from the Harefield Road through enclosures numbered 258 and Pt. 605 on Plan, and thence over the roadway through the Homestead to this Lot (see footnote to Lot 53).

LOT 61

(Coloured Blue on Plan)

A Very Useful Accommodation Holding

known as

SPRINGWELL MEADOWS

situate to the West of Lot 53, abutting the road from Mill End to Harefield, and lying between the River Colne and the Grand Junction Canal.

The Lot comprises well-watered Meadow Lands, a small Spinney, and a timber and galvanised-roofed Cowshed for nine. In all it extends to an area of about

32 A. 3 R. 34 P.

and is Let, as to part, to Mr. William Kibbles under Yearly Michaelmas Tenancy, determinable at two years' notice at a Rent of £75 per annum, the remainder comprising the Spinney being in hand. The Shooting over the Lot is Let to Donald A. Stewart, Esq., until February 2nd, 1920.

All the Buildings other than that above described are claimed by the Tenant.

SCHEDULE.

No. on Plan.	Tenant.	Description.	Quantity.	Total Quantity.
	PARISH OF HAREFIELD (MIDDLESEX).			
Pt. 656	Mr. W. Kibbles .	Ditch	.220	
657		Pasture	4.638	
658		Do.	1.533	
659		Do.	4.774	
659A		Buildings and Yard . .	.402	
Pt. 660		Stream	.320	
669		Pasture	9.879	
669A		Watercress Bed . . .	.237	
	PARISH OF RICKMANSWORTH RURAL (Det. 3).			
238		Pasture	5.862	
239		Do.	4.248	
				32.113
	PARISH OF HAREFIELD (MIDDLESEX).			
Pt. 656	In hand. . .	Spinney		.850
			Total .	A.32.963

LANDLORD'S OUTGOINGS.

Commuted Tithe Rent Charge £2 4 7

The Timber on this Lot has an estimated value of £35 and is included in the Sale.

LOTS 62, 63 and 64 WILL FIRST BE OFFERED TOGETHER.

Failing a Sale in this manner, the Lots will then be submitted separately.

SUMMARY OF LOTS 62, 63 AND 64.

LOT.	HOLDING.	TENANT.	QUANTITY.
62	Colne Mead	R. F. Myddelton, Esq., and Mr. R. S. V. Ayre . .	4.389
63	Meadow Land . . .	Mr. R. S. V. Ayre . .	15.236
64	Market Garden Land . .	Do. . .	37.851
		TOTAL . . .	A 57.476

LANDLORD'S OUTGOINGS.

Commuted Tithe Rent Charge	£13	4	10
Land Tax	3	10	0
TOTAL	£16	14	10

The Timber on these three Lots has an estimated value of £61, and is included in the Sale.

LOT 62

(Coloured Blue on Plan)

A pretty little Residential Property

known as

"COLNE MEAD"

situate at Mill End lying between the River Colne and the road from Uxbridge to Rickmansworth, and being about a mile-and-a-half from the latter station.

The House, Gardens, Stabling, Buildings, Orchard and Paddock, with that Stretch of the River Colne which abuts on the same, in all extend to an area of about

4A. 1R. 22P.

Held, as to part, by Richard F. Myddleton, Esq., under Lease expiring at Midsummer, 1920, Rent £65, the Lessee being responsible for repairs, and as to a further part (the Farmbuildings) Let to Mr. R. S. V. Ayre, together with other Lands, under Yearly Michaelmas Tenancy, apportioned Rent, £10.

THE RESIDENCE

occupies a very pleasant position about 150 ft. above sea level, is built of brick with slated roof, and contains

ON THE GROUND FLOOR: Hall, Dining Room (North) having tiled fireplace and hearth and measuring about 17 ft. 6in by 12 ft. 9 in. by about 10 ft. in height, Drawing Room (North and West) also having tiled fireplace and hearth, casements opening to the lawns, and measuring about 22 ft. 6 in. by 13 ft. 3 in. and 10 ft. in height; Kitchen with range, Scullery with copper and sink (h. and c.), Pantry, China Pantry with large underground Coal Cellar; and Tradesmen's Entrance.

ON THE FIRST FLOOR are three Best Bedrooms, the two largest measuring about 17 ft. 6 in. by 13 ft. each; Dressing Room, Maid's Bedroom, Bathroom with fireplace, porcelain-lined bath and lavatory basin, each having hot and cold services and W.C. with valve apparatus. Company's Water and Gas are laid on; modern Sanitary Arrangements; Main Drainage.

At the back of the House is brick and tiled Stabling consisting of two Stalls, one having a loft over, Harness Room with fireplace, Coach House and Store Shed.

THE GROUNDS

are a feature of the Property and while they are of a delightful character they are quite inexpensive to keep up. There is a neat Lawn on the West of the House and a small Front Garden shaded by a Deodara. Further West there is an Apple Orchard, Tennis Lawn and Paddock; these stretch down towards the River along which a River Walk has been formed flanked by Herbaceous Borders, and whence pretty views are obtained across the intervening meadows to the wooded hills beyond. The River affords Boating and Fishing and as a whole the amenities of the Lot are quite exceptional. Such part of the Fishery in so much of the Mill Stream as is included in the Lot, is included in the Sale.

COLNE MEAD. (LOT 62.)

MONEYHILL HOUSE. (LOT 68.)

THE FARMBUILDINGS

included in this Lot, and which could readily be Let off if desired, comprise timber and tiled two-bay Barn or Shed for young Cattle, timber and slated Implement Shed, and three Cowsheds each for six.

SCHEDULE.

No. on Plan.	Tenant.	Description.	Quantity.	Total Quantity.
	PARISH OF RICKMANSWORTH URBAN.			
556	R. F. Myddelton, Esq.	Paddock	1.830	
557		Garden	.285	
558		Orchard	.564	
Pt. 576		River	.625	
Pt. 577		House and Garden . .	.320	
	PARISH OF RICKMANSWORTH RURAL (Det 3).			
Pt. 294		River	.465	
				4.089
	PARISH OF RICKMANSWORTH URBAN			
Pt. 577	Mr. R. S. V. Ayre .	Buildings and Yard . .		.300
			Total .	A.4.389

LANDLORD'S OUTGOINGS.

Commuted Tithe Rent Charge £0 16 6

The Timber on this Lot has an estimated value of £23 and is included in the sale.

The Lot is Sold and will be conveyed subject to a Right of Way for all usual and necessary purposes in favour of Lot 63 over the accommodation roadway and bridge leading from the Public Road to Lot 63 (see footnote to Lot 63).

LOT 63

(Coloured Brown on Plan)

TWO ENCLOSURES OF RICH MEADOW LAND

situate at Mill End, lying to the South of the foregoing Lot and bounded on two sides by the River Colne.

The Lot extends to an area of about

15A. 0R. 38P.

and is Let together with other Lands, to Mr. R. S. V. Ayre, under Yearly Michaelmas Tenancy, at an apportioned Rent of £18.

SCHEDULE.

No. on Plan.	Description.	Quantity.
	PARISH OF RICKMANSWORTH RURAL (Det. 3).	
290	Pasture	8.011
295	Pasture	7.225
	Total	A.15.236

LANDLORD'S OUTGOINGS.

Commuted Tithe Rent Charge £3 16 4

The Lot is Sold with a right of way for all usual and necessary purposes over the accommodation roadway and bridge on Lot 62, leading from the Public Road to this Lot (see footnote to Lot 62). No part of the River Colne is included in the Sale of this Lot.

LOT 64

(Coloured Pink on Plan)

AN ENCLOSURE OF MARKET GARDEN LAND

and a small area of Land adjoining occupied as Allotment Gardens, situate at Mill End, abutting the road from Uxbridge to Rickmansworth, and also having a frontage to Long Lane.
The Lot extends to an area of about

37A. 3R. 16P.

and is Let, together with other Lands, to Mr. R. S. V. Ayre under Yearly Michaelmas Tenancy, at an apportioned Rent of £47.

SCHEDULE.

No. on Plan.	Description.	Quantity.
	PARISH OF RICKMANSWORTH URBAN.	
421	Arable	34.982
560	Allotments	2.156
561	Do.	.713
	Total .	A.37.851

LANDLORD'S OUTGOINGS.

Commuted Tithe Rent Charge	£8	12	0
Land Tax	3	10	0
Total .	£12	2	0

The Timber on this Lot has an estimated value of £38 and is included in the sale.

LOT 65

(Coloured Yellow on Plan)

A PAIR OF COTTAGES AND GARDENS

situate at Drayton Ford, near Mill End. They cover an area of about

0A. 1R. 7P.

and are Let respectively under Weekly Tenancies to Mr. Thomas Jordan and Mr. Charles W. Collins.

THE COTTAGES

are brick and slated and each contains Living Room, Scullery and two Bedrooms. Each Cottage has a lean-to Shed in one of which is a copper. Well Water.

The Rates are discharged by the Landlord.

LANDLORD'S OUTGOINGS.

Commuted Tithe Rent Charge £0 0 6

No part of the River Colne is included in the Sale of this Lot.

LOT 66

(Coloured Yellow on Plan)

A Valuable Area of

ACCOMMODATION AND BUILDING LAND

now occupied as Allotment Gardens, etc., situate off Church Road, Mill End. The Lot extends to an area of about

12A. 3R. 14P.

and the Gardens are Let to some 22 tenants at 3d. per pole per annum, under Yearly Michaelmas Tenancies, the total income so derived from the Lot amounting to about £20 10s. 9d. per annum.

Provision has been made for developing the Land for building purposes by a roadway running out of Church Road, and the Lot also lends itself to development in connection with a roadway made on adjoining Land to the South of the Lot.

The Lot contains valuable deposits of Gravel, some of which have already been worked. The mines referred to in General Remark No. 11 are execpted from the Lot. This Lot is subject to certain restrictions on buildings fronting Church Lane and the maintenance of fences on part of the southern boundary of No. 580 in an Indenture dated July 1st, 1909.

SCHEDULE.

No. on Plan.	Description.	Quantity.
	PARISH OF RICKMANSWORTH URBAN.	
563	Pasture	3.388
564	Old Gravel Pit	3.057
571	Allotments	.511
572	Do.	.227
573	Do.	3.720
580	Pasture	1.932
	Total .	A.12.835

LANDLORD'S OUTGOINGS.

Commuted Tithe Rent Charge £1 12 10

The Rates are also discharged by the Landlord.
Any Timber on this Lot will be included in the Sale.
The mines referred to in General Remark No. 11 are excepted from this Lot.
This Lot is subject to certain restrictions on buildings fronting Church Lane, and the maintenance of fences on part of the Southern boundry of No. 580 in an Indenture, dated July 1st, 1909.

LOT 67

(Coloured Green on Plan)

TWO VALUABLE ENCLOSURES OF MEADOW LAND

situate at Mill End, and approached from the main road by an accommodation roadway. The Lot is bounded on two sides by the River Colne, extends to an area of about

2A. 1R. 12P.

and is Let, as to part, together with other Lands, to Mr. Henry Giles under Yearly Michaelmas Tenancy, at an apportioned rent of £1, and as to the remainder to Mr. William Humphrey under Yearly Michaelmas Tenancy, at a rent of £5 10s.

SCHEDULE

No. on Plan.	Tenant.	Description.	Quantity.	Total Quantity.
	PARISH OF RICKMANSWORTH RURAL (Det. 3).			
Pt. 279	Mr. W. Humphrey .	Meadow		1.260
278	Mr. H. Giles . .	Meadow	1.000	
	PARISH OF RICKMANSWORTH URBAN			
Pt. 577		Roadway	.070	1.070
			Total .	A. 2.330

LANDLORD'S OUTGOINGS.

Commuted Tithe Rent Charge	£0	5	7
Land Tax	0	6	0
Total	£0	11	7

The Lot is Sold and will be conveyed subject to such rights of way as exist (if any) from and over the accommodation roadway to adjoining or neighbouring Property. The mines mentioned in General Remark No. 11 are excepted from this Lot.

LOTS 68 AND 69 WILL FIRST BE OFFERED TOGETHER.

Failing a Sale in this manner, Lot 68 will next be offered alone, and if not so Sold, Lot 69 will be withdrawn.

SUMMARY OF LOTS 68 AND 69.

Lot.	Holding.	Tenant.	Quantity.
68	Moneyhill House . .	Messrs. Franklin & Son and in hand	21.555
69	Land adjoining . .	Messrs. Franklin & Son	2.828
		Total . . .	A. 24.383

LANDLORD'S OUTGOINGS.

Commuted Tithe Rent Charge	£7	3	1
Land Tax	9	0	9
Total .	£16	3	10

The Timber on these two Lots has an estimated value of £51 and is included in the Sale.

LOT 68

(Coloured Blue on Plan)

MONEYHILL HOUSE

A VALUABLE RESIDENTIAL PROPERTY

of about

21A. 2R. 9P.

unusually compact and self contained, situate abutting the Road to Uxbridge and about three-quarters of a mile from Rickmansworth Station.

It comprises a Red Brick RESIDENCE with Stabling, Garage, Chauffeur's Quarters, Cottage, Laundry, Small Farmery, pretty Gardens, Orchard, and well timbered Parklands.

Let, as to part (No. 410 and Pt. 595 on Plan) together with other lands to Messrs. Franklin & Sons under Yearly Michaelmas tenancy, at an apportioned rent of £48 10s., the remainder being in hand, and of this latter part Vacant Possession will be given on completion of the Purchase.

THE RESIDENCE

is built of brick with part tiled and part slated roof, its southern front being ivy clad. It stands at a short distance back from the road from which it is separated by a high wall, has south-west as its principal aspect, and contains :—

ON THE GROUND FLOOR: Hall about 21 ft. 3 in. by 10 ft. 6 in., panelled in dark oak and with oak-beamed ceiling, and having a Lavatory leading off on the right, fitted with W.C.; Dining Room about 23 ft. 9 in. by 17ft. 6 in., with serving hatch to the kitchen; Drawing Room measuring about 19 ft. 6 in. by 15 ft. 6 in., and having statuary marble mantel, both of the foregoing rooms open on to a Conservatory (heated); Morning Room having marble mantel and measuring about 16 ft. 6 in. by 12 ft.; Ante Room fitted with telephone; Billiard Room measuring about 27 ft. by 22 ft. 3 in. and about 12 ft. in height, and having statuary marble mantel. The room is heated by means of iron grids in the floors, and has French casements opening to the lawns. Smoking Room about 15 ft. by 10 ft. 3 in; Housekeeper's Room about 15 ft. 9 in. by 14 ft.; Kitchen about 16 ft. by 15 ft. 3 in. with double-oven range and hot plate at the side; Butler's Pantry with glazed ware sink (h. and c.) and ample cupboard room; Scullery with sink (h. and c.); Larder and Store Place; and outside are Dairy, Coal House and two W.C.'S.

ON THE FIRST FLOOR, reached by principal and secondary Staircases, the former having oak-panelled dado and handrail, are :—

Six Principal Bedrooms measuring respectively about 23 ft. by 21 ft. 9 in.; 24 ft. 3 in. by 17 ft. 6 in.; 21 ft. 3 in. by 13 ft. 9 in.; 16 ft. 6 in. by 15 ft. 6 in.; 16 ft. by 12 ft. 3 in.; and 13 ft. 6 in. by 10 ft. 6 in.; Secondary Bedroom about 14 ft. 9 in.

by 8 ft.; two Dressing Rooms, Bathroom with porcelain lined bath (h. and c.); two W.C.'S, Lobby with large Linen Cupboard; Housemaids' Sink (h. and c.), and two Maids' Bedrooms, each having fireplace and measuring respectively about 16 ft. 6 in. by 12 ft. and 15 ft. 3 in. by 14 ft.

SUMMARY OF ACCOMMODATION.

Hall.	Housekeeper's Room.
Dining Room.	Domestic Offices.
Drawing Room.	Six Best Bedrooms.
Conservatory.	Secondary Bedroom.
Morning Room.	Two Dressing Rooms.
Ante Room.	Bathroom.
Billiard Room.	Two Maids' Bedrooms.
Smoking Room.	Five W.C.'S.

Gas and Company's Water are laid on, and there is also a Well on the Premises. Main Drainage.

THE STABLING AND GARAGE

are contained in a substantial Building of red brick with slated roof and having central covered Archway and Campanile. The Laundry, Home Farmery and Chauffeur's Quarters are also contained in this block of buildings.

The Stables comprise three-stall Stable, two large Loose Boxes, Harness Room with fireplace, Garage (or Coach House) for three cars, and there are also Fowl House, Coal House and three Kennels.

The Laundry consists of fitted Ironing Room, Wash-house, with Copper and Pump and Stoke Hole.

The Home Farmery includes Cowshed for about eight Cows, two Loose Boxes and Trap House, and the

Chauffeur's Quarters consist of Living Room, Pantry, and two Bedrooms; and adjoining the latter are two Lofts with separate Staircase outside down to the Stable Yard.

The Stable and Buildings are drained into a cesspool.

THE PLEASURE GROUNDS

lie on the Northern and Western sides of the House, a sunk fence forming an invisible division between them and the Park.

They are fully matured and well timbered, high yew hedges and shrubberies adding to their seclusion and making a break between the Flower Gardens and Lawns.

The timbering includes a large Acacia and Plane, while features in the Gardens are a walled Rose Garden, Grotto Summer House with shell-studded walls and pointed arch doorways, and Rock Garden. There are Lawns for Tennis and Croquet.

The Kitchen Garden is productive, walled on one side and planted with Apricot Trees ; adjoining is an Orchard of Apple, Pear and Cherry Trees.

The Glasshouses include Circular Conservatory or Greenhouse with domed roof, and a sunk Pit in two divisions. There is also a fitted Fruit Room.

The Gardener's Cottage, situate at the South-West corner of the Lot, is built of red brick with tiled roof and contains Living Room, Kitchen, Scullery with sink having Water laid on, Coal Shed, and two Bedrooms.

The Park contains some finely-grown timber, and in it is a useful timber and galvanised half-open Shed for Cattle or Horses. It is screened on the West by a belt of Timber.

SCHEDULE.

No. on Plan.	Tenant.	Description.	Quantity.	Total Quantity.
	PARISH OF RICKMANSWORTH URBAN.			
411	In hand. . .	Spinney	.579	
Pt. 577		Cottage and Garden . .	.084	
588		Orchard	.747	
589		Kitchen Garden and Paddock.	.810	
590		House, Buildings and Garden.	2.776	4.996
410	Messrs. Franklin and	Pasture	16.499	
Pt. 595	Sons. . .	Do.	.060	16.559
			Total	A 21.555

LANDLORD'S OUTGOINGS.

Commuted Tithe Rent Charge		£6	2	4
Land Tax		9	0	9
	Total	£15	3	1

The Timber on this Lot has an estimated value of £45 and is included in the Sale.

A Purchaser of the Lot will be required to take to and pay for by Valuation in addition to his purchase money the Tenant's Fixtures and Fittings, planned and Fitted Furniture on the Premises according to an inventory to be prepared or approved by the auctioneers in accordance with General Remark and Stipulation No. 4.

The fencing off of the small Plot at the North Eastern corner of the Gardens shall be carried out within six months of the completion of the purchase, and maintained by the Purchaser of this Lot, the new length of fencing to be in a straight line with and of similar construction to the existing fence, forming the Western boundary of Lot 69.

LOT 69

(Coloured Yellow on Plan)

An Enclosure of

ACCOMMODATION PASTURE LAND

situate on the Eastern side of Lot 68 and being only just over half-a-mile from Rickmansworth Station. It has a frontage of about 350 ft. to the Uxbridge Road, a depth of about 330 ft., and is RIPE FOR IMMEDIATE DEVELOPMENT.

The frontage is sewered and Company's Water and Light are available. The aspect is South-East, and the height above sea level, about 165 ft.
The Lot extends to an area of about

2A. 3R. 12P.

and is Let, together with other Lands, to Messrs. Franklin and Son under Yearly Michaelmas Tenancy at an apportioned Rent of £8 10s. Power is reserved to the Landlord to resume possession of any part of the Land for building purposes.

LANDLORD'S OUTGOINGS.

Commuted Tithe Rent Charge	£1 0 9

The Timber on this Lot has an estimated value of £6 and is included in the Sale.

LOT 70

(Coloured Brown on Plan)

A Detached Block of

THREE BRICK AND TILED COTTAGES

of attractive elevation and ivy clad. They are numbered 111 to 113 in the Uxbridge Road, situate on the opposite side of the road to Moneyhill House, and their Gardens, over 200 ft. in length, slope down to the River Colne.
The Lot extends to an area of about

0A. 1R. 10P.

and the Cottages are Let under Weekly Tenancies as under :—Nos. 111 and 112 to Mrs Bartlett, and No. 113 to Mr. William Green.

No. 111 contains Living Room, back Kitchen with range and sink having water laid on, and two Bedrooms.

No. 113, Lobby and one Room upstairs and one down, and

No. 112, two Rooms on the Ground Floor and two above.

At the back in a timber and tiled Shed are three W.C.'s. Company's Water. Main drainage.

The Rates and Water charges are paid by the Landlord.

LANDLORD'S OUTGOINGS.

Commuted Tithe Rent Charge	£0 2 0
Land Tax	0 8 0
TOTAL	£0 10 0

N.B.—IF DESIRED, LOTS 71 and 72 WILL FIRST BE OFFERED TOGETHER

LOT 71

(Coloured Green on Plan)

A very useful Area of

ACCOMMODATION PASTURE LAND

situate half-a-mile from Rickmansworth Station, bounded on the East by an accommodation roadway, and having an outlet for a development roadway running direct into the Uxbridge Road.

The Land possesses a high prospective building value, and the herbage is of excellent quality.

The Lot extends to an area of about

15A. 0R. 37P.

and is Let to Mr. William E. Franklin under Yearly Michaelmas Tenancy.

There is a Right of Way to this Lot, in common with other Property, over the accommodation roadway on the East of the Lot.

In No. 383 on plan is a timber and galvanised Cattle Shed.

SCHEDULE.

No. on Plan.	Description.	Quantity.
	PARISH OF RICKMANSWORTH URBAN.	
383	Pasture	6.137
387	Old Gravel Pit	.427
406	Pasture	2.020
408	Do.	1.210
Pt. 409	Do.	5.436
	Total	A.15.230

LANDLORD'S OUTGOINGS.

Commuted Tithe Rent Charge £4 13 1

The Timber on this Lot has an estimated value of £120 and is included in the Sale.

LOT 72

(Coloured Pink on Plan)

Two Enclosures of

ACCOMMODATION ARABLE LAND

and a Valuable Gravel Pit situate to the North of Lots 68 and 71, and abutting on Berry Lane.

There is also a Right of Way to the Lot over the accommodation roadway bounding Lot 71 on the East, and which roadway is continued along the North-Eastern boundary of Enclosure No. 383 (Lot 71), and so to Enclosure No. 368 of this Lot.

The Lot extends to an area of about **38A. 2R. 3P.**

and is Let as to part to Mr. R. S. V. Ayre under Yearly Michaelmas Tenancy, as to a further part to Mr. William Kibbles under Yearly Michaelmas Tenancy, the remainder comprising the Gravel Pit workings being in hand. The Shooting over the Lot is in hand.

An excavated part of the Gravel Pit is being filled in by permission of the Vendor by the Rickmansworth Urban District Council.

SCHEDULE.

No. on Plan.	Tenant.	Description.	Quantity.
	PARISH OF RICKMANSWORTH URBAN		
368	Mr. R. S. V. Ayre .	Arable.	28.720
381	Mr. W. Kibbles .	Do.	3.420
382	In hand. . .	Gravel Pit	6.381
		Total .	A.38.521

LANDLORD'S OUTGOINGS.

Commuted Tithe Rent Charge	£10 19 11
Land Tax	3 10 0
Total	£14 9 11

The Timber on this Lot has an estimated value of £40 and is included in the Sale.

LOT 73

(Coloured Brown on Plan)

An Enclosure of

ACCOMMODATION ARABLE LAND

Situate to the North of the foregoing Lot and abutting on Berry Lane.

The Lot extends to an area of about **5A. 0R. 0P.**

and is Let with other Lands to Mr. Henry Giles under Yearly Michaelmas Tenancy at an apportioned Rent of £5 10s.

A part of the boundary of the field on its Southern and Western sides, where indicated by a dotted line on the Plan, is not defined by a fence.

LANDLORD'S OUTGOINGS.

Commuted Tithe Rent Charge	£1 6 1
Land Tax	3 0
Total .	£1 9 1

Any Timber on this Lot will be included in the Sale.

LOT 74

(Coloured Yellow on Plan)

A Very Valuable Accommodation Property

known as

THE BURY MEADOWS

situate adjoining the town of Rickmansworth, abutting in part on Bury Lane and Church Street, and having another road access on the North to Ebury Road.

The Lot comprises a DWELLING HOUSE AND DAIRY FARM BUILDINGS for 21 cows, a small area of Allotment Gardens and Watercress Beds, and rich well-watered Pastures, the whole extending to an area of about

20A. 0R. 7P.

The Land is Ripe for Building Development, and a system of Sewers has been laid in the position approximately shown on the Sale plan.

Let as to part to Mr. Frederick Barton under yearly Michaelmas Tenancy, as to a further part (the allotments) to the Rickmansworth Urban District Council, rent £5 18s., and as to a further part (Garden and Watercress Beds) to Mr. Charles H. Sansom under Yearly Michaelmas Tenancy, rent £30.

Power is reserved to the Landlord to resume possession of any part of the Land for building purposes.

THE HOUSE

is brick and slated, and contains two Sitting Rooms, Scullery with sink having water laid on, and copper ; Pantry; and three Bedrooms, and adjacent to the House are Wash-house with pump from well and supply from the local Company's mains ; brick and tiled Dairy with cemented floor.

THE BUILDINGS

are mostly timber and tiled and comprise Loose Box, Stable for three, Fowl House with Loft over, Coal House, Loose Box, Root House, Grain Pit, Cowhouse for fifteen with Calf Pen at end, and another Cowhouse for six. The drainage from the Cowhouses is connected with the Public Sewer.

At the rear of the Buildings is a Plot of Vegetable Garden.

The outlet roadway at the North-West corner of the Lot has to be made up and kept in repair by the Rickmansworth Urban District Council.

SCHEDULE.

No. on Plan.	Tenant.	Description.	Quantity.	Total Quantity.
	PARISH OF RICKMANSWORTH URBAN.			
Pt. 602	Mr. F. Barton .	Stream	.075	
Pt. 606		Pasture	2.745	
610		Do.	2.702	
Pt. 611		Garden	.256	
Pt. 612		House, Buildings, etc. . .	.616	
Pt. 614		Stream	.260	
Pt. 614		Do.	.164	
Pt. 615		Pasture	7.784	
Pt. 617		Do.	1.446	
				16.048
609	Mr. C. H. Sansom .	Watercress Bed	.783	
Pt. 611		Garden	.379	
Pt. 612		Watercress Bed	.100	
				1.262
Pt. 343	Rickmansworth U.D.C.	Allotments		2.000
Pt. 400	In hand . .	Roadway	.300	
Pt. 616		Pathway	.047	
Pt. 625		River	.384	.731
			Total .	A.20.041

LANDLORD'S OUTGOINGS.

Land Tax £2 10 0

The Timber on this Lot has an estimated value of £15 and is included in the sale.

There is an amount of Rectorial Tithe of 13s. 6d. apportioned to No. Pt. 606 and owned by the Vendor. This Tithe is included in the sale of the Lot.

The Lot is Sold and will be conveyed subject to a Right of Way for all purposes in favour of Lot 50 during the existing Lease thereof, between the points marked U and V on the Sale Plan (see reference to this under paragraph (*a*), Lot 50).

The Lot is Sold and will be conveyed subject to such rights of access to, and other easements (if any) as are enjoyed by the present Tenant of " The Bury," an adjoining property belonging to the Vendor.

The Lot is Sold and will be conveyed subject to the continued use and existence, as at present, of the lines of sewers following under the proposed development roadways to the Rickmansworth Pumping Station, with a right in favour of the Rickmansworth Urban District Council to enter the Lot for all necessary purposes in connection with the sewers.

The Lot is Sold and will be conveyed subject to a right in favour of Lot 50, until the termination of the Lease of the Lake to Mr. W. H. Walker, to enter enclosures Nos. Pt. 606 and Pt. 615 for the purpose of fishing and bathing therefrom along the River Bank; no part of the River is included in the Sale of this Lot (74), see footnote to Lot 50.

This Lot is Sold and will be conveyed subject to a liability with other Property in the former Parish of Rickmansworth to a liability to contribute towards the repair of Batchworth Bridge.

LOT 75

(Coloured Brown on Plan)

Two capital Enclosures of

MARKET GARDEN LAND

and a belt of Larches and mixed Conifers situate abutting Tolpits Lane and only a little over half-a-mile from Watford West Station and the outskirts of the Town. The Lot extends to an area of about

46A. 2R. 5P.

and is Let, as to part, to Mr. James Watts under Yearly Michaelmas Tenancy, the remainder, comprising the Plantation and the Shooting over the Lot being in hand.

The Right of Way to the East of the Lot is not the property of the Vendor.

SCHEDULE.

No. on Plan.	Tenant.	Description.	Quantity.	Total Quantity.
	PARISH OF WATFORD RURAL (Det.)			
Pt. 1000	Mr. J. Watts . .	Arable	24.059	
Pt 1001		Do.	19.300	
				43.359
1020	In hand. . .	Plantation		3.175
			Total	A.46.534

LANDLORD'S OUTGOINGS.

Commuted Tithe Rent Charge £13 1 7

The Timber on this Lot has an estimated value of £37 and is included in the sale.

LOT 76

(Coloured Blue on Plan)

A valuable property comprising about fifteen-and-a-half acres of

MARKET GARDEN LAND

and a Gravel Pit bounded on the South by the Rickmansworth Branch of the London and North Western Railway, abutting on Tolpits Lane, and being only half-a-mile from Watford West Station and the outskirts of the Town. The Lot extends to an area of about

16A. 0R. 31P.

and is Let, as to part, to Mr. Herbert J. Woodward under Yearly Michaelmas Tenancy, rent £42 15s., as to a further part (the Gravel pit) to Messrs. Walter and Dudley Wilkins under Yearly December 24th Tenancy determinable by either party by three months' notice at any Quarter Day, rent £25 per annum, the Shooting over the Lot being in hand.

The Land is of good quality and the Gravel Pit is close to the high road. The Gravel commands a good market and is believed to extend over a considerable area of the Lot. The Gravel is worked at the rate of 2s. 9d. per superficial yard for every yard or part of a yard of Land opened, but the rental paid in no case to be less than £6 5s. per quarter.

SCHEDULE.

No. on Plan.	Tenant.	Description.	Quantity.	Total Quantity.
	PARISH OF WATFORD RURAL. (Det.)			
Pt. 1017	Mr. H. J. Woodward	Arable	13.980	
1017A		Do.	1.528	15.508
Pt. 1017	Messrs. W. & D. Wilkins .	Gravel Pit		.683
			Total	A.16.191

LANDLORD'S OUTGOINGS.

Commuted Tithe Rent Charge £5 4 11

The Timber on this Lot has an estimated value of £16 and is included in the sale.

The Lot will be Sold with a Right of Way over that part of the accommodation roadway abutting on the North and East of this Lot and forming the approach roadway to Lot 8 (see footnote to Lot 8).

It will be Sold with a right to lay a 6 in. Pipe beneath any part of the length of the accommodation roadway above referred to for the purpose of a conduit from the Holywell Sewage Works on making proper compensation for any damage so caused (see footnote to Lot 8).

LOT 77

(Coloured Green on Plan)

This Lot comprises nearly

SIXTEEN ACRES OF MARKET GARDEN LAND

and a Gravel Pit situate adjacent to Lot 76, but at a somewhat shorter distance from Watford West Station and the Town. The Lot extends to an area of about

18A. 2R. 12P.

and is Let as to part, together with other Lands, to Mr. Thomas J. Simmons under Yearly Michaelmas Tenancy subject to two years' notice by either party at an apportioned rent of £27 5s., and also as to a part (the Gravel Pit) to Mr. Thomas J. Simmons under Yearly Lady Day Tenancy, determinable by either party, by three months' notice at any Quarter Day giving him the right to dig for gravel, the Shooting over the Lot being in hand.

The Land has a long frontage to the public road. On the East it lies adjacent to the Holywell Sewage Works, the effluent from which could be made available by arrangement for irrigation purposes.

The Gravel is of capital quality and the working thereof is let at the rental of 2s. 9d. per superficial yard for every yard or part of a yard of Land opened but the rental paid in no case to be less than £25 per annum.

SCHEDULE.

No on Plan	Description.	Quantity.
	PARISH OF WATFORD RURAL (Det.)	
Pt. 1004	Arable	15.698
Pt. 1004	Gravel Pit	2.000
1004A	Old Gravel Pit	.870
Pt. 1006	Gateway	.008
	Total	A.18.576

LANDLORD'S OUTGOINGS.

Commuted Tithe Rent Charge £5 1 0

The Timber on this Lot has an estimated value of £70 and is included in the Sale.

The Lot is Sold with a Right of Way over that part of the accommodation roadway abutting on the South of this Lot and forming the approach roadway to Lot 8 (see footnote to Lot 8).

LOT 78

(Coloured Yellow on Plan)

A valuable block of

MARKET GARDEN LAND

situate to the North of the foregoing Lot, having a frontage of about 300 ft. to the road to Watford and being only about half-a-mile from Watford West Station and the outskirts of the Town. The Lot extends to an area of about

8A. 3R. 32P.

and is Let to Mr. F. W. Clark under Lease for 14 years from September 29th, 1905, at a rent of £34, the Shooting over the Lot being in hand.

The Land on its Eastern Boundary lies adjacent to the Holywell Sewage Works, the effluent from which could be made available by arrangement for irrigation purposes. The frontage is suitable for Factory or similar purposes. Company's water mains are laid along the road.

LANDLORD'S OUTGOINGS.

Commuted Tithe Rent Charge £3 14 11

The Timber on this lot has an estimated value of £12 and is included in the Sale.

LOT 79

(Coloured Brown on Plan)

A Similar Block of

MARKET GARDEN LAND

situate to the North of Lot 78 and enjoying like advantages of position. It is only a quarter-of-a-mile from Watford West Station and the outskirts of the town. It has a frontage of about 450 ft. to the public road, extends to an area of about

8A. 2R. 10P.

and is Let to Mr. David Cook under Lease for 14 years from 29th September, 1905, at a rent of £36, the Shooting over the Lot being in hand.

The frontage Land is suitable for factory or similar purposes. The back Land lies adjacent to the Holywell Sewage Works, the effluent from which is available by arrangement for irrigation purposes.

SCHEDULE.

No. on Plan.	Description.	Quantity.
	PARISH OF WATFORD URBAN	
Pt. 101	Market Garden	3.240
102	Do.	5.322
	Total .	A. 8.562

LANDLORD'S OUTGOINGS.

Commuted Tithe Rent Charge £3 0 7

The Timber on this Lot has an estimated value of £4 10s. and is included in the Sale.

LOT 80

(Coloured Blue on Plan)

Another Block of

MARKET GARDEN LAND

situate to the North of Lot 79 and being only a quarter-of-a-mile from Watford West Station and the outskirts of the town. It has a frontage of about 80 ft. to the public road and extends to an area of about

8 A. 1 R. 18 P.

Let as to part to Mr. Thomas Clark under Yearly Michaelmas Tenancy, as to a further part together with other Land to Mr. Thomas J. Simmons under Yearly Michaelmas Tenancy, subject to two years' notice, at an apportioned rent of £2, and as to further parts together with other Lands to Mr. William Smith, Mr. Arthur Tibbles, and Mr. William Tibbles respectively, under separate Leases expiring Lady Day, 1920, the Shooting over the Lot being in hand.

Power is reserved to the Vendor to resume possession of any part of the Land for building purposes.

The back Land lies adjacent to the Holywell Sewage Works, the effluent from which could be made available by arrangement for irrigation purposes.

SCHEDULE.

No. on Plan.	Tenant.	Description.	Quantity.	Total Quantity.
	PARISH OF WATFORD URBAN.			
98	Mr. T. J. Simmons	Pasture . . .	.863	
Pt. 99		Do.	.496	
				1.359
Pt. 101	Mr. W. Tibbles .	Market Garden . . .		1.235
Pt. 101	Mr. W. Smith .	Do. . . .		3.940
Pt. 101	Mr. T. Clark .	Do. . . .		1.730
Pt. 101	Mr. A. Tibbles .	Do. . . .		.100
			Total	A 8.364

LANDLORD'S OUTGOINGS.

Commuted Tithe Rent Charge £2 8 6

Any Timber on this Lot will be included in the Sale.

LOT 81

(Coloured Pink on Plan)

COLE KING'S HOUSE

an old-fashioned Residence with modern appointments standing in its own Grounds and occupying a very convenient position within five minutes' walk of Watford West Station, and about one-and-a-half miles from Watford Junction.

The Lot extends to an area of about

2 A. 1 R. 23 P.

and is occupied as by part by R. H. Bindloss, Esq., under a Lease granted to Major E. W. Monro for a term of fourteen years, from 25th December, 1913, at a rent of £80, and as to a further part together with other Land by Mr. Thomas J. Simmons, under Yearly Michaelmas Tenancy, subject to two years' notice, at an apportioned rent of £25.

THE HOUSE

is built of brick faced with rough-cast and with slated roof, and stands about 220 ft. above sea level with principal aspect of South-East.

It is approached by a short Carriage Drive and contains :—

ON THE GROUND FLOOR : Hall, about 27 ft. by 13 ft., having lincrusta dado and fitted for heating by gas ; Dining Room with tiled grate and mahogany mantel, and measuring about 19 ft. (inclusive of a bay), by 14 ft. 3 in. ; Drawing Room, having tiled grate ; French Casement to the Lawn and measuring about 21 ft. 6 in. (including a bay) by 15 ft. ; Study about 15 ft. 6 in. by 12 ft. ; Kitchen, with double-oven range about 19 ft. 3 in. by 11 ft. 9 in. ; Scullery with two sinks each having h. and c. services, and two Larders.

ON THE FIRST FLOOR, reached by principal and secondary staircases, are three Best Bedrooms, measuring respectively about 19 ft. 6 in. by 14 ft. 3 in., 17 ft. by 14 ft., and 15 ft. 6in. by 13 ft. ; Dressing Room, Bathroom with bath and lavatory basin (h. and c.), W.C., and two Maidservants' Bedrooms.

Outside are a brick and slated Larder, Wood and Store Shed, and W.C.

The principal Rooms on the Ground Floor are about 10 ft. 6 in. high, and those on the First Floor about 10 ft.

Electric Light, Gas, and Company'sWater are laid on ; the Drainage is on modern principles and taken into the Public Sewer.

At the end of the House is a range of brick and slated

COLE KING'S HOUSE. (LOT 81.)

STABLING

the accommodation comprising two good Loose Boxes, Harness Room with fireplace, Corn Room, Coach House, another Loose Box or Bicycle House, Harness Room, and Fowl House.

Water is laid on outside the Stabling.

THE PLEASURE GROUNDS

are well timbered and shrubbed, and on the Eastern Lawn is a large Wellingtonia and an Araucaria. They also include a Tennis Lawn, Rock Garden, and Vegetable Garden, span-roofed Greenhouse and Vinery, and an eight-light brick pit.

There is also a small Paddock, and a Plot of Ground with some large Walnut Trees.

At the back of the House is a small Set of

FARMBUILDINGS

built of brick or timber with tiled, slated and iron roofs, and comprising Loose Box Cart Horse Stable for five, large Loose Box, Barn, Granary, old thatched Stable, Barn with Chaff House and Loft, three Loose Boxes, six-stall Stable, two Loose Boxes, covered Shed and Workshop.

There is a separate entrance to these Buildings from Hagden Lane, and Water and Gas are laid on to some of them.

SCHEDULE.

No. on Plan.	Tenant.	Description.	Quantity.	Total Quantity.
	PARISH OF WATFORD URBAN.			
Pt. 84	R. H. Bindloss, Esq.	House and Garden . .	.805	
85		Garden and Paddock . .	1.001	
				1.806
Pt. 84	Mr. T. J. Simmons.	Buildings and Yard . .		.590
			Total .	A.2.396

LANDLORD'S OUTGOINGS.

Commuted Tithe Rent Charge £1 7 1

The Timber on this Lot will be included in the Sale.

This lot is sold and will be conveyed subject to a right of way in favour of Lot 82 until the termination of the present lease of this Lot with or without horses and carts across the paddock as at present existing (see footnote to Lot 82).

LOT 82

(Coloured Green on Plan)

A very Valuable

BLOCK OF BUILDING LAND

situate immediately adjoining the South-Western outskirts of the town of Watford, and lying between same and Watford West Station.

It is bounded on two sides by the public thoroughfare known as Hagden Lane, to which it has frontages of about 800 ft. and 600 ft. respectively. Hagden Lane is sewered and the frontages facing this Lot are almost entirely built over.

The Lot extends to an area of about

14A. 1R. 30P.

and is Let, together with other Lands, to Mr. Thomas J. Simmons, under Yearly Michaelmas Tenancy, subject to two years' notice, at an apportioned rent of £21.

Power is reserved to the Landlord to resume possession of any part of the Land for building purposes.

The Land is rectangular in shape and lends itself to economical development both as regards its own lay out and in connection with the road systems adjoining it.

SCHEDULE.

No. on Plan.	Description.	Quantity.
	PARISH OF WATFORD URBAN.	
86	Pasture	4.204
Pt. 87	Arable	10.233
	Total . . .	A.14.437

LANDLORD'S OUTGOINGS.

Commuted Tithe Rent Charge £4 3 0

The Timber on this Lot has an estimated value of £25 and is included in the Sale.
This Lot has the benefit of a right of way during the existence of the present lease of Lot 81 with or without horses and carts across the paddock of Lot 81 as at present existing.

LOT 83

(Coloured Yellow on Plan)

Another Enclosure of

BUILDING LAND

occupying an important corner Site and situate immediately adjoining Watford West Station, and having frontages to the Station Road and Hagden Lane of about 400 ft. and 150 ft. respectively.

The Lot extends to an area of about

1A. 3R. 17P.

and is ripe for immediate Development.

Let together with other Lands to Mr. Thomas J. Simmons under Yearly Michaelmas Tenancy, subject to two years' notice, at an apportioned rent of £2 15s.

Power is reserved to the Landlord to resume possession of any part of the Land for building purposes.

LANDLORD'S OUTGOINGS.

Commuted Tithe Rent Charge £0 11 8

Any Timber on this Lot will be included in the Sale.

CHAPTER NINE

1959 Auction

(Reproduction of the original Auction Document. Prices realised are quoted next to Lot numbers)

IN THE GREEN BELT, NEAR LONDON

Between Rickmansworth and Moor Park, Hertfordshire

18 miles from Marble Arch 2 miles from Northwood 4 miles from Watford Junction

Particulars, Plans and Conditions of Sale of the

VALUABLE FREEHOLD

Residential and Agricultural Estate

MOOR PARK ESTATE

occupying a KEY POSITION on the outskirts of Rickmansworth and Moor Park, including

HOME FARM HOUSE WITH VACANT POSSESSION
6 ACRES

(with extra land available if required), undoubtedly one of the finest sites for a First Class Residence in the Outer London Area, protected at the rear by Moor Park Golf Course and **with hundreds of acres of rolling green belt land forming the whole of the splendid vista to the South**

TWENTY-FOUR SEPARATE LOTS OF VERY VALUABLE ACCOMMODATION LAND

in Moor Park, Batchworth Heath, London Road, Rickmansworth, etc., mostly

WITH VACANT POSSESSION

and varying from 1 acre to 20 acres

Four Farms

MOOR PARK FARM BATCHWORTH HEATH FARM STOCKER'S FARM PIPERS FARM

let at very low rents and occupying most important positions, and

SEVERAL SMALL AREAS OF WOODLAND

the whole extending to about

611 acres

To be offered for Sale by Auction "unless sold by private treaty" in 37 Lots by

BERNARD THORPE & PARTNERS

at THE SWAN HOTEL, RICKMANSWORTH
on THURSDAY, 14th MAY, 1959
at 3 o'clock.

Auctioneers: **BERNARD THORPE & PARTNERS,** 1 Buckingham Palace Road, London, S.W.1 (Telephone: VICtoria 3012)
and at Mayfair, Hereford, York, Darlington, Hexham, Newcastle upon Tyne, Edinburgh and Oxted, Surrey
Solicitors: BATTEN & CO., Church House, Yeovil (Telephone: 685)

Foreword

There can be very few Estates of 600 *acres within* 18 *miles of Marble Arch and in such a valuable residential district as the Moor Park Estate. Practically the whole of the land for sale is in the Metropolitan Green Belt, and is the last great expanse of open country on the road to London before reaching Hyde Park.*

Lot 1, *the Home Farm House and Walled Garden—with extra land if required—bounded on one side by Moor Park Golf Course and on the other by open "Green Belt" lands, is a site without equal in this much favoured district where, owing to the "Green Belt", sites are so scarce.*

The Sale also includes numerous areas of land where planning permission has been refused but, possibly in years to come, with the flexibility of planning, these areas may be available particularly where they are situated close in to existing development.

Agricultural Investments

As will be seen from the Particulars there are four tenanted farms which singly or as a group will form a very good agricultural investment.

These properties have not been kept up in line with modern requirements and as a result a Purchaser can remodel, repair and modernise these farms and take advantage of the Income Tax Sections inducing agricultural owners to do so. On the one hand there is the Maintenance Claim for repairs, insurance and management on which there is no limitation to the Schedule A assessment (as with other classes of property), any excess amount of claim being carried forward or set off against other income; and on the other hand there is the Capital Expenditure Claim whereby the cost of improvements can be set off against tax liability over a 10 year period and again if agricultural Schedule A is inadequate, the claim may be set off against other income.

Add to this the availability of Government grants for work of this class, and the result is that for the Sur-Tax payer in particular great improvements can be brought about at far less cost than if such work did not rank for relief. The result should be a considerable capital appreciation in the investment quite apart from the likelihood of such appreciation due to the position of the land.

The rents are very low and will therefore allow of considerable increase by way of return on such improvements.

With these important advantages there remains the final attribute of the investment in agricultural land for the well-to-do man wishing to conserve his estate as much as possible, namely the 45% saving in Estate Duty in respect of the agricultural value.

GENERAL REMARKS

SITUATION

The Estate, whether for residential purposes, agricultural investment or for the selection of areas of accommodation land is most beautifully situated, covering a most important section of the undeveloped land between Batchworth Heath and Rickmansworth, at present zoned as **Metropolitan Green Belt,** together with small areas of land into Moor Park.

Marble Arch is 18 miles; Watford is 4 miles; Northwood 2 miles; while Aylesbury is about 20 miles to the North West. Rickmansworth adjoins the Estate. Practically the whole estate is in Hertfordshire, one or two enclosures being over the Middlesex Border.

TRAIN SERVICE

A feature of this area is the first class train service to London. Trains from Moor Park to Baker Street are about five every hour with a similar return service and the fast train takes 28 minutes. Some trains, particularly at the peak hours, go on to Liverpool St. (44 mins.) from Moor Park.

GOLF

The district is particularly well served by first class Golf Courses.

Moor Park Golf Course (two courses in addition to the Municipal Course); Sandy Lodge Golf Course (close to Moor Park Station); Haste Hill and Northwood Golf Courses (within one mile).

OUTGOINGS

Tithe Redemption Annuity £98 0s. 9d per annum on the whole Estate.

TOWN PLANNING

All the Lots offered for sale are within the Green Belt zoning (with the exception of the North West corner of Lot 12 and the frontage land to Kewferry Drive (Lot 35)) and applications for development have been refused. The Vendor has received any claims for loss of development value under the Town Planning Acts 1947 and 1954 and so far as it is aware there are no "unexpended balances" on any of the Lots.

RESIDENTIAL SITE

In view of the Green Belt zoning the Auctioneers draw particular attention to Lot 1 and its surrounds, as whether by way of conversion of the existing house, or replacement with a modern residence, a first class site is available within the Green Belt and bordered by the Golf Course; a unique position and set of circumstances in this most favoured residential area.

LOCAL AUTHORITIES and SERVICE AUTHORITIES

Local Authority:	Rickmansworth U.D.C., High St., Rickmansworth.
Planning Authority:	Hertfordshire C.C., County Hall, Hertford.
Water Company:	Rickmansworth and Uxbridge Valley Water Co., Batchworth, Rickmansworth, *or*
	Colne Valley Water Co., Aldenham Road, Watford.
Electricity:	Eastern Electricity Board, 1 Love Lane, Pinner.
Gas:	Eastern Gas Board, 48 High Street, Rickmansworth.

AREA

The Estate has a total area of 611 acres and will be offered in 37 Lots.

SPORTING

The sporting over the Estate is in hand and will be included in the Sale of each Lot.

VIEWING

Lots 1 to 3 can be viewed by applying to Moor Park Estate Office (Tel.: Northwood 2343) for the key. All other Lots can be viewed at any time on production of these Particulars, and any enquiries made to the Estate Office during the visit. Tenanted Lots can be viewed by appointment through the Estate Office, or at any time by courtesy of the tenants.

NO INGOING VALUATION ON VACANT PROPERTIES

There will be no Ingoing Valuation or Tenant Right Valuation of any kind and any such matters and items in the way of Tenants' Fixtures will be included in the Sale, in the case of Vacant Possession Lots.

PRIVATE ROADS

Lots 5, 6, 7, 8, 9, 10, 11, 12, 16, 17, 18, 19 adjoin private estate roads maintained by Moor Park (1958) Limited, but all these Lots being within the green belt are exempt from annual payments of any sort.

The only Lots on which annual payments are made are:

Lot 20: £1 per annum.
Lot 35: £6 per annum.

TIMBER

All timber is included in the sale and in the purchase price (*See Special Condition No.* 41).

SUMMARY OF LOTS

Lot No.	*Description*	*Area*	*Present Income*	*Tenant's Name if Let*	*Remarks*
1	Home Farmhouse and Walled Garden ...	5·923	—	—	Vacant Possession.
2	Accommodation Land adjoining	3·999	—	—	Vacant Possession.
3	Part of Walled Garden, Home Farm House ...	2·185	—	—	Vacant Possession.
4	Accommodation Land, adjoining	4·540	—	—	Vacant Possession.
5	do. Farm Road ...	4·040	—	—	
6	do. do.	1·092	—	—	Let on a Grazing licence to
7	do. do. ...	6·116	—	—	W. Nichols.
8	do. Batchworth Lane ...	1·426	—	—	1 month's notice required.
9	do. do. ...	1·601	—	—	
10	do. Russell Road ...	3·154	—	—	Vacant Possession.
11	do. Bedford Road ...	3·536	—	—	Vacant Possession.
12	do. do. ...	1·464	—	—	Vacant Possession.
13	Tolpits Plantation, Tolpits Lane	3·400	—	—	Vacant Possession.
14	The Withy Bed, Moor Lane	9·000	—	—	Vacant Possession.
15	Green Knoll, Moor Lane	1·032	—	—	Vacant Possession.
16	Land at Hamper Mills	6·433	£7 10 0	—	Grazing licence to S. A. Brazier. 1 month's notice.
17	do.	·800	—	—	Vacant Possession.
18	Plot in Wolsey Road	·309	—	—	Vacant Possession.
19	do.	·620	—	—	Vacant Possession.
20	Plot on South Approach	·128	—	—	Vacant Possession.
21	Moor Park Farm	97·261		A. J. F. Holloway	
22	Accommodation Land, London Road ...	2·641	£225 0 0	do.	
23	Plot of Land, London Road	·352		do.	
24	Batchworth Heath Farm	106·732	£196 13 5	A. Nichols	
25	The Brickfield, London Road	26·000	£53 18 6	A. Nichols	
26	Accommodation Land, London Road ...	15·694	—	—	Vacant Possession.
27	do. do. ...	8·156	—	—	Vacant Possession.
28	Orchard and Pasture, London Road ...	·582	£10 0 0	Mrs. Chalk	
29	do. do.	1·103		do.	
30	Stocker's Farm, Rickmansworth	123·036			
31	Accommodation Land, Rickmansworth ...	2·506	£144 0 0	J. H. Wheaton.	
32	Pasture Land, Harefield Road, Rickmansworth	34·288			
33	The Sewage Field, Harefield Road, do.	26·715	—	—	Vacant Possession.
34	Pipers Farm, Rickmansworth	91·885	£150 4 3	W. Timms.	
35	Building and Accommodation Land, Kew-ferry Drive	7·887	—	W. Nichols	Grazing Licence—1 month's notice.
36	Manorial Rights				
37	Fishing Rights, etc.				
	TOTALS	611·150	£733 7 8		

A view of Home Farm House

LOT 1 (£8,000) (Coloured *blue* on Plan)

The Georgian Farmhouse Residence

HOME FARM HOUSE

MOOR PARK

occupying what is undoubtedly

One of the Finest Residential Sites within 18 miles of London

extending in all to nearly

6 ACRES

and including, in addition to the House

A Picturesque set of Farm Buildings

which, because of their matured appearance and setting, can be utilised as **Stablings,** Farm Buildings or Outbuildings, while at the same time forming a Courtyard approach to the House

and

The Secluded Walled Kitchen Garden

at present uncultivated, but forming a really superb site for the pleasure grounds secluded within the brick wall

the whole property

Bounded on the North by the Moor Park Golf Course
and, to the South, enjoying

Uninterrupted Views over the extensive and undulating areas of the Outer London Green Belt, between Moor Park and Rickmansworth while the Eastern and Western boundaries adjoin Lots 2 and 3 which are also within the Green Belt area.

The feature of this Lot, whether a Purchaser decides to modernise, improve and repair the Farmhouse, or to build a new Country House in place of it, is that there is the opportunity of

Providing a First Class Residence in such an exceptional position within the Green Belt

in an area where building Sites of even moderate size are at such a premium.

Home Farm House

faces South and is about 90 yards back from the public road. It is constructed of mellowed brickwork and tiled roof and has the following accommodation:—

On the GROUND FLOOR:

Dining Room, 14 ft. by 14 ft., fitted cupboard.
Sitting Room, 14 ft. by 15 ft.
Work Room, 14 ft. by 11 ft. 3 in.
Reception Room, 17 ft. 9 in. by 17 ft. 9 in.
Kitchen, Scullery, Larder, Cellar, Bathroom and W.C.

On the FIRST FLOOR (two Staircases):

Three Bedrooms, 14 ft. 9 in. by 12 ft. 4 in.; 14 ft. 9 in. by 14 ft.; and 14 ft. by 16 ft.
Boxroom, 8 ft. 3 in. by 6 ft. 9 in.
Tank Room, 16 ft. 9 in. by 12 ft. 4 in.

SERVICES: MAIN WATER AND ELECTRICITY

There is a carriage sweep and lawns in front of the house with a path from the public road; brick and tiled outbuilding adjoining Garden Wall.

The Walled Garden

is situated to the West of the House and has an area of about 2 acres and there is also a wide area of Verge between the Garden and the public road.

The Farm Buildings

to the South East of the House, are of considerable age, and attractive appearance in brick, weatherboarding, and tiled roofs, and comprise:—

Cowstall for 16 (to modern standard) with drinking bowls; **Barn and Store** with concrete floor, and sliding doors, and with fitted 6 h.p. electric motor, switchgear, shafting, cornmill and hopper; **Meal House** adjoining with concrete floor; Dairy; Store Room; **Fine Granary;** Loose Box; and Tractor Shed.

3-Bay open Cattle Shed with concrete yards; Pig Yard (corrugated iron roof) and Implement Shed.

Stable providing **Four Loose Boxes and Harness Room;** Old Piggeries (in disrepair) and Silage Pit.

MAIN WATER AND ELECTRICITY

VACANT POSSESSION

SCHEDULE

No. on Ordnance Sheet (1935 Edition)	*Description*	*Area*
	Parish of Rickmansworth Urban	
Pt. 171	Pasture, etc. ... ... estimated	1·060
264	Pond	·240
Pt. 265	House, Garden, Kitchen Garden and Farm Buildings ... estimated	4·223
Pt. 310	Woodland ... ... estimated	·400
	Total Acreage ...	**5·923**

Rates:—19*s.* 2*d. in the* £.

Fences on East of Entrance Road and North East of Buildings (between Lots 1 and 2):—*The fence shall be the property of the Purchaser of Lot* 1.

Sheds, Etc. rear of Kitchen Garden:—*These various Sheds are the property of Moor Park Golf Club who have no tenancy in respect of the land, and agree to the removal on request.*

Garden Wall between Lots 1 and 3:—*The wall shall be the property of the Purchaser of Lot* 1.

Rights of Way:—*There are no rights of way over this Lot and the apparent or actual use of tracks at the rear of the buildings is as a result of the Moor Park Golf Club use of the buildings referred to above or previous use for agricultural purposes.*

Electricity Cable:—*This Lot is sold with the benefit of an easement in respect of an underground electricity cable* (*see* Remarks *under Lot* 2).

Overflow from Pond:—*This Lot is sold with the benefit of an easement for the overflow or drainage from the pond to Lot* 4 *as at present existing.*

LOT 2 (£2,000) (Coloured *brown* on Plan)

A VALUABLE AREA OF

Accommodation Land

East of HOME FARM, MOOR PARK

extending to about

4 ACRES

This land is heavily timbered and is bounded on the South by the London Road (from which there is access by a field gate), and on the North by Moor Park Golf Course.

Timber Valuation: £247

VACANT POSSESSION

AREA:—*This Lot comprises Ordnance No.* 263, *Parish of Rickmansworth Urban* (1935 *Edition*). *Area* 3.857 *acres and Part of Ordnance No.* 265, *area estimated at* .142 *acres. Total area* 3.999 *acres or thereabouts.*

TITHE REDEMPTION ANNUITY:—11*s.* 3*d. per annum.*

FENCES BETWEEN LOTS 1 AND 2:—*The fences shall be the property of the Purchaser of Lot* 1. *There shall be no right for the Purchaser of Lot* 2 *to use the gateway to the field from Home Farm Road.*

WATER PIPE LINE:—*There is an underground water pipe line running South to North across the field serving Moor Park Golf Club. No easement rental is paid. Lot* 2 *is sold subject to the easement in favour of Moor Park Golf Club.*

ELECTRICITY CABLE:—*An underground electricity cable from Park Close crosses the land from West to East, serving Lot* 1. *Lot* 2 *is sold subject to an easement for the continuation of the use of this cable for the benefit of the Purchaser of Lot* 1 *together with the right of entry for repairs and maintenance.*

FUTURE DEVELOPMENT OF LOT 2:—*If Building Development takes place on Lot* 2 *there is a responsibility to construct the sewer so that the property "Deep Hollow" (on the North East) can be connected.*

LOT 3 (£1,450) (Coloured *pink* on Plan)

THE WESTERN PORTION

of the

Walled Kitchen Garden

with an area of nearly

$2\frac{1}{4}$ ACRES

Having a doorway entrance from the London Road beyond which to the South is the Green Belt Land.

There was originally a cottage on this Site and although the present Town Planning Scheme prevents any development, attention is drawn to the excellence of the Site should a future revision of the Planning Scheme include this area for development

VACANT POSSESSION

AREA:—*This Lot comprises Part of Ordnance No.* 265, *Parish of Rickmansworth Urban* (1935 *Edition*), *area estimated at* 2·185 *acres.*

WALL BETWEEN LOTS 1 AND 3:—*This wall shall be the property of Lot* 1.

LOT 4 (£900) (Coloured *green* on Plan)

A FURTHER AREA OF

Accommodation Land

to the South of HOME FARM, MOOR PARK

adjoining the main London Road and with a concrete apron and steel field gate access therefrom, having an area of about

4½ ACRES

VACANT POSSESSION

AREA:—*This Lot comprises Part of Ordnance No.* 266, *Parish of Rickmansworth Urban* (1935 *Edition*), *area estimated at* 4·540 *acres.*

TITHE REDEMPTION ANNUITY:—11*s.* 11*d. per annum.*

DRAINAGE RIGHT FOR LOT 1:—*The Pond O.S.* 264 (*Lot* 1) *has an overflow or drain to the North West corner of Lot* 4 *and Lot* 4 *is sold subject to an easement in favour of the Purchaser of Lot* 1 *for the continuance of such overflow or drain as at present existing.*

LOT 5 (£1,100) (Coloured *blue* on Plan)

A VALUABLE AREA OF

Accommodation Land

on the West Side of FARM ROAD, MOOR PARK

approached by a gate from Farm Road (leading off Batchworth Lane), having an area of about

4 ACRES

and with frontage to Rickmansworth Road.

This land is occupied by Mr. W. Nichols of Park Farm, Duckshill Road, Northwood, under licence, determinable by **one month's notice.**

MAIN WATER AND SEWER

AREA:—*This Lot comprises Part of Ordnance No.* 43, *Parish of Ruislip* (1935 *Edition*), *area estimated at* 4·040 *acres.*

MOOR PARK ESTATE ROADS:—*Farm Road is a private road maintained by Moor Park* (1958) *Ltd.* (*see Special Condition No.* 20).

SEWER EASEMENT:—*There is a sewer across this land and the owner of the land West of Rickmansworth Road has the right to connect thereto for the development of his land.*

OVERHEAD CABLE:—*The Vendor has made a claim against the Central Electricity Authority in respect of the pylons and overhead cable and this claim is reserved to the Vendor.*

LOT 6 (£500) (Coloured *pink* on Plan)

A SMALL CONVENIENT AREA OF

Accommodation Land and Woodland

West of FARM ROAD, MOOR PARK

having an area of about

1 ACRE

and with access by a gate from Farm Road

This land is occupied by Mr. W. Nichols of Park Farm, Duckshill Road, Northwood, under license, determinable by **one month's notice.**

AREA:—*This Lot comprises parts of Ordnance Nos.* 175 *and* 177, *Parish of Rickmansworth Urban* (1935 *Edition*), *areas estimated at* ·920 *acres and* ·172 *acres respectively. Total* 1·092 *acres or thereabouts.*

TITHE REDEMPTION ANNUITY:—4*s.* 11*d. per annum.*

MOOR PARK ESTATE ROADS:—*Farm Road is a private road maintained by Moor Park* (1958) *Ltd.* (*see Special Condition No.* 20).

LOT 7 (£1,300) (Coloured *brown* on Plan)

A FURTHER WELL SITUATED AREA OF

Accommodation Land

on the East Side of

FARM ROAD, MOOR PARK

and also adjoining the continuation of Farm Road on the South boundary, extending to over

6 ACRES

This land has access from Farm Road, and there is a short frontage to Batchworth Road at the North East.

This land is occupied by Mr. W. Nichols of Park Farm, Duckshill Road, Northwood, under license, determinable by **one month's notice.**

AREA:—*This Lot comprises Part of Ordnance No.* 175, *Parish of Rickmansworth Urban and Ordnance No.* 44, *Parish of Ruislip* (1935 *Edition*), *areas* ·876 *acres estimated and* 5·240 *acres respectively. Total area* 6·116 *acres or thereabouts.*

TITHE REDEMPTION ANNUITY:—1*s.* 4*d. per annum.*

MOOR PARK ESTATE ROADS:—*Farm Road is a private Road maintained by Moor Park* (1958) *Ltd.* (*see Special Condition No.* 20).

SEWER EASEMENT:—*There is a sewer across this field continuing from Lot* 5 *and an easement to connect thereto* (*see Remarks under Lot* 5).

OVERHEAD CABLE:—*The Vendor has made a claim against the Central Electricity Authority in respect of the overhead cable and pylons and this claim is reserved to the Vendor.*

LOT 8 (£300) (Coloured *yellow* on Plan)

AN AREA OF

Accommodation Land

with access from and frontage to

BATCHWORTH LANE, MOOR PARK

having an area of nearly

$1\frac{1}{2}$ ACRES

This land is occupied by Mr. W. Nichols of Park Farm, Duckshill Road, Northwood, under license, determinable by **one month's notice.**

AREA:—*This Lot comprises Part of Ordnance No.* 175, *Parish of Rickmansworth Urban* (1935 *Edition*), *area* 1·426 *acres or thereabouts.*

OVERHEAD CABLE:—*The Vendor has made a claim against the Central Electricity Authority in respect of the pylons and overhead cable and this claim is reserved to the Vendor.*

LOT 9 (£1,400) (Coloured *blue* on Plan)

AN AREA OF

Accommodation Land

BATCHWORTH LANE, MOOR PARK

having about 310 feet frontage to the public road and an area of about

$5\frac{1}{2}$ ACRES

This land is occupied by Mr. W. Nichols of Park Farm, Duckshill Road, Northwood, under license, determinable by **one month's notice.**

SCHEDULE

No. on Ordnance Sheet (1935 *Edition*)	*Description*		*Area*
	Parish of Rickmansworth Urban		
Pt. 10	Rough	estimated	1·736
	Parish of Ruislip		
Pt. 20	Pasture	estimated	·368
Pt. 25	do.	estimated	1·951
Pt. 26	do.	estimated	·760
Pt. 27	do.	estimated	·699
		Total Acreage ...	**5·514**

ELECTRICITY CABLE:—*The Eastern Electricity Board have the right to lay an underground cable within the Western Boundary.*

SEWER EASEMENT:—*This Lot is sold subject to an easement in respect of a sewer crossing the land in an East to West direction.*

BOUNDARY BETWEEN LOT 9 AND LOT 35:—*See remarks under Lot* 35.

LOT 10 (£1,000) (Coloured *green* on Plan)

A PARTICULARLY WELL SITUATED AREA OF

Accommodation Land

RUSSELL ROAD, MOOR PARK

but also fronting Batchworth Lane. There is a frontage of about 465 feet to Russell Road and about 250 feet to Batchworth Lane.

The land is level pasture, and has an area of nearly

3¼ ACRES

VACANT POSSESSION

AREA:—*This Lot comprises Part of Ordnance No. 24, Parish of Rickmansworth Urban (1935 Edition), area estimated at 3·154 acres.*

BOUNDARY AT NORTH:—*The owner of the land to the North of this Lot is responsible to fence the boundary between his land and Lot 10.*

BOUNDARY ON EAST:—*There is at present no division between Lots 10 and 11, and the boundary is the original ordnance hedge or fence. The Purchaser of Lot 10 shall be responsible for the erection of a stock-proof fence on this boundary within three months of receiving written notice to fence from the Purchaser of Lot 11.*

MOOR PARK ESTATE ROADS:—*Russell Road is a private road maintained by Moor Park (1958) Ltd. (see Special Condition No. 20).*

OVERHEAD CABLE:—*The Vendor has made a claim against the Central Electricity Authority in respect of the pylons and the overhead electricity cable and this claim is reserved to the Vendor.*

LOT 11 (£1,000) (Coloured *pink* on Plan)

A SIMILAR AREA OF

Accommodation Land

BEDFORD ROAD, MOOR PARK

adjoining Lot 10 and also with frontage to Batchworth Lane. There is about 540 feet frontage to Bedford Road and about 265 feet frontage to Batchworth Lane.

The land is level and has an area of about

3½ ACRES

VACANT POSSESSION

AREA:—*This Lot comprises Part of Ordnance No. 25, Parish of Rickmansworth Urban (1935 Edition), area estimated at 3·536 acres or thereabouts.*

BOUNDARY ON WEST:—*See Remarks under Lot 10.*

BOUNDARY ON NORTH:—*There is at present no division between Lots 11 and 12. The Purchaser of Lot 11 shall be responsible to erect a stock-proof fence within three months of receiving written notice to fence from the Purchaser of Lot 12.*

MOOR PARK ESTATE ROADS:—*Bedford Road is a private road maintained by Moor Park (1958) Ltd. (see Special Condition No. 20).*

OVERHEAD CABLE:—*The Vendor has made a claim against the Central Electricity Authority in respect of the pylons and the overhead electricity cable and this claim is reserved to the Vendor.*

LOT 12 (£600) (Coloured *yellow* on Plan)

A VERY CONVENIENT AREA OF

Accommodation Land

BEDFORD ROAD, MOOR PARK

Situated to the North of Lot 11 and with a frontage of about 200 feet to the road, and an area of nearly

1½ ACRES

VACANT POSSESSION

Note: The North West corner is not in the Green Belt, but application for permission to erect a dwellinghouse has been refused.

AREA:—*This Lot comprises Part of Ordnance No.* 25, *Parish of Rickmansworth Urban* (1935 *Edition*), *area estimated at* 1·464 *acres or thereabouts.*

BOUNDARY ON WEST:—*The owner of the land on the West is responsible for the erection of a fence between this Land and Lot* 12.

BOUNDARY ON SOUTH:—*See Remarks under Lot* 11.

MOOR PARK ESTATE ROADS:—*Bedford Road is a private road maintained by Moor Park* (1958) *Ltd.* (*see Special Condition No.* 20).

OVERHEAD CABLE:—*The Vendor has made a claim against the Central Electricity Authority in respect of the pylons and the overhead electricity cable and this claim is reserved to the Vendor.*

LOT 13 (£500) (Coloured *blue* on Plan)

AN AREA OF WOODLAND

known as

Tolpits Plantation

TOLPITS LANE, MOOR PARK

extending to nearly

3½ ACRES

Bounded on the North by the public road, on the South by the River Colne and on the East by the Railway, and containing some

GOOD SALEABLE TIMBER

TIMBER SCHEDULE

No. of Trees	*Species*	*Estimated Content*
10	Beech	486
12	Sycamore	140
25	Ash	734
6	Oak	160
7	Elm	212
1	Cherry	40
2	Alder	56
7	Scots Pine	542
70	TOTAL	2,370 cubic feet

VACANT POSSESSION

AREA:—*This Lot comprises Part of Ordnance No.* 476, *Parish of Rickmansworth Urban* (1935 *Edition*), *area estimated at* 3·400 *acres or thereabouts.*

IRRIGATION AND FISHING:—*See Special Condition No.* 10.

LOT 14 (£900) (Coloured *pink* on Plan)

The Withey Bed

MOOR LANE, MOOR PARK

having an area of about

9 ACRES

and long frontage to and access from Moor Lane.

VACANT POSSESSION

AREA:—*This area comprises Part of Ordnance No.* 165, *Parish of Rickmansworth Urban* (1935 *Edition*), *area estimated at* 9 *acres or thereabouts.*

TITHE REDEMPTION ANNUITY:—£1 7*s.* 5*d. per annum.*

IRRIGATION AND FISHING:—*See Special Condition No.* 10.

LOT 15 (£300) (Coloured *yellow* on Plan)

A SMALL WOODLAND AREA

known as

Green Knoll

MOOR LANE, MOOR PARK

having an area of about

1 ACRE

and long frontage and access from Moor Lane.

VACANT POSSESSION

AREA:—*This Lot comprises Part Ordnance No.* 460, *Parish of Rickmansworth Urban* (1935 *Edition*), *area estimated at* 1·032 *acres.*

IRRIGATION AND FISHING:—*See Special Condition No.* 10.

LOT 16 (**Sold prior to auction**) (Coloured *pink* on Plan)

A VERY CONVENIENTLY SITUATED AREA OF

Accommodation Land

known as

LAND AT HAMPER MILLS, MOOR PARK

With access off the track leading from the main road (Sandy Lane) and from Sandy Lodge Lane, having an area of nearly

6½ ACRES

and a frontage of about 330 feet to Sandy Lodge Lane.

This Lot is occupied under grazing license only (one month's notice) by S. A Brazier of Carpenters Park Dairy, Oxley Lane, Watford, who pays 12s. 6d. per month.

SCHEDULE

No. on Ordnance Sheet (1934 Edition)	*Description*	*Area*
	Parish of Rickmansworth Urban	
124	Pasture	4·949
	Parish of Watford Rural	
286	do.	·543
Pt. 287	do. ... ... estimated	·941
	Total Acreage ...	**6·433**

RIGHT OF WAY:—*There is a right of way over the lane leading from Sandy Lane to the East of this Lot (see Special Condition No.* 23).

FOOTPATH:—*The footpath running East to West across this Lot is used by Merchant Taylors School as a short cut from the public path to the boundary of the School property.*

MERCHANT TAYLORS' SCHOOL:—*See Special Condition No.* 12 *regarding rights vested in Merchant Taylors' School.*

MOOR PARK ESTATE ROADS:—*Sandy Lodge Lane is a private road maintained by Moor Park* (1958) *Ltd. (see Special Condition No.* 20).

RESTRICTIVE COVENANTS FOR THE BENEFIT OF LOT 16:—*There are certain restrictive covenants over the property adjoining on the West for the benefit of Lot* 16.

LOT 17 (£450) (Coloured *yellow* on Plan)

A Small Area of Land

at

HAMPER MILLS, MOOR PARK

Situated south of Lot 16 and West of the Garage Site, having a frontage to Sandy Lodge Lane of about 200 feet and an area of about

¾ ACRE

VACANT POSSESSION

AREA:—*This Lot comprises Part of Ordnance No.* 96, *Parish of Rickmansworth Urban* (1934 *Edition*), *area estimated at* ·800 *acres.*

MERCHANT TAYLORS' SCHOOL:—*See Special Condition No.* 12 *regarding rights vested in Merchant Taylors' School.*

LOT 18 (£200) (Coloured *yellow* on Plan)

A Plot of Land

in

WOLSEY ROAD, MOOR PARK

Having a frontage of 94 feet, a width at rear of 122 feet, and a depth of 157 feet (average) with an area of about

SQUARE **1,884** YARDS

The overhead cable is partly over this Lot and partly on Lot 19 (*see note beneath*)

VACANT POSSESSION

AREA:—*This Lot comprises Part of Ordnance No.* 62, *Parish of Rickmansworth Urban* (1935 *Edition*), *area estimated at* ·309 *acres.*

BOUNDARY ON SOUTH:—*The Purchaser of this Lot will be responsible to erect a stockproof fence between this Lot and Lot* 19 *within three months of receiving written notice to fence from the Purchaser of Lot* 19.

MOOR PARK ESTATE ROADS:—*Wolsey Road is a private road maintained by Moor Park* (1958) *Ltd.* (*see Special Condition No.* 20).

OVERHEAD CABLE:—*The Vendor has made a claim against the Central Electricity Authority in respect of the overhead cable and this claim is reserved to the Vendor.*

LOT 19 (£350) (Coloured *blue* on Plan)

A Plot of Land

in

WOLSEY ROAD, MOOR PARK

Adjoining Lot 20 on the South, having a frontage of 186 feet, a width at the rear of about 158 feet and a depth of 157 feet (average), with an area of about

SQUARE **3,000** YARDS

The overhead cable is partly over this Lot and partly over Lot 18 (*see note beneath*).

VACANT POSSESSION

AREA:—*This Lot comprises parts of Ordnance Nos. 28 and 62 parish of Rickmansworth Urban (1935 Edition) area estimated at ·574 acres and ·046 acres respectively. Total ·620 acres or thereabouts.*

BOUNDARY ON NORTH:—*See notes under Lot* 18.

MOOR PARK ESTATE ROADS:—*Wolsey Road is a private road maintained by Moor Park* (1958) *Ltd.* (*see Special Condition No.* 20).

OVERHEAD CABLE:—*The Vendor has made a claim against the Central Electricity Authority in respect of the overhead cable and this claim is reserved to the Vendor.*

WATER MAIN:—*This Lot is sold subject to an easement in respect of a water main (above and underground).*

FOOTPATH:—*There is a footpath along the Northern boundary which is in substitution for an old diverted footpath.*

LOT 20 (£150) (Coloured *green* on Plan)

A Plot of Land

in

SOUTH APPROACH, MOOR PARK

Having a frontage of 40 feet (including the 6 feet footpath on the South), a depth of about 150 feet, and an area of about

SQUARE **666** YARDS

VACANT POSSESSION

AREA:—*This Lot comprises Part of Ordnance No.* 61, *Parish of Rickmansworth Urban* (1935 *Edition*), *area estimated at* ·128 *acres.*

SEWER EASEMENT:—*This Lot is sold subject to an easement in respect of a sewer passing under the land, in an East to West direction.*

FOOTPATH ON SOUTH:—*See Special Condition No.* 13.

SURFACE WATER DRAIN EASEMENT:—*There is a pipe along the Northern boundary taking service water from the footpath and Lot* 20 *is sold subject to this easement.*

LOT 21 (£8,750) (Coloured *brown* on Plan)

The Valuable Compact Dairy Farm

MOOR PARK FARM

occupying a very important position on the immediate outskirts of the town of Rickmansworth, having an area of

97¼ ACRES

or thereabouts

and comprising:—

Small Dwellinghouse

cob and tiled, comprising:—
Two Sitting Rooms; Kitchen with Sink (H. and C.); Washhouse and W.C.; Two Bedrooms; and Bathroom. Main Electricity and Water. Externally there is a timber garage and a Store.

The Farm Buildings

are close to the main road and include Timber, brick and tiled Range, comprising:—
Tractor Shed; Four Loose Boxes; Barn; and Store Shed.

Timber, brick and tiled range comprising:—
Workshop; Fodder Store with concrete floor and sliding doors; **Main Cowstall for 28** with tubular divisions and concrete floor and fitted drinking bowls, connecting to **Cowstall for 8; Range of Calf Pens** (old Cowstall and Stable) with Loft over; **Large Dairy;** Large Wash-up Room and Boiler House.

MAIN WATER AND ELECTRICITY

In O.S. 289: Brick and corrugated asbestos building—Stock Shed and Store (main water).

The Agricultural Land

is undulating with a varying soil, the South part being generally a light soil, with stronger land on the North and East.

Let to Mr. A. J. F. Holloway on a yearly Michaelmas tenancy under an agreement dated 24th November, 1950, at a rent of £225 (to include Lots 22 and 23) the rent apportioned to Lot 21 for the purpose of Sale being

PER £218 5s. 0d. ANNUM

Timber Valuation: £172.

Tithe Redemption Annuity: £16 5s. 6d.

SCHEDULE

No. on Ordnance Sheet (1935 Edition)	*Description*		*Area*
	Parish of Rickmansworth Urban		
289	Pasture		12·578
297	do.		21·198
Pt. 298	do.	estimated	7·828
Pt. 331	House, Buildings, etc. ...	estimated	1·186
Pt. 332	Pasture	estimated	6·646
Pt. 338	Arable	estimated	9·123
Pt. 355	do.	estimated	14·558
356	12 acres Arable, 12 acres Pasture ...		24·144
	Total Acreage ...		**97·261**

LICENSES IN RESPECT OF JUNIPER HILL:—*There are three licenses in respect of wicket gates rear of Houses in Harefield* **Road** *for recreational access to Juniper Hill. Each licensee pays 2s. 6d. per annum and the licenses are determinable on one month's notice.*

WATER PIPE EASEMENT FOR BUILDING ON JUNIPER HILL:—*There is a 1 in. service pipe through a plot fronting Harefield* **Road**, *giving water supply to the Building on Juniper Hill and* **Lot** *21 is sold with the benefit of this easement.*

RIGHT OF WAY:—*There is a right of way over the farm road and an easement for a water pipe line, and also a 12 ft. right of way over the track marked A—B on plan for the benefit of the owner of Batchworth Hill House and* **Lot** *21 is sold subject to these easements.*

SEWER PIPE ACROSS O.S. 297:—*A 9 in. sewer pipe is laid under* **Lot** *25 and thence across O.S. 297, with five* **manholes**, *leading to the tank in Sandfield Spring and takes the drainage from the houses in London Road.* **Lot** *21 is sold subject to this easement.*

CELLAR DRAINAGE—BATCHWORTH HILL HOUSE:—*Lot 21 is sold subject to the right of the owner of Batchworth Hill* **House** *to discharge water from the* **House** *Cellar via a drain to discharge into the Farm Cowstall drainage and thence to field.*

BOUNDARIES OF LOTS 22 AND 23:—*See Remarks under these Lots.*

WATER MAIN:—*A water* **main** *crosses this Lot in a North to South direction and* **Lot** *21 is sold subject thereto.*

RIGHT OF WAY FOR THE GROVE:—*This Lot is sold subject to a 15 ft. right of way for all purposes between* **the points** *L—M—N* **on** *Plan, as access to the wood known as The Grove (see Special Condition No. 25).*

LOT 22 (£1,700) (Coloured *yellow* on Plan)

AN IMPORTANT AREA OF

Accommodation Land

LONDON ROAD, RICKMANSWORTH

Having a frontage to the road of about 450 feet and a depth of about 250 feet and an area of over

2½ ACRES

This land is included in Moor Park Farm tenancy (*see reference under Lot* 21) and the rent apportioned to Lot 22 for Sale Purposes is

PER £6 ANNUM

TITHE REDEMPTION ANNUITY:—*7s. 1d. per annum.*

AREA:—*This Lot comprises Part of Ordnance No.* 338, *Parish of Rickmansworth Urban* (1935 *Edition*), *area estimated at* 2·641 *acres.*

BOUNDARY ON WEST:—*The Purchaser of this Lot shall be responsible to erect a stockproof fence on the West boundary within three months of receiving written notice to fence from the owner of Lot* 21.

RIGHT OF WAY FOR THE GROVE:—*This Lot is sold subject to a* 15 *ft. right of way for all purposes between the points N—O on plan as access to the wood known as The Grove* (*see Special Condition No.* 25).

LOT 23 (£400) (Coloured *blue* on Plan)

A Plot of Land

LONDON ROAD, RICKMANSWORTH

Having a frontage of about 75 feet and a depth of about 200 feet with an area of about

SQUARE 1,700 YARDS

This land is included in the Moor Park Farm tenancy (*see reference under Lot* 21) and the rent apportioned to Lot 23 for Sale purposes is

PER 15s. ANNUM

TITHE REDEMPTION ANNUITY:—1*s. per annum.*

AREA:—*This Lot comprises Part of Ordnance No.* 332, *Parish of Rickmansworth Urban* (1935 *Edition*), *area estimated at* ·352 *acres.*

BOUNDARY ON WEST:—*The Purchaser of this Lot shall be responsible to erect a stockproof fence on the West boundary within three months of receiving written notice to fence from the owner of Lot* 21.

LOT 24 (£15,500) (Coloured *yellow* on Plan)

A Valuable Dairy and Pig Farm

BATCHWORTH HEATH FARM

situated about equi-distant between Moor Park and Rickmansworth, adjoining the main London Road, having an area of

106¾ ACRES

or thereabouts

and comprising:—

Dwellinghouse

situated on Batchworth Heath, semi-detached, brick and tiled, containing: Sitting Room, Kitchen, Three Bedrooms, outside Coal Store and W.C. (W.C. installed by Tenant). Electricity and Main Water (installed by Tenant).

Farm Cottage

adjoining Farm Entrance, brick and tiled, containing: Two Bedrooms, Sitting Room, Kitchen. The Tenant has installed Water and Electricity; sink in the Kitchen and W.C.

The Farm Buildings

which are approached by a short farm road leading off Batchworth Heath comprise:—

Brick and tiled **Granary;** Brick weatherboard and tiled **Barn;** and a **Barn** adjoining of similar construction; Brick and tiled **Store Shed** (adjoining Chicken House is a Tenant's building); Timber and iron **Boiler House;** Timber and tiled **Pig House;** Timber and iron **Pig House.** Concrete and iron range of **Four Pig Sties;** Boarded and tiled **Swill House and Two Sties.** Range of **Three** boarded and tiled **Pig Sties** (end sty is a Tenant's addition); Boarded and tiled range of **Three Sties** (end addition is Tenant's); Boarded and tiled **Cowstall for 9** with concrete floor and divisions; Boarded and tiled **Cowstall for 16** with concrete floor and divisions; Boarded and tiled Stable used as Calf Shed and Loose Box.

In addition to the above: a Garage, Dutch Barn, Open Hovel, Two brick and iron Pig Sties, Open Shed, Pig Sty and Garage, all erected by the Tenants.

The Agricultural Land

is within a ring fence, all on the South of the main road, is in a number of enclosures of moderate and useful size, and includes some good arable and pasture land of medium texture with heavier land at the South.

Let to Mr. A. Nichols of 9 Batchworth Heath, on a Michaelmas tenancy under an agreement dated 17th June, 1921, at a rent of

PER **£196 13s. 5d.** ANNUM

Timber Valuation: £603.

Tithe Redemption Annuity: £19 14s. 2d.

SCHEDULE

No. on Ordnance Sheet (1935 Edition)	*Description*		*Area*
	Parish of Rickmansworth Urban		
Pt. 178	Dwellinghouse	estimated	·128
Pt. 179	Cottage and Buildings ...	estimated	·200
180	Pasture	... ...	·823
181	do.	... ...	10·429
182	do.	... ...	13·149
183	do.	... ...	6·598
192	do.	... ...	17·643
233	Arable	... ...	11·137
234	Shaw	... ...	·249
235	Arable	... ...	5·694
236	Wood—Whipping Spring	... ...	1·166
237	Pasture	... ...	7·649
238	Wood—Howard Spring	... ...	1·217
239	Arable	... ...	7·509
240	Buildings	... ...	·966
Pt. 241	Arable	estimated	4·086
242	Buildings, etc.	... ...	·477
Pt. 267	Pasture	estimated	17·612
		Total Acreage ...	**106·732**

NOTE:—**The woodland areas** Ordnance Nos. 234, 236 and 238 are not included in the tenancy and are sold **with Vacant Possession.**

FARM ENTRANCE ROAD:—*There is a right of way in favour of the owner of Batchworth Heath House.*

DRAINAGE FROM NOS. 1 AND 2 GROSVENOR VILLAS:—*Lot 24 is sold subject to the right of the owners of these two Cottages to discharge drainage in field No.* 267 *as heretofore.*

LOT 25 (£3,500) (Coloured *pink* on Plan)

A VERY CONVENIENT AND WELL-SITUATED AREA OF ARABLE LAND

known as

THE BRICKFIELD

LONDON ROAD, RICKMANSWORTH

with about 1,100 feet frontage thereto, having an area of about

26 ACRES

This land is slightly undulating with a South Westerly slope and apart from its important position so close to Rickmansworth, is a very good arable field with a medium soil. There is a water point close to the main road.

Let to Mr. A. Nichols of 9 Batchworth Heath on a tenancy under an agreement dated 31st August 1939 at a rent of

PER £53 18s. 6d. ANNUM

Timber Valuation: £86

TITHE REDEMPTION ANNUITY:—£4 0*s.* 8*d. per annum.*

AREA:—*This Lot comprises Part of Ordnance No.* 302, *Parish of Rickmansworth Urban* (1935 *Edition*), *area estimated at* 26·000 *acres.*

SEWER PIPE AND MANHOLES:—*A* 9 *in. sewer pipe and five manholes are laid across Lot* 25 *and part of Lot* 21, *taking drainage from the houses on the East side of London Road to the tank in Sandfield Spring and Lot* 25 *is sold subject to this easement.*

WATER TROUGH:—*The trough between this Lot and Field* 298 (*Lot* 21) *is the property of the tenant or Purchaser of Lot* 21 *and no rights of water are included in the sale of Lot* 25.

WATER MAIN:—*A water main crosses this Lot in a North to South direction and Lot* 25 *is sold subject to this easement.*

LOT 26 (£4,000) (Coloured *brown* on Plan)

A CONVENIENT ENCLOSURE OF

Accommodation Land

LONDON ROAD, RICKMANSWORTH

Having a frontage to the main road of about 440 feet, and an area of about

15½ ACRES

The Entrance is by a gate from the lane off the main road (*see note beneath as to right of way*)

This is a very good enclosure of pasture, with a main water tank

VACANT POSSESSION

Timber Valuation: £103

Tithe Redemption Annuity: £2 1s. 11d. p.a.

AREA:—*This Lot comprises Part of Ordnance No.* 271, *Parish of Rickmansworth Urban* (1935 *Edition*), *area estimated at* 15·694 *acres.*

RIGHT OF WAY:—*This Lot is sold with the benefit of a right of way over that portion of the lane* (*No.* 306 *on Plan—Part of Lot* 27) *required as access to the existing gateway to Lot* 26.

WATER MAIN:—*A water main crosses this Lot in a North to South direction close to the wood and Lot* 26 *is sold subject to this easement.*

LOT 27 (£800) (Coloured *blue* on Plan)

A FURTHER AREA OF

Accommodation Land

adjoining Lot 26, having a total area of about

8 ACRES

The Entrance is by a grass lane leading from the public road.

VACANT POSSESSION

Tithe Redemption Annuity: £1 1s. 9d. p.a.

AREA:—*This Lot comprises Ordnance Nos.* 270 *and Part* 305, *Parish of Rickmansworth Urban* (1935 *Edition*), *area* 8·061 *acres and* ·095 *acres respectively. Total area* 8·156 *acres.*

RIGHTS OF WAY:—*This Lot is sold subject to rights of way in addition to the public footpath) over the lane, No.* 306(*a*) *in respect of the portion as far as the existing gateway in favour of the Purchaser of Lot* 27 *and* (*b*) *over the whole length in favour of the Purchaser of Lot* 29.

LOT 28 (£200) (Coloured *green* on Plan)

A SMALL ENCLOSURE OF

Orchard and Pasture

LONDON ROAD, RICKMANSWORTH

adjoining Primrose Cottage, having an area of just over

½ ACRE

This Orchard is included with Lot 29 in a tenancy to **Mrs. Chalk** of Primrose Cottage, London Road, Rickmansworth (yearly tenancy following the expiry of lease) at a rent of £10 p.a.) and for sale purposes the rent apportioned to Lot 28 is

PER £4 ANNUM

AREA:—*This Lot comprises Part of Ordnance No.* 308, *Parish of Rickmansworth Urban* (1935 *Edition*), *area estimated at* ·582 *acres.*

TITHE REDEMPTION ANNUITY:—1*s.* 6*d. per annum.*

LOT 29 (£200) (Coloured *pink* on Plan)

A FURTHER AREA OF

Orchard and Pasture

off LONDON ROAD, RICKMANSWORTH

(Rear of Primrose Cottage and approached by a lane leading from London Road), extending to just over

1 ACRE

This Orchard is included with Lot 28 in a tenancy to **Mrs. Chalk** of Primrose Cottage, London Road, Rickmansworth (yearly tenancy following the expiry of lease), at a rent of £10 per annum and for Sale purposes the rent apportioned to Lot 29 is

PER £6 ANNUM

AREA:—*This Lot comprises Ordnance Nos.* 268 *and* 269, *Parish of Rickmansworth Urban* (1935 *Edition*), *areas* ·821 *acres and* ·282 *acres respectively. Total area* 1·103 *acres or thereabouts.*

TITHE REDEMPTION ANNUITY:—4*s.* 6*d. per annum.*

RIGHT OF WAY:—*This Lot is sold with the benefit of a right of way over the lane No.* 306 *on Plan* (*part of Lot* 27).

LOT 30 (£9,000) (Coloured *pink* on Plan)

STOCKER'S FARM

RICKMANSWORTH

situated just on the outskirts of the town, with the Grand Union Canal as the farm boundary on the North, having an area of

123 ACRES

or thereabouts

comprising:—

An Attractive Farmhouse

built of brick with tiled roof, containing:

On the GROUND FLOOR:
Two large Reception Rooms; Cloakroom and W.C.; Kitchen; Scullery; Cellar; Dairy.

On the FIRST FLOOR:
Five Bedrooms; Bathroom; Boxroom.

SERVICES: MAIN WATER

Good lawns and flower garden.

The Farm Buildings

are grouped in various ranges close to the house and are mainly of weatherboarding construction on brick dwarf walls, with tiled roofs:—

Barn Timber and iron **Cowstall** (partitions removed) **Barn arranged as 24 Stalls** Small Cattle Shelter

On the Second Side of Yard:—

Cowstall **Loose Box** **Barn** **Loose Box**

On the Third Side of Yard:—

Old Stable with Loft over **4-Bay open Cattle Shed** **2-Bay Cart Shed** **Shed** **Implement Shed**

The above three ranges of buildings are grouped around a good concrete yard.

A second set of Buildings close by comprises:—

4-Bay Cattle Shed **Two Loose Boxes** **Large Stable** (partitions removed)

and to the South of the House is:—

Cattle Shed **Loose Box** **Hen House**

A Pair of Farm Cottages

close to the public road known as Stocker's Cottages, brick and tiled, each containing: Two Bedrooms; Boxroom; Kitchen and Sitting Room. Gas and Main Water. Outside Privy and Outhouse.

The Agricultural Land

is for the most part undulating pasture with a light soil over the underlying chalk, and suitable for Stock rearing, and there is some stronger grazing land towards the Canal.

This Lot (with the exception of the woods which are in hand), together with Lots 31 and 32 is let to Mr. J. H. Wheaton on an annual Michaelmas tenancy under an agreement dated 17th July, 1933, at a rent of £144 p.a. and the rent apportioned to Lot 30 for Sale purposes is

PER **£110 18s. 6d.** ANNUM

Timber Valuation: £103.

Tithe Redemption Annuity: £24 7s. 4d. per annum.

SCHEDULE

No. on Ordnance Sheet (1935 Edition)	*Description*		*Area*
	Parish of Rickmansworth Urban		
Pt. 286	Shaw	estimated	·348
366	Cottages and Garden ...	.. ...	·128
Pt. 500	Pasture adjoining Cottages	estimated	·300
Pt. 500	Pasture	estimated	19·138
Pt. 502	do.	estimated	32·116
Pt. 509	do.	estimated	20·784
509a	do.	.. ...	7·579
510	do.	... ...	26·606
511	Woodland	... ...	9·136
512	do.	... ...	·219
552	Old Orchard and Pasture	... ...	3·989
553	Pit and Shaw	... ...	·961
Pt. 555	House, Buildings and Yard	estimated	1·732
		Total Acreage ...	**123·036**

TRUNK SEWER:—*A trunk sewer is laid in No. 510 South of the Canal running West to East, South of Buildings and across No. 502, and Lot 30 is sold subject to an easement in respect thereof.*

MAIN WATER:—*This Lot is sold with the benefit of an easement in respect of the main water connection by the Pumping Station, this being the 1 in. supply pipe for the House and Buildings and two troughs.*

RIGHT OF WAY AND OTHER RIGHTS OF DEVELOPMENT OVER CONCRETE ROAD TO PUMPING STATION:—*The Vendor has a right of way over the Concrete road between points D and D(1) and certain other rights (see Special Condition No. 9). In the event of Lot 31 being sold separately to Lot 30 this right of way shall, as always intended, become the farm entrance in substitution for the farm road to the North, and Lot 30 will not be conveyed with any right of way over Lot 31. (See Note under Lot 31.)*

RIGHT OF WAY TO STOCKER'S LOCK HOUSE:—*See Special Condition No. 9.*

RIGHT OF WAY FOR LOT 31:—*Lot 30 is sold subject to a right of way over the farm road forming part of the land with the two Cottages, in favour of the Purchaser of Lot 31 until such time as Lot 31 is developed and access obtained on to the concrete road, when this particular right of way will cease.*

FENCING AGAINST LOT 31:—*See remarks under Lot 31.*

LOT 31 (£800) (Coloured *green* on Plan)

A VALUABLE AREA OF

Accommodation Land

OFF HAREFIELD ROAD, RICKMANSWORTH

extending to about

2½ ACRES

Entered by the Stocker's Farm road and **with about 350 feet frontage to the concrete road to the South** (over which there is a right of way and other rights in the event of development), and 150 feet depth. This Lot is included in the letting of Stocker's Farm (Lots 30, 31 and 32) and the rent apportioned to Lot 31 for Sale purposes is

PER **£2 5s. 0d.** ANNUM

Tithe Redemption Annuity: 11s. 6d. p.a.

Timber Valuation: £70

AREA:—*This Lot comprises Part of Ordnance No.* 500, *Parish of Rickmansworth Urban* (1935 *Edition*), *area estimated at* 2·506 *acres or thereabouts.*

FENCING:—*The Purchaser of this Lot shall be responsible to erect a stock-proof fence on the North and West boundaries adjoining Lot* 30 *within three months of receiving written notice to fence from the Purchaser of Lot* 30.

RIGHT OF WAY AND OTHER DEVELOPMENT RIGHTS OVER CONCRETE ROAD TO PUMPING STATION:—*The Vendor has a right of way over the concrete road between Points D and D*(1) *on Plan and certain other rights* (*see Special Condition No.* 9).

In the event of Lot 31 *being sold separately to Lot* 30 *there shall be no right of way for the benefit of Lot* 30 *over the existing farm road through Lot* 31, *but Lot* 31 *is sold subject to whatever rights the tenant may have over the farm road until he uses the concrete road instead.*

RIGHT OF WAY OVER LOT 30:—*Lot* 31 *is sold with the benefit of a right of way over the farm road, North of Stocker's Cottages, until such time as Lot* 31 *is developed and direct access made on to the concrete road.*

INTERVENING STRIP OF GROUND:—*This strip of Ground which does not belong to the Vendor is marked out on Site but the Vendor has access over the farm road.*

LOT 32 (£2,500) (Coloured *blue* on Plan)

A COMPACT BLOCK OF

Pasture Land

HAREFIELD ROAD, RICKMANSWORTH

extending to

34¼ ACRES

or thereabouts

and comprising four very convenient and healthy enclosures of grazing land, with a fairly light gravelly soil on the underlying chalk. There are main water troughs in two fields. This area of land is part of Stocker's Farm letting (*see details under Lot* 30) and the rent apportioned to Lot 32 for Sale purposes is

PER **£30 16s. 6d.** ANNUM

Timber Valuation: £111

Tithe Redemption Annuity: £7 4s. 0d. p.a.

SCHEDULE

No. on Ordnance Sheet (1935 Edition)	*Description*		*Area*
	Parish of Rickmansworth Urban		
Pt. 223	Pasture	estimated	4·122
280	Arable (ley)	... ...	11·268
506	Pasture	... ...	9·434
Pt. 507	Shaw	estimated	·075
508	Pasture	... ...	9·389
	Total Acreage	...	**34·288**

RIGHT OF WAY TO SEWAGE FIELD AND SHEPHERDS CLOSE DELL:—*This Lot is subject to a right of way 15 ft. wide over the track marked EF on Plan, for the Purchaser of Lot 33, together with a right of way over the track between Point F and Harefield Road, in so far as this track may form any part of Lot 33; and to a similar right for all purposes as access to the wood known as Shepherds Close Dell.* (*see Special Condition No.* 25.)

NORTH EAST CORNER OF NO. 230 ON PLAN:—*This small area of land is occupied by an adjoining Cottage tenant at 2s. 6d. per annum, acknowledgment rent.*

LOT 33 (£1,750) (Coloured *yellow* on Plan)

A COMPACT AREA OF

Arable Land

formerly the

SEWAGE FARM, HAREFIELD ROAD RICKMANSWORTH

extending to about

26¾ ACRES

with an approach from Harefield Road.

This Lot comprises a good level enclosure which, after an initial cleaning (the land was not cultivated in 1958, but was sprayed to control weeds) should still benefit from the previous sewage treatment.

VACANT POSSESSION

Tithe Redemption Annuity: £5 3s. 6d. p.a.

AREA:—*This Lot comprises Part of Ordnance No.* 507 *and Ordnance No.* 508A (*Shaw*), *Parish of Rickmansworth Urban* (1935 *Edition*), *areas* 25·642 *acres, estimated, and* 1·073 *acres respectively. Total area* 26·715 *acres or thereabouts.*

RIGHT OF WAY:—*This Lot is sold with the benefit of a right of way over a 15 ft. track part of Lot 32, marked by the letters EF on Plan, and thence over the track from Point F to Harefield Road.*

RIGHT OF WAY TO SHEPHERDS CLOSE DELL:—*This Lot is sold subject to a 15 ft. right of way between the points E and G as access to the wood, Shepherds Close Dell, from the track EF previously referred to.* (*See Special Condition No.* 25.)

LOT 34 (£10,500) (Coloured *green* on Plan)

A Stock and Arable Farm

PIPER'S FARM

WOODCOTE HILL, RICKMANSWORTH

having an area of about

$91\frac{3}{4}$ ACRES

The Homestead is centrally situated within the curtilage of the farm and the approach is by a good road from the North-West part of the farm.

There is a

Detached Farmhouse

brick and tiled comprising:—

On the GROUND FLOOR:
Two Reception Rooms, Kitchen, Scullery, Pantry, and Cellar.

On the FIRST FLOOR Three Bedrooms, Bathroom, and W.C.
(Two Staircases):
Two attics in addition.

SERVICES: MAIN WATER

The Farm Buildings

are close by and well arranged around a good yard, and a very useful set, including:—
Brick and tiled **Dairy; Timber Shed;** Boarded and tiled **Cowstall for 11** (to T.T. Standard but not at present used for milking); Boarded and tiled **Barn; 3-Stall Stable.**

3-Bay **Cart Shed;** Boarded and tiled **good Barn; Cowstall for 7** with Loft and **Two Loose Boxes;** Lean-to Shed; **Four Pig Sties.** Corrugated Hay Shed is a Tenant's building.

The Agricultural Land

is within a ring fence and comprises for the most part enclosures of pasture with easy slopes, and a few fields under the plough. There are main water points in three fields.

Let to Mr. W. Timms on a yearly Michaelmas tenancy under an agreement dated 28th July, 1942, at a rent of

PER **£150 2s. 2d.** ANNUM

Timber Valuation: £112.

Tithe Redemption Annuity: £13 19s. 6d.

SCHEDULE

No. on Ordnance Sheet (1935 Edition)	*Description*		*Area*
	Parish of Rickmansworth Urban		
194	Arable		8·107
195	do.		4·342
Pt. 205	do.	estimated	6·070
230	Pasture		9·466
232	Bush Spring		1·077
272	Pasture		13·654
273	do.		14·595
274	Old Orchard and Pasture		·809
275	House, Buildings, etc.		1·516
276	Arable		3·205
277	do.		8·624
Pt. 292	do.	estimated	5·307
Pt. 293	do.	estimated	9·522
295	Garden and Rough		·600
296	Arable		4·991
		Total acreage ...	**91·885**

EASEMENT FOR WATER:—*This Lot is sold with the benefit of an easement for the water supply pipe along the track South of the Brickworks to the boundary of the farm.*

WATER MAIN:—*A water main crosses the Eastern portion of No.* 273 *in a North to South direction and Lot* 34 *is sold subject to the easement.*

RIGHT OF WAY TO LONG SPRING:—*This Lot is sold subject to a* 15 *ft. wide right of way for all purposes between the points marked J—K as access to the wood, Long Spring.* (*See Special Condition No.* 25.)

LOT 35 (£6,750) (Coloured *pink* on Plan)

A VALUABLE AREA OF

Building Land and Accommodation Land Kewferry Drive, Moor Park

having a total area of about

7¾ ACRES

and

with Planning Consent for the Erection of Four Houses

The land on which Planning Consent has been given is the Kewferry Drive frontage (**about 240 feet**) to a depth of about 160 feet at the East and 190 feet at the West.

NOTE:—There is an underground chalk working under part of this building land: it is situated to the West of the frontage and the excavated area goes back about 100 feet from the frontage. At the East (adjoining the house "Wynchfield") is an area of about 90 feet frontage which is not affected by these underground workings. For the benefit of prospective purchasers the depth between the surface of the ground and the top of the workings is about 40 feet and a plan can be inspected at the Moor Park Estate office or the Auctioneers' offices.

This land is occupied by Mr. W. Nichols of Park Farm, Duckshill Road, Northwood, under license determinable by **one month's notice.**

AREA:—*This Lot comprises Parts of Ordnance Nos.* 20 *and* 27 *Parish of Ruislip* (1935 *Edition Ordnance Sheet*), *areas* ·604 *acres and* 7·283 *acres respectively* (*estimated*). *Total area* 7·887 *acres or thereabouts.*

SEWER EASEMENTS:—*A sewer crosses this land in a West to East direction* (*continuing from Lots* 5 *and* 7—*see remarks under Lot* 5) *and the sewer in Farm Road continues across this land to join the first mentioned sewer and continues to the East boundary and this Lot is sold subject to this easement.*

LICENCE:—*Mr. G. V. Tottle of Wynchfield is a tenant at will in respect of the small area of land adjoining his house* (*part of the Kewferry Drive frontage*).

OVERHEAD CABLE:—*The Vendor has made a claim against the Central Electricity Authority in respect of the pylons and overhead cable and this claim is reserved to the Vendor.*

BOUNDARY BETWEEN LOT 9 AND LOT 35:—*The Purchaser of Lot* 35 *shall be responsible to erect a stockproof fence on this boundary within three months of receiving written notice to fence from the owner of Lot* 9.

LOT 36 (£500)

The Lordship of the Manor

appertaining to

The Moor Park Estate

and described in the Land Registry under Absolute Title No. 6407 as "The Incorporeal hereditaments known as the Manor or reputed Manor of Moor in the County of Hertford, registered on the 8th December, 1902".

LOT 37 (Not sold at auction)

Fishing, Sporting and Certain Navigation Rights

This Lot comprises such **Rights of Fishing, Sporting and otherwise** in portions of the **River Colne** and of the **Grand Junction Canal** and in the bed of the River Colne as are vested in the Vendor on the day of the Sale.

NOTE:—*Prospective Purchasers are strongly advised to instruct their Solicitors to contact the Auctioneers or the Vendor's Solicitors before the Sale in order to inspect such records as are available as to definition and extent of these rights. An office copy of the entry in the Register and of the filed plan of this Title would then be produced.*